Rea

BROWNING'S RING METAPHOR AND TRUTH

by

Paul A. Cundiff

The Scarecrow Press, Inc.
Metuchen, N.J.   1972

Library of Congress Cataloging in Publication Data

Cundiff, Paul A
    Browning's ring metaphor and truth.

    1. Browning, Robert, 1812-1889. The ring and the
book. I. Title.
PR4219.C8   821'.8   79-189092
ISBN 0-8108-0478-6

1692818

For their encouragement and help

W. B. Jones
L. L. Dantzler
George R. Coffman
William C. DeVane
Finley Foster
Charles F. Harrold
Maurice B. Cramer
Frederic E. Faverty

CONTENTS

Page

v

The search for Truth is in one way hard and in another easy. For it is evident that no one can master it fully nor miss it wholly. But each adds a little to our knowledge of Nature, and from all the facts assembled there arises a certain grandeur.

Aristotle, The Metaphysics

INTRODUCTION

The seven essays in this volume are intended to form a continuous and unified study. Four are new essays, three are reprinted with relevant supplementary material, and all speak primarily to contemporary thought on Browning's long poem. The scheme, though it eventually embraces reference to most of the recorded critical attitudes on the poem, is deliberate in its constant focus on the Ring metaphor and the poet's use of the word truth and truth itself.

It was through Essay One that Dean DeVane was persuaded to believe "the moral purpose and the various approaches to the evolution of The Ring and the Book, if not the intricate final division, were reached upon Browning's first reading the Old Yellow Book in 1860." And I believe that Browning's earlier organization of the poem, his permanent involvement with Pompilia's story once he learned of it, and his inspiration as revealed in Book I for creating the poem find considerable acceptance.

Essay Two is my interpretation of the Ring metaphor, and without its inclusion Essay Four, which treats of other interpretations of the metaphor, would of course need to be much longer.

Essay Three tells one side of the controversy over truth, a controversy which is beset with theoretical and practical difficulties, and largely explains why the four new essays were written. Its insistence upon Browning's faith in an absolute truth of God and, particularly, upon his unfavorable appraisal of human knowledge evoked among relativists and factualists a warm disapproval. Their objections and my continuing belief that Browning cannot convincingly be separated from his idealistic temperament and his idealistic poetic practice account for a large part of three of the four new essays.

In Essay Four all of the serious interpretations of the Ring metaphor, save my own, are discussed and proof of their continuity is undertaken. My reasons for thinking them deficient, especially in reliance upon obvious technical errors, are further elaborated on, even when the interpretations sometimes depend upon my interpretation for a starting point. Essay Four is also a logical place to present additional metallurgical information, to expand upon available information which many critics think unimportant and ignore or continue to misinterpret whenever they resort to the Ring analogy.

Essay Five deals with influential and representative interpretations of Browning's view of truth. In two of the three interpretations offered, the validity of the points of view and of the arguments, insofar as the poem and the poet are concerned, is challenged; a desire that the thought of these two critics be fairly represented weighed heavily in the decision not to slight substantive quotations.

Essay Six seemed necessary for two reasons: popularly and persuasively advanced comments on The Ring and the Book often appear, not in their original or seminal form, but in derivative essays and introductions which add almost permanently to the substance or error, as the case may be, of the initial undertaking. Thus a fair variety of thought from eclectic essays is included.

At the beginning of this present study, Essay Seven was contemplated as a working synthesis of the pros and cons on Browning's Ring metaphor and his use of the word truth. I disliked the social criticism which more and more was being attributed to the poem, but I could not satisfactorily rationalize its intensity or popularity. Nor could I reconcile my thought on the poem with a critical belief that Browning, a very conscious artist, would implicitly or explicitly condemn the Catholic Church as he so freely was being advanced as doing. The closer I looked into modern essays the more I found them tailored of one fabric, and that fabric A. K. Cook, not the poet, had supplied. In response to the relativists in Essay Five I had been compelled, virtually word by word, to re-read or re-interpret the last five hundred lines (1630-2135) of Book X. So Essay Seven, rather than becoming a synthesis even the reader may now have to delay, became a new reading of the Pope's monologue, that is, down through Euripides' speech and the Pope's foreboding thoughts on a new era of doubt (1850). Critics have always had good reason for taking seriously the appearance of Euripides in The Ring and the Book, and their thoughts have been additionally confirmed by Browning's words to Isa Blagden, September 19, 1864: "For me, I have got on by having a great read at Euripides--the one book I brought with me." And I believe critics have still better reason for attempting to find an organic purpose of dignified dimension for the Euripides so evidently welcomed by Pope Innocent. It is therefore hoped that yet another interpretation of the Pope's monologue may prove proportionate to the cause.

I am especially indebted to my University for a sabbatical leave of absence; to Director Jack Herring and the Armstrong Browning Library of Baylor University, where I worked for four very pleasant months; to the staffs of the libraries at the University of Texas, the Henry E. Huntington Estate, and the University of Delaware; and to the many individuals to whom I have importunately turned for information or aid on metallurgy, Aristotelian Greek, Plato, Coleridge, St. John, St. Paul, and repetitive typing and proof-reading. The quotations from Browning's poetry are from The Centenary Edition of The Works of Robert Browning, edited by F. G. Kenyon (London, 1912).

P.A.C.
Newark, Delaware

1

THE DATING OF BROWNING'S CONCEPTION OF THE PLAN OF THE RING AND THE BOOK

Reprinted with permission from Studies in Philology, XXXVII (1941), 543-551. Supplementary material is indicated by brackets.

The generally accepted date for Browning's earliest composition on The Ring and the Book is 1864.[1] In August of that year Browning visited the Pass of Roland, a mountain gorge in the French Pyrenees, and, according to W. M. Rossetti, "laid out the full plan of his twelve cantos, ac-curately carried out in the execution."[2] Contemporary critics[3] have accepted these words as evidence that Brown-ing conceived the full plan of the poem at the pass and be-gan composition immediately. I believe, however, that re-cently published letters discredit both the date 1864 and the inspiration at the pass, and help establish the conclusions that Browning was seriously concerned with the poem as early as 1862; that he probably began to write it in 1864; and that the Pass of Roland was connected in no way with the conception of the poem. Moreover, the opening book of the poem and the heretofore dismissed evidence of Rudolf Lehmann[4] indicate that Browning conceived the plan as well as the moral purpose of the poem upon first reading the Old Yellow Book in 1860.

The history of the actual composition of The Ring and the Book has become more involved as new allusions to it from Browning appear. William Michael Rossetti recorded in his diary March 15, 1868, immediately after visiting with Browning:

> Browning's forthcoming poem exceeds 20,000 lines:... He began it in October '64. Was staying at Bayonne, and walked out to a mountain-gorge traditionally said to have been cut or kicked

> out by Roland, and laid out the full plan of his
> twelve cantos, accurately carried out in the exe-
> cution. (pp. 299, 302)

Up to 1941, Browning scholars have agreed that Rossetti's statement is the most accurate and the most thorough
account of the composition of the poem. They think Browning
had reached the point at which he wanted to write a poem
about the content of the Old Yellow Book in 1862, but they
are convinced he was not in a position to start the poem
until after the publication of Dramatis Personae in 1864.[5]
Their reason is that Browning was so involved with publication that he had no time to begin the composition of so extended a poem. Mr. Raymond writes of the Biarritz letter,
composed September 19, 1864:

> Browning speaks in this letter as if his 'new poem
> that is about to be' were very much in the fore-
> front of his thoughts. The whole of it, he informs
> Miss Blagden, [6] is pretty well in his head. This
> points to a time when he seriously addressed him-
> self to the composition of The Ring and the Book.
> (p. 366; Infinite Moment, p. 84)

And Mr. DeVane suggests:

> As we know, the edition of old things came first,
> in 1863, and actually by its success, delayed the
> publication of the new poems, Dramatis Personae.
> It was probably not until this last volume was
> published on May 28, 1864, that Browning felt free
> to address himself to the task his Roman murder-
> case presented. (p. 284; 2d ed., p. 321)

Yet it is now evident that Browning originally planned to
write a much shorter poem, which would partially account
for an earlier composition. He told Miss Wedgwood in 1864
that he would write the twelve books in six months.[7] And
he wrote Isa Blagden in October 1864 that he hoped "to have
a long poem ready by the summer, my Italian murder
thing."[8] In addition, it seems to me, Mr. Raymond has
misunderstood Browning's intention when he interprets
Browning's request for the Baker manuscript to mean that
the poet had only a growing interest in the subject of the
Old Yellow Book in 1862.[9] When Browning asked, on
September 19, 1862, for Mrs. Baker's account of "the trial
of Count Francesco Guidi," he wrote: "I am anxious to

collate [it] with my own collection of papers on the subject...
I should greatly like to see it. "[10] Taken alone, these words
do indicate little more than the desire of a collector, but the
poet was to express his intentions definitely and positively a
month later, October 18, 1862, in his second allusion to the
subject of The Ring and the Book:

> Thank you most truly for attending to my request
> so promptly, in the matter of the Account of the
> Murder &c. which I found on my return--pray thank
> Mrs Baker for her kindness, & say it will be par-
> ticularly useful to me: it would be of little use to
> anybody without my documents, nor is it correct in
> several respects, but it contains a few notices of
> the execution &c. subsequent to my account that I
> can turn to good: I am going to make a regular
> poem of it. (Letters to Isa Blagden, pp. 68-69;
> McAleer, p. 128)

This letter establishes conclusively that Browning was
no longer merely considering the subject of the Old Yellow
Book for a poem.   Here, in October 1862, his decision is
definitely reached to make a poem of it.   One month later,
November 19, 1862, he tells Isa Blagden that his plans for
the spring are these: "Early in Spring, I print new poems,
a number: then, a new edition of all my old things, corrected: then begin on my murder-case" (pp. 73-74; Mc-
Aleer, p. 134).   And two months later, December 19,
1862,[11] his words constitute irrefutable proof that he was
deeply concerned over the outcome of The Ring and the Book:
"In the spring I print the new poems, & a new edition of my
things in four vols... I am about a long poem to be
something remarkable--work at it hard.   May it please you!"
(Letters to Isa Blagden, pp. 79, 82; McAleer, pp. 142, 212)

Does Browning mean he was actually writing The Ring
and the Book, or does he mean he was casting the material of
the Old Yellow Book into shape for poetical treatment?   Few
would question that "long poem" means The Ring and the Book,
because there are innumerable references to it as such; but the
poet was so often "about" the poem and for so long that these
terms became commonplace.   Notice should be taken, however, of his words of December 19, 1862 [1864[11]], when he
says "I work at it hard."   The excerpts given above from
the poet's letters of 1862-64 convey the impression that
Browning was going through a period similar to that of
Milton three years before the composition of Paradise Lost.

He was reading, studying, and perhaps writing about the content of the Old Yellow Book as early as 1862.   There are
statements in subsequent letters to show that the poet had
written to or talked with friends about the book before the
earliest days of writing on the poem.   He wrote Isa Blagden,
September 19, 1864, of "the Roman murder story you
know,"[12] which he had mentioned first to her by letter in
September 1862.   But of more importance are the words to
Miss Wedgwood, October 3, 1864:   "I have got the whole of
that poem, you enquire about, well in my head, shall write
the twelve books of it in six months" (p. 79).

Although Browning had been occupied with the story
of the Old Yellow Book since 1862, perhaps 1860 when he
found it, the actual writing of The Ring and the Book was
probably not started until the fall of 1864.   It was from
Biarritz, September 19, 1864, that Browning wrote of a
definite scheme for the poem and of plans to begin writing
at once:

> For me, I have got on by having a great read at
> Euripides--the one book I brought with me, besides
> attending to my own matters, my new poem that is
> about to be; and of which the whole is pretty well
> in my head--the Roman murder story you know. [12]

Fourteen days later, in a letter from Biarritz, he describes
the final division of the poem to Miss Wedgwood when he
says, "I shall write the twelve books of it in six months."
Moreover, he was to tell W. M. Rossetti in March 1868 that
he began the poem in October 1864.   Additional evidence also
exists in the poem itself to suggest it was not until 1864 that
Browning really devoted his full energies to the writing of
the poem.   In Book XII he addresses the Old Yellow Book:

> How will it be, my four-years'-intimate,
> When thou and I part company anon?   (XII. 227-228)

The upshot is that Browning was both preoccupied with
publication and reluctant to tackle the actual writing of the
poem, or that he wished to deceive his public about the time
required to write it.   I leave interpretation of the following
passage, spoken by Tennyson and recorded in Allingham's
Diary, to the judgment of the reader, simply because a
charge of willful deception on the part of Browning would
be gratuitous: "Browning must think himself the greatest
man living.   I can't understand how he should care for my

poetry.   His new poem has 15,000 lines--there's copious-
ness!"[13]   Allingham wrote these words November 1, 1865.
Browning's own first[14] recorded statement about the number
of lines he had composed came on April 23, 1867: "I want
to get done with my Poem, sixteen thousand lines!"[14]   If,
as Browning, Rossetti, and the critics say, the earliest writing on the poem occurred in October 1864, Browning wrote
15,000 lines between October 1864 and November 1, 1865--
just over 12 months--and 1,000 lines between November 1,
1865 and April 23, 1867--nearly 18 months.   Moreover, between April 23, 1867 and October 10, 1868 (the date the
poem went to press, DeVane, p. 286)--nearly 18 months--
he wrote 5,000 lines.   It is only fair to add that Browning
wrote, according to the record, 2,000 lines from April 23,
1867 to May 17, 1867 (Wedgwood Letters, p. 126).   Any
further discussion at this point would be merely conjectural,[15]
but there is a probable suggestion to account for Browning's
indecision with the Old Yellow Book from 1860 to 1864.   The
story of Pompilia became for Browning, the day he found it,
an obsession.   No subject had offered him so complete an
opportunity to explain his theories of life and poetry.   In it
were the Andromeda myth, the St. George legend, the slip-
pery villain, and a repetition of the story of his own life.
In addition, he had always selected out-of-the-way incidents
with which to present his reading of life.   Do what he could,
the story continued to haunt him.   So, after he found he
could not interest his friends in it,[16] he finally concluded
that the only way to rid himself of it was to begin the poem.

Despite the mist which has gathered around the genesis
of the poem, one inescapable conclusion can be drawn from
Browning's correspondence of 1862.   The Ring and the Book
did not burst upon the poet in all its complexity at the pas de
Roland, and it is doubtful that it even occurred to him there.
Following Rossetti, Mr. Raymond says of Browning: "Standing beside the historic pas de Roland, in the latter part of
August, his imagination received a fillip and 'the full plan'
of the twelve cantos of The Ring and the Book was actually
conceived" (p. 368; Infinite Moment, p. 86).   Mr. DeVane
proposes the same: "The pass of Roland may well have been
vivid in his consciousness, for there on August 27[17] the
great conception of The Ring and the Book seems finally to
have sprung into Browning's mind" (p. 284; 2d ed. p. 322).

For evidence to determine whether the full plan of the
poem was conceived at the Pass of Roland, there are four
accounts of Browning's visit to the pass and a dated etching

of the pass by Browning's sister. [18] The first reference to
the pass is in a letter to Miss Wedgwood, August 20, 1864:

> I went this morning to see the mountain-pass called
> 'Le pas de Roland'--the tradition being that he
> opened a way through a rock that effectually blocked
> it up, by one kick of his boot, and so let Charle-
> magne's army pass: it is a striking little bit of
> scenery, with the clear green river between the
> mountain-walls, not unlike Lima at Lucca; but I
> think I liked best of all a great white-breasted
> hawk I saw sunning himself on a ledge, with his
> wings ready. (Wedgwood Letters, p. 43)

The second notice is in the undated Story letter, which can
be dated with certainty (since the trip was made on the 20th),
August 22, 1864:

> I went two days ago to see a famous mountain-
> pass, le pas de Roland, so called because that
> paladin kicked a hole in a rock, which blocked
> the way, to allow Charlemagne's army to pass. [19]

Browning, on returning to London in the fall of 1864, used
the pass as a figure to characterize Tennyson's "Boadicea":

> 'Boadicea,' the new metre is admirable, a paladin's
> achievement in its way. I am thinking of Roland's
> Pass in the Pyrenees, where he hollowed a rock
> that had hitherto blocked the road, by one kick of
> his boot. [20]

And lastly, there are the words which William Michael Rossetti recorded in his diary March 15, 1868, immediately
after conversation with Browning:

> [Browning] was staying at Bayonne, and walked out
> to a mountain-gorge traditionally said to have been
> cut or kicked out by Roland, and laid out the full
> plan of his twelve cantos, accurately carried out
> in the execution. (p. 302)

Of all the information now available on the conception
of the poem, the quotation taken from Rossetti's diary contains the only statement, oral or written, which places
Browning at the Pass of Roland when he envisioned a plan
of twelve cantos for The Ring and the Book. Save in two

instances, its trustworthiness has not been questioned. Rossetti says that the visit was made from Bayonne in October,
whereas it was really made from Cambo on August 20. But
more seriously, there is a contradictory account of Browning's division of the poem which has been given by Rudolf
Lehmann in his An Artist's Reminiscences:

> When I first read the book, my plan was at once
> settled. I went for a walk, gathered twelve peb-
> bles from the road, and put them at equal distance
> on the parapet that bordered it. These represent-
> ed the twelve chapters into which the poem is
> divided and I adhered to that arrangement to the
> last. (p. 224)

Lehmann[21] does not say when Browning spoke these words
to him, but his statement, though a recollection published in
1894, cannot be discarded, as A. K. Cook has done, by
merely saying Rossetti recorded his words immediately after
conversation with the poet (Commentary, p. 278). Since
Rossetti was inaccurate enough to mistake the date of the
visit to the pass and the place from which it was made, it
is also likely that he could have further misunderstood
Browning. Perhaps Browning's own memory failed him.
Moreover, Browning may have told Rossetti the same thing
that he was thinking of when he called the poem his "four-
years'-intimate." That is, he probably took into the account
only the actual time of final composition, ignoring the preparatory period. Lehmann may also have been thinking of
the following passage from the poem itself, but nowhere else,
except in Lehmann's memoirs, can there be found such a
vivid description of the final division of the poem:

> Till, by the time I stood at home again...
> I had mastered the contents, knew the whole truth....
> Before attempting smithcraft, on the night
> After the day when--truth thus grasped and gained, --
> I turned, to free myself and find the world,
> And stepped out on the narrow terrace,...
> And paced its lozenge-brickwork sprinkled cool;...
> Over the roof o' the lighted church I looked
> A bowshot to the street's end, north away
> Out of the Roman gate to the Roman road
> By the river, till I felt the Apennine....
> There lay Arezzo!...
> Whence I went on again, the end was near,
> Step by step, missing none and marking all,...

> The life in me abolished the death of things,
> Deep calling unto deep: as then and there
> Acted itself over again once more
> The tragic piece.
>   (I. 113, 117, 470f, 478f, 481, 497ff, 505,
>   516f, 520ff)

The long passage from which the above verses were
taken contains some of the most vivid poetry of the poem,
and in it Browning is writing of the day on which he found
the Old Yellow Book.   Does it not seem strange that he
would prefer as poetic material this first day's experience
with the Old Yellow Book to the experience at the Pass of
Roland, if he did actually reach the final conception of The
Ring and the Book at the pass?   It is improbable that Browning could have had the experience at the Pass of Roland
which was recorded by Rossetti without mentioning it to even
one of the correspondents for whom he described the visit
immediately following the experience.   Although he describes
the visit in detail to Miss Wedgwood, Mrs. Story, and Tennyson, he does not mention the subject of the poem.   The only
thing of sufficient interest at the pass to cause Browning to
write of it, other than the legend of Roland, is mentioned in
the letter to Miss Wedgwood: "I think I liked best of all a
great white-breasted hawk I saw sunning on a ledge, with his
wings ready. "   Surely Browning would not have told Miss
Wedgwood this on August 20, only a few hours after the
visit to the pass, if his great plan for the poem occurred at
the same hour he was enjoying the take-off of a hawk, and
have waited until October 3 to tell her "the whole of that
poem, you enquire about" is well in my head.   Since the
poet had already discussed the poem with Miss Wedgwood
and Miss Blagden, and since they had become interested
enough in the projected poem to inquire about it, it is most
doubtful that Browning would not have forsaken all else to
depict the unusual event recounted by Rossetti on the day it
occurred.   Browning was not a secretive person.   He told
his correspondents, especially the women, almost everything
of any consequence in his life.   Furthermore, the statement
to Rossetti is not at all unlike some other of Browning's
after-thoughts, all of which demonstrate that he was not reluctant to exercise the poet's inclination for the picturesque.

The substance of Lehmann's words--which is that the
moral purpose and the various approaches to the evolution of
The Ring and the Book, if not the intricate final division,
were reached upon Browning's first reading the Old Yellow

Book in 1860--is in accord with the whole opening book of
the poem.   The large portion of Book I devoted to the discovery of the book illustrates how completely Browning visu-
alized the plan and purpose of the poem on the first day of
his acquaintance with Pompilia.   Though it is only hypothetical, I believe Browning's words to Rossetti constitute no
more than a desire to romanticize the inception of the poem
with a legendary setting of natural beauty, as he had otherwise romanticized the discovery of the Old Yellow Book in
the introduction to The Ring and the Book.   Mr. Raymond's
belief that the poem was started in 1864 is probably correct
insofar as it goes, but it does not take into consideration
two years of both sporadic and intensive preparation.
Browning never really got his mind off the story of Pompilia
from his first reading of it in 1860.   Unable to pass his attachment to the Old Yellow Book on to his fellow writers,
he began to study the book in 1862 in earnest, but probably
did not start the actual writing of the poem until 1864.
Whereas Rossetti's statement stands alone, every other
piece of evidence strengthens the argument against any possible connection between the Pass of Roland and the poem.
Finally, Lehmann's words and Browning's effective poetical
treatment of his initial acquaintance with Pompilia's tragic
story substantiate the belief that, from a memorable June
day in 1860, Browning carried in his mind the germ of the
organization and of the moral purpose of The Ring and the
Book.

Notes

1.   W. O. Raymond, "New Light on the Genesis of The Ring
and the Book, " Modern Language Notes, XLIII (1928),   357-
368.   Also available in The Infinite Moment (Toronto,   1965),
pp. 75-88.   Composition, in Mr. Raymond's article,   means
preparation--reading and studying--as well as writing.

2.   W. M. Rossetti, Rossetti Papers 1862 to 1870 (London,
1903), p. 302.

3.   W. C. DeVane, A Browning Handbook (New York, 1935),
p. 284; 2d ed. (1955), pp. 321-323; Raymond, "New Light, "
pp. 357-368; A. K. Cook, A Commentary upon Browning's
"The Ring and the Book" (London, 1920), pp. 275-278.

4.   Rudolf Lehmann, An Artist's Reminiscences (London,
        1894), p. 224.

5. Raymond, "New Light, " pp. 365-367; Infinite Moment,
p. 86; DeVane, Handbook, p. 284; 2d ed. , p. 320; Cook,
Commentary, pp. 277-278.

6. Mrs. Sutherland Orr, Life of Robert Browning (London,
1891), II, 377-378.

7. Robert Browning and Julia Wedgwood ... Their Letters,
ed. Richard Curle (New York, 1937), p. 79.

8. Letters of Robert Browning, ed. T. L. Hood (New
Haven, 1933), p. 82.

9. In a letter to me, Mr. Raymond has since expressed
the opinion that Browning was working on the poem earlier
than 1864.

10. Letters of Robert Browning to Miss Isa Blagden, col-
lected by A. J. Armstrong (Waco, 1923), pp. 63-65. Also
available in Dearest Isa: Robert Browning's Letters to Isa-
bella Blagden, ed. E. C. McAleer (Austin, 1951), p. 124.

11. [As DeVane and Raymond have moved closer to my
position on earlier preparation for the poem, I have moved
closer to their position on later composition. Because the
second half of the quotation--"I am about a long poem to be
something remarkable... work at it hard"--was mistakenly
attached by A. J. Armstrong to letter (57), December 19,
1862, my documentary argument was weakened. McAleer
has shown that the fragment from which the quotation was
taken properly belongs to letter (78), March 18, 1865.]

12. Orr, Life, II, 377-378; McAleer, p. 193.

13. William Allingham: A Diary, ed. H. Allingham and D.
Radford (London, 1907), pp. 127-128.

14. Letters to Isa Blagden, p. 140; McAleer, p. 263. [A
mistake in the first reference by Browning, but a more complete account of the whole matter may now be given. Browning began writing the poem in October 1864 (Rossetti, p. 302).
He himself first recorded on July 8, 1865, that "since au-
tumn" he had composed 8, 400 lines (Hood, p. 85). By November 1, 1865, the number of lines had reached 15, 000
(Allingham, pp. 127-128), scarcely over a year, and by May
19, 1866, 16, 000, "less than two years" (McAleer, p. 239).
Apparently, though Browning was surely estimating lines,

nothing more was written before April 23, 1867, when the
report was still 16,000 lines (McAleer, p. 263). But in
May 1867 an additional 2,000 lines made the total 18,000
(Curle, p. 126). And the poem exceeded 20,000 lines by
July 19, 1867 (Hood, p. 114), a jump of 4,000 lines in three
months, although it was not until March 15, 1868, that Browning told Rossetti the number of lines was 20,000 (Rossetti,
p. 302). Without a title as late as July 30, 1868, by September 2, 1868, the poem was planned for publication in
four monthly volumes. It went to press on October 10, 1868,
and the first volume was ready for the public on November
21, 1868 (DeVane). As DeVane says, it would be an error
to believe that Browning wrote the poem straight through
without considerable later alterations. For example, it
would have been impossible for the first 8,400 lines, com-
prising the first five books, or the first 15,000 lines, com-
prising a little more than the first nine books but short of
the Pope's monologue, not to suffer radical change in the
subsequent three years of composition.]

15.   [Circumstantial evidence suggests that Browning may
have written as many as twice 21,116 lines for The Ring and
the Book. When complaining to Julia Wedgwood that he "had
to do all this scribbling" on the completed poem without her
as an accustomed amanuensis, Browning adds: "And how
much more that you will never see!" (Curle, p. 162; italics
added) But, independent of this statement, it is the unim-
peded flow of Browning's words of which I am thinking. Almost casually we accept the report that 15,000 lines were
composed between October 1864 and November 1, 1865--just
over twelve months from the first reported composition--
without bothering about the long lapses of time thereafter before new lines were added. Certainly the ease with which
the poet enters into elaborate, often irrelevant digressions
as well as the rapid movement forward of his narrative confirms a mind steeped in research of every imaginable range,
a mind so eager for expression the three hours allotted early
each morning to composition seem insufficient floodgates.
At a time when so much favorable criticism is appearing on
The Ring and the Book, are we not also obliged to seek reasons for the rough transitions, undeveloped passages, and
disjointed parts which may be attributed to desired but un-
skillful excising?
     No one has tried more admirably to justify the or-
ganization of The Ring and the Book than B. R. McElderry,
Jr. , "The Narrative Structure of The Ring and the Book, "
Research Studies of the State College of Washington, XI

(1943), 193-233.   But if one were to offer a qualification to
his thesis it might best be the hypothesis that Browning
chanced on as well as planned on the distribution of his materials so that no episode would be excessively labored.
One of McElderry's strongest arguments centers on the
skillful economy Browning imposed on his twelve essential
episodes: for example, Caponsacchi greatly enlarges upon
the flight; Pompilia briefly mentions it.   But what if in initial composition Browning had allowed both characters to
expand upon the flight, later to decide Caponsacchi's words
far surpassed Pompilia's in dramatic poignancy?   He could
thus have improved upon the total effect of the poem by elimi-
nating the repetitiveness of Pompilia's words while tightening
the overall organization of the poem.   If Browning chose to
write as many as forty to fifty thousand lines over a period
of four to eight years, he thereby sought an unequalled opportunity to select the best poetic treatment of which he was
capable for almost every incident in the Old Yellow Book.
In so doing, however, he also courted the inevitable hazard
of leaving noticeable gaps in the continuity of individual monologues.
        The only known manuscript copy of The Ring and the
Book offers little or no assistance in speculation of the above
order; and until variant manuscripts or work sheets (not
likely under Browning's watchful eye) are found, one would
do well to go on believing with McElderry that "if Browning
has not altogether succeeded in achieving a consistent whole,
he has not altogether failed," rather than believing with De-
Vane that Browning's "artistry is final and consummate."
When the demand was on Browning, he was, as we know
from the many incomparably effective passages in The Ring
and the Book, capable of distilling his thoughts, but the la-
bors of distillation went mightily against his mental patterns.
Moreover, Browning sometimes simply gave up--as in Book
XII--just when the greatest demands were placed on his talent.   Perhaps through nagging weariness and "pretty financial
offers" he was persuaded not to take the additional years he
had promised to bring the poem to a satisfactory conclusion.
Whatever the cause, it is only that we would have a strong
poem made stronger that we speculate on why Browning did
not go still farther in excising or improving upon other lines
of irrelevance, tautology, melodrama, and prolixity.   Even
Browning himself seems to have anticipated and attempted to
answer the question for us when he wrote, "Out of the long
twenty [some thousand lines] aforesaid I honestly don't think
and cannot but hope, as an artist, that not a paragraph is
extractable as an episode or piece complete in itself" (Hood,

p. 128). But in a not uncommon circumlocution, Browning
is really not talking about excising or improving.]

16. Griffin and Minchin, The Life of Robert Browning (London, 1910) pp. 229-231; Orr, Life, II, 379.

17. August 20: Wedgwood Letters, p. 43; corrected in De-
Vane's Handbook, 2d ed. , p. 322.

18. This etching does not help in the present case, but it
gives rise to questions which as yet cannot be answered.
Professor Hood's use of the etching to fix the date of Browning's visit to the pass on the 27th is no longer acceptable,
unless there were two visits. It has been suggested that the
sister returned to sketch the pass, but she could have
sketched it from memory. As for the handwriting on the
sketch it appears to be Browning's, and it could have been
written later. There was little at the pass to draw Browning back for a visit within a week, judged by the etching and
the comments on the first visit. Apparently the etching is
misdated, or it was drawn a week later.

19. Henry James, W. W. Story and his Friends (Boston,
1903), II, 154-155.

20. Alfred Lord Tennyson, A Memoir by his Son (New York,
1897), II, 16.

21. [Although DeVane, in his revised Handbook (pp. 321-
323), suggested a possible reconciliation between Rossetti's
and Lehmann's accounts for the genesis of The Ring and the
Book, it is quite clear he as well as Raymond (The Infinite
Moment, pp. 84-87) continued to reject Lehmann's reminis-
cence that Browning reached a decision to divide the poem
into twelve chapters in Florence in 1860. But DeVane did
sense my reason for reviving Lehmann's remarks and wrote
accordingly:

> With what avidity Browning read the book, and how
> ... his imagination reconstructed the whole tragedy,
> ... he has told vividly in the first part of the poem.
> But from the history of the composition of The Ring
> and the Book as we know it, it would be a mistake
> to think that the whole conception of the gigantic
> poem came to him in that moment. Browning's
> moral judgments upon the characters and their ac-
> tions were probably made as soon as he read the

> Old Yellow Book, but his method of telling his
> story and his detailed plan were probably not ar-
> rived at until 1864, when the actual writing began.
> (Handbook, p. 320)

Most satisfactory with one exception, DeVane's position on
the genesis of the poem may be taken by almost anyone who
is also permitted to believe the "method of telling the story
and the detailed plan" could have been devised any time between 1860 and 1864.

It is understandable why neither DeVane nor Raymond
wished to sacrifice the association of le pas de Roland with
Browning's decision to write twelve cantos.   But it is not so
evident why they minimize the early investigations Browning
made in Arezzo and Rome; all references in the poem, dia-
ries, and the letters to the inspiration except Rossetti's;
and the unbroken interest Browning evinced in the Old Yellow
Book from the day he found it.   DeVane recognized Rossetti's
unreliability, if not his propensity for editorializing, and
balanced this flaw with Browning's unsure memory.   But we
do not know when Browning spoke to Lehmann, and it may
not have been Browning's memory at all.   So, from the
known history of the composition, there seems to be no conclusive reason for not believing that Browning conceived the
plan of his poem in 1860 as Lehmann reported, or in 1864
as Rossetti reported, or at any time between these two
specified dates, a span which would conform with the normal
functioning of the poetic mind.]

2.

THE CLARITY OF BROWNING'S RING METAPHOR

Reprinted with permission from Publications of The Modern Language Association of America, LXIII (1948), 1276-82. Supplementary material is indicated by brackets.

Browning's Ring metaphor has remained for seventy-nine years one of the most baffling figures of speech in English poetry. [1] His critics do not differ concerning either the formation of a gold ring or the poet's intention in his metaphor, but they differ greatly on the applicability of the metaphor. One group believes Browning to have said that the contribution made by his fancy disappeared at the completion of the poem. Its members therefore insist that Browning, in The Ring and the Book, reproduced faithfully the facts of the Old Yellow Book. They have attempted to explain that he was at once a scientific historian in his treatment of fact and a poet in his treatment of truth. They have been unwilling to discredit his historical accuracy or to admit that he was not first of all a poet. The best illustration and the apparent foundation for all other similar comments is supplied by Mrs. Sutherland Orr:

> The story of the Franceschini case, as Mr. Browning relates it, forms a circle of evidence to its one central truth; and this circle was constructed in the manner in which the worker in Etruscan gold prepares the ornamental circlet which will be worn as a ring. The pure metal is too soft to bear hammer or file; it must be mixed with alloy to gain the necessary power of resistance. The ring once formed and embossed, the alloy is disengaged, and a pure gold ornament remains. Mr. Browning's material was also inadequate to his purpose, though from a different cause. It was too hard. It was 'pure crude fact,' secreted from the fluid being of the men and women whose experience it had formed.

> In its existing state it would have broken up under
> the artistic attempt to weld and round it. He sup-
> plied an alloy, the alloy of fancy, or--as he also
> calls it--of one fact more: this fact being the echo
> of those past existences awakened within his own.
> He breathed into the dead record the breath of his
> own life; and when his ring of evidence had re-
> formed, first in elastic then in solid strength,
> here delicately incised, there broadly stamped
> with human thought and passion, he could cast
> fancy aside, and bid his readers recognize in
> what he set before them unadulterated human
> truth. (Handbook to Browning's Works [London,
> 1899], pp. 76-77)

The other group also accepts Browning's apparent literal meaning, but its members do not believe that Browning's
fancy disappeared with the renovating wash. They are familiar with his method of using the material of the old book
in a free manner, never allowing it to hamper his invention;
they know that it is impossible for a poet's imaginative contribution to be isolated and expelled from his poetry. Consequently, they do not believe that Browning reproduced faithfully the facts of his source. Though uniformly overlooked
by later critics in this group who were also finding a discrepancy in the metaphor, probably the best illustration by
an early moderate critic appeared as an anonymous review,
"Mr. Browning's Latest Poetry, " The North British Review,
LI (October 1869), 97-126:

> Bottini is no more astray... than the poet himself
> is in his comparison between ring-making and
> poetry.... The gold is the dead matter of the
> poem; the alloy is the 'surplusage of soul,' which
> the poet projects into the dead matter to make it
> malleable; the embossing and shaping is the poetic
> form; the spirt of acid by which the alloy is washed
> away is some final act of the poet, by which he re-
> moves all traces of himself, and leaves the poem
> quite impersonal. This Mr. Browning claims to
> have done.... But the reader, who will see that each
> speaker in these idyls talks unmistakeable Brown-
> ingese,... will justifiably wonder what spirt it is
> which has caused that which was only just now al-
> loy suddenly to have become pure unalloyed gold.
> ... For in truth, we cannot find that Mr. Browning
> makes any special spirt to clear away his own ad-

ditions to the story, except an argument to prove
that the alloy is no alloy, but spirit and life. According to him, historical facts are gold, but gold
in the ingot. The gold is unformed; the fact un-
vivified, lifeless, unremembered. An old and dead
fact can only be re-created by being infused, trans-
fused, inspired, by the living force of a creative,
or rather re-creative, fancy, which is related to
fact as alloy is related to gold in making the ring--
necessary to prepare it for the hammer and file
which are to give it artistic shape and imagery....
However true all this may be, it does not seem to
account for any double action of the poet. The alloy is added by one act.... But whatever alloy the
poet first contributes remains in the perfect poem,
unless he writes it all over again. There are not
two distinct acts--first of infusing surplusage of
soul, and next of washing it away. Here, as elsewhere, Mr. Browning seems, of set purpose, to
let an element of incompleteness, or even error,
remain in his similes. [2]

Extremists of this group think that the poet has been flagrant-
ly dishonest and unjust, whereas the remainder conclude that
he has unconsciously reversed his meaning or has "pressed
too hard his admirable metaphor" (Cook, Commentary, p. 2).
The best illustration of vitriolic opposition to Browning's
metaphor and one generally unaccepted is provided by Frances Theresa Russell. In writing about the "poet's word for
the relation of his epical production to its inspiring source, "
she says:

And that word he made emphatic and unequivocal....
His reconstructing fancy was declared... no irresponsible guesswork, but a thorough and honest
quest in search of the hidden truth; an entirely
successful quest, we are assured, a triumphant
pursuit and capture of those shrouded verities that
had hitherto defied investigation. That is to say,
the 'ring' presented the facts of the 'book' without
wrenching or falsification, but with the just explanation that rewards patient study and clear insight. It is not fiction but authentic history, poetic
in form and spirit but as truthful as any encyclopedia....   All of which leads up to and requires
this present, if not final ironic situation--that in
the interests of that very truth to which Browning

offers such eloquent lip-service, we are obliged to
declare that... he did in paying his homage to reality say it with words rather than deeds....   That
Browning's headstrong emotionalism should have
betrayed him into flagrant injustice is not strange,
but it is curious indeed that the whole flock of critics should have trotted along so docilely after him.
They... permit him... to weave a conscienceless
web of falsity....

In the first place, Browning muddles his own metaphor until it becomes a treacherous quagmire,...
[and] in this gratuitous performance he so thoroughly
misinterprets himself and misleads his readers that
practically the reverse of his assertions constitutes
the actual case.   (One Word More on Browning
[Palo Alto, 1927], pp. 110-111, 113, 122, 114; "Gold
and Alloy, " Studies in Philology, XXI [July 1924],
467)

Browning compares his method of creation with the
process involved in the formation of a gold ring. [3]   Pure gold
is soft and not subject to permanent embossing.   The artificer must mix with the unworkable gold an alloy [metal], [4] so
that he may have a manageable mass susceptible of tempering.   As soon as he has worked his gold and alloy metal into
a homogeneous mixture, he then molds them into a delicately
designed ring (I. 458-463, 141-145).   As gold is dug or
gained from the earth before ring-making may begin, Browning first dug from the book the pure and unadulterated facts
(I. 458-463).   The facts, however, were no more serviceable
to him than pure gold is to the artificer before he adds an
alloy metal.   So Browning mixed with his source material
"something else surpassing" the facts of the book, to make
them malleable and firm to file. [4]   His comparison means
that whatever he found in the book was to him what pure
gold is to the artificer.   As the metal, before the ring was
forged, "lay gold,... / So, in this book lay absolutely truth,
/ Fanciless fact" (I. 141-145).   It should be noted that
Browning does not say "absolute truth, " a reading which
probably misled Hodell, but either "absolutely [free from
mixture; pure] truth, fanciless fact" or "absolutely [certainly]
truth. "

Before explaining the last act of the artificer, we
should mark a distinction in Browning's use of the word
truth.   What the critics call Browning's claim to "fidelity

to truth" hinges solely upon the meaning Browning attached
to the word truth, and upon one passage in Book I.   Browning used the word in at least two different ways.   First, he
applies it to mere statement of fact or alleged fact.   He considers any statement found in the book to be a fact or truth.
No statement is necessarily represented as true or false,
but each is indisputably a part of the source.   Secondly, he
applies truth to the conclusion he or any one else might draw
from the total evidence of the book.   The critics have not
called attention to this distinction.   Yet, in Book I, the poet
uses truth almost exclusively in the sense of fact or factual
evidence--age, date, action, broken wall, rough road, boy
baby, elopement, trial, execution.   Before referring to the
contents of the book as "absolutely truth, " Browning calls
the book "pure crude fact" (I. 35, 86) and says, "I had mastered the contents, knew the whole truth / Gathered together,
bound up in this book" (I. 117-118).   He further says, "This
is the bookful; thus far take the truth, / The untempered
gold, the fact untampered with, / The mere ring-metal ere
the ring be made!"   (I. 364-366) Six words have now been
used synonymously by the poet: book, fact, truth, contents,
ring-metal, gold.   Browning moreover reveals that he took
his book to Rome to try "truth's power / On likely people"
(I. 423-429).   "Have you met such names? / Is a tradition
extant of such facts?"   The Romans responded, "Why, you'll
waste / Your pains... [on] names and facts thus old. "   Here
is evidence of a pattern which pervades the first book and
echoes throughout the poem--a pattern of indiscriminate exchange of the words fact and truth.

When asked by the Romans whether his narrative was
from the book or mere poetry, Browning answered with one
statement which tells specifically how much of his poem is
from the book:

> This [the OYB] was it from, my fancy with those facts,
> I used to tell the tale;... such alloy,
> Such substance of me interfused the gold [fact]
> Which, wrought into a shapely ring [poem] therewith,
> Hammered and filed,...
> Lay ready for the renovating wash
> O' the water.   "How much of the tale was true?"
> I disappeared; the book grew all in all;
> The lawyers' pleadings swelled back to their size, --...
> Lovers of dead truth [fanciless fact], did ye fare the
> worse?

> Lovers of live truth [fanciful fact], found ye false
>   my tale?
>
> (I. 679-697)

At the beginning of Book I, Browning says that the artificer,
after effecting a "manageable mass" with gold and gold's
alloy metal, [copper], works it into a delicately designed
ring.   But then,

> Oh, there's repristination [restoration to an ori-
>   ginal state]! Just a spirt
> O' the proper fiery acid o'er its face,
> And forth the alloy unfastened flies in fume;
> WHILE SELF-SUFFICIENT NOW, THE SHAPE
>   REMAINS.
>
> (I. 23-26; capital letters added)

This passage explains the last act involved in the formation
of a gold ring.   A fiery acid is spurted over the face of the
ring to remove the alloy metal, copper. [5] Browning would
have us think that he similarly removed himself from the
FACE of the poem.   He cannot, I think, mean that he disappeared entirely from the poem; and critics have probably
gone astray in speculating on how he could have disappeared.
Just as the artificer restores to the FACE or surface of a
gold ring a film of pure gold, so Browning as an artist restored to the surface of the poem a pure narrative of the
book, knowing however that his fancy had contributed to the
interior structure the quality which makes the poem durable
and shapely.   He explains:

> so I wrought
> This arc, by furtherance of such alloy,
> And so, by one spirt, take away its TRACE
> Till, justifiably golden, rounds my ring.
>
> (I. 1386-89; capital letters added)

Browning liked to believe that no TRACE of his fancy
was discernible on the surface of the poem.   The notion of
the poet's complete disappearance from the poem is based
upon faulty knowledge of ring-making.   If an artificer takes
a ring, made of gold and copper, and entirely removes the
copper from it with an acid, he is clearly back right where
he started.   The gold again becomes soft and not subject to
tempering, and the ring becomes a mere spongy mass of
pure gold less serviceable than solid gold.   No miracle is
known to metallurgy which will remove the alloy metal and

leave the ring just as if the alloy metal were still present.
If the ring is to remain serviceable, tempered, and durable,
the copper must be retained. To give the appearance of
pure gold, a spurt of acid on the surface will remove all
external copper and leave a film of pure gold.

By the same token, Browning could not have written
his poem, mixing with the facts of the book "something of
his own, " and then disappear, leaving no part of himself:

> From the book, yes; thence bit by bit I dug
> The lingot truth [fact], that memorable day,
> Assayed and knew my piecemeal gain was gold, --
> Yes; BUT FROM SOMETHING ELSE SURPASSING
>   THAT,
> SOMETHING OF MINE WHICH, MIXED UP WITH
>   THE MASS,
> Made it bear hammer and be firm to file.
>   (I: 458-463; capital letters added)

To Browning the facts as they appeared in the book became,
upon the completion of the poem, merely the pure gold surface.   His insistence upon the figure of gold does not show
how highly he valued the contents of the old volume.   On the
contrary, it demonstrates how little he valued them. [6]   It was
his fancy which provided the "surpassing" value.   The word
gold, with its usual meaning of precious, has no doubt added
to our confusion.   Edward Dowden was the first to say, "We
are compelled to reverse the meaning of the metaphor...the
gold is contributed by Browning's imagination, the alloy is
the fact. "[7]   But to Browning gold meant no more than any
other pristine metal.   Throughout Book I he warns us to remember that gold is unserviceable until mixed with an alloy
metal.   In his poem the copper, [his imaginative and interpretive addition], is of surpassing value.

Knowing that Browning's poem presents upon the surface of the printed page almost every fact of the Old Yellow
Book, we are asked only to think of those facts as we think
of the gold surface of a ring.   The facts are supported beneath by an alloy metal (his fancy) which remains hidden in
the gold ring (his poem), but which gives the facts both durability and fixed shape.   Pure gold on the surface of a ring
is actually a camouflage, but the inexperienced purchaser
may never know it, if he is not told.   Browning, however,
immediately tells his reader that he will find the poet's fancy
beneath the surface of the poem, giving both form and sub-

stance to the narrative.

As the contradictory facts of any trial come to the
surface, so do the contradictory facts of the poem come to
the surface.   Never once, [it may be argued], does Browning say that he was faithful to the facts.   He or his character reiterates that such and such is a truth, but the poet
never says that he believes it to be a finally trustworthy
fact.   His purpose was to present the facts in as many different lights as they could be presented.   He realized that
regardless of how greatly he "wrenched" the facts, they
could not be harmed as much as the witnesses and the lawyers had harmed them.

Browning accepts ART as the one possible way of
speaking truth.   His artistic way is through the addition of
fancy or imagination, which is God-given, like the gift of
prophet and seer, and possessed only by those "called of
God. "   Final truth, which God alone is capable of revealing,
is, for Browning, the only goal worth striving toward.   Mere
[human] knowledge, though not rejected in the poem, is partially incapacitated because of its restricted use and falls
before the potency of divine truth as revealed through love.
Man, with his limited love and his dependence upon knowledge
or fact, is incapable of seeing or knowing the final truth.
But, with the assistance of art, which in this poem is the
art of Browning, mankind may feel the partial or diluted
truth which proceeds from God.   In their search for facts
all the characters of the poem, including the Pope, 8 missed
the one agent which might have revealed the final truth.   Because they were still relying upon knowledge, looking for
facts, they were unable to feel truth.

Browning profoundly believed that mankind could find
in the poets inspiration and illumination leading to beauty and
truth.   He considered poetry an art expressing mankind's
deepest convictions concerning the most important interests
of life.   In poetry the mind not only sees truth but feels it.
It is not when Browning argues or presents facts that he
proves, but when he sees as a poet and conveys his vision
to the reader through a poetic medium.   In poetry the fact
itself is comparatively unimportant, since there is hardly
any fact so insignificant that it does not grow poetic under
the intensity of emotion.

The Ring and the Book is an artistic creation, not, as
has been asserted, because it is "authentic history, poetic in

form and spirit but as truthful as any encyclopedia, " but because Browning created it as other poems are created.   He
thought that in transforming "dead truth" (fanciless fact) into
"live truth" (fanciful fact) he was revealing the "inmost glint"
of the facts of his source.   His fancy did not need to search
for hidden truth, because it had received a revelation of truth
from the source [itself].   His fancy was capable of "lifting to
very heaven. "9   From that transcendent point of vantage,
he was capable of feeling truths no "mortal ever in entirety
saw. "   Mere "patient study and clear insight" could never
have rewarded Browning with a "capture of those shrouded
verities. "   For him a God-given divination "lighted his eye,
and let him have his way with the characters of the Book. "
He recognized no verities within the Old Yellow Book; they
were within the heart, his own and the hearts of his readers.
Browning was therefore justified in using the figure of the
gold and alloy.   The experience of the poet was the alloy
which, added to the crude fact, made The Ring and the Book
one of the supreme studies of human nature in the literature
of the world. 10

Notes

1.   [Submitted in 1940 as part of a doctoral thesis under the
direction of W. C. DeVane and read before the Victorian
Group of MLA in Detroit in 1947, Essay Two was published
in PMLA in 1948.   Its impetus and initial substance were
derived from a chance remark by a graduate student in
chemistry at Cornell University.   A reversal of my master's
thesis at the University of Kentucky, in which Browning was
accused of not understanding his own figurative language and
of not being faithful to the facts of the Old Yellow Book, the
new interpretation, with its metallurgical basis, necessitated
a rejection of all antecedent interpretations, including A. G.
Drachmann's serious spadework.   Its acceptance and rejection in subsequent critical essays by others provide the materials for Essay Four.   That Essay Two, among other
things, was an attempt to vindicate intelligence in a poet
who often despaired of human intelligence, therefore a refutation in part of a very important theme of The Ring and the
Book, has generally been overlooked.]

2.   [As might be expected, the same shrewd but sometimes
contentious author also writes discerningly and at length on
almost all other matters which loom large in current criticism of The Ring and the Book.   To the original note the

following quotations are consequently being added:

> With a timely consciousness that has hitherto
> failed to be generally understood, he has set him-
> self...to repeat what he had to say in a tongue
> more comprehensible. (pp. 97-98) With a second-
> ary sympathy for creeds which he does not profess,
> and for habits which he disallows, he takes a spe-
> cial pleasure, and shows an extraordinary facility,
> in throwing himself into the states of mind of the
> professors of such creeds, or the thralls of such
> habits. (p. 100) Mr. Browning thinks in blocks,
> by images and pictures, not by abstract notions,
> and forms his ideas not by clearing away the super-
> fluous, but by conglomerating all possible details.
> (p. 101) Truth, he tells us, comes out, not in
> the long-drawn collections of reason, but in the
> sudden interjections of feeling. (p. 102) Life then,
> made up as it is of the empty contrivances of rea-
> son, and the imperfect utterances of passion, be-
> comes itself vanity, and would be merely a failure
> and a jest if it were not for its teleological con-
> sequences. (p. 103) He jumbles up its comic and
> tragic sides, and illustrates them by the first
> metaphors which come to hand. (pp. 103-104) The
> concluding canto of the present poem is like the
> conclusion of a firework--an empty tube and a
> stick. (p. 106) The satirical element in Mr.
> Browning's mind is strong; but he is too serious
> a theologian and moralist to be a genuine satirist.
> (p. 107) Mr. Browning, in analysing as he does
> the processes and the characters of men's minds,
> attributes to himself a kind of infallibility. (p. 107)
> He considers that the artist is the real and only
> truth-teller. For him the fictions of art, combined
> with the facts of nature, are a higher grade of
> truth than the facts themselves. Moreover, all
> human attempts, by means of logic or theories of
> probabilities, or criticism, to sift and tell the
> truth, are failures. (p. 108) Hitherto he had not
> ventured on dealing thus with any of the more ar-
> ticulate and defined characters of history.... But
> in the present poem he has introduced a person as
> well known as Pope Innocent XII, and has assigned
> him a long and searching soliloquy. The main out-
> lines of the character show a careful regard of
> Ranke; the fillings-up smack rather of the poet's

surplusage of soul than of any probable opinions of
any Pope. Innocent XII would hardly have pro-
pounded as part of his creed the opinions of modern Universalism, not have gone far towards iden-
tifying God with Nature; nor, because he was the
first of his line who exhibited either justice or
mercy to the Jansenists, would he necessarily have
proceeded to compare an 'irregular noble scape-
grace,' whom he meant to praise, with Augustine,
or a 'fox-faced horrible priest,' whom he abhorred,
with Loyola; nor, without the gift of prophecy,
would he have alluded to and joined in the condemnation of modern civilisation in the Syllabus of
Pius IX; nor, without a kind of presentiment of
Hegel's doctrine of the genesis of being out of not-
being, would he have formulated his fine theory of
the restoration of faith in the latter days through
the antagonism of doubt. (pp. 108-109) For, after
all, the truth which the artist contends for is
his own ideal--himself. (p. 109) Perhaps the spirt
of acid which he speaks of is this suppression of
the individual and secret personality which, after
so many efforts, he had found to be incommuni-
cable, and the determination only to communicate
so much of himself as he can render intelligible
in the common tongue. (p. 110) He always tried
to be a dramatist; but he is, and ever will be, a
critical poet. (p. 110) The main characteristics
of the poet... show how it is that, in spite of his
theological bias and undeniable Christianity, he is
acceptable to the materialistic and positivist thought
of the day.... his decided contempt for reason in
comparison with the sentiments must endear him
to all friends of Comte's law, 'que l'esprit doit
être subordonné au coeur.' (p. 110-111) Another
trait of this poem is its hybrid character.... The
monologues are dramatic, because the speakers are
placed in dramatic situations, where the event depends upon their suasive power. They are narrative; for they set before us the history, not the
actual development, of an event. But they are
eminently lyric, because their chief interest is
reflective, lying not in the deed or narrative itself, but in the psychological states of the speakers,
and in the various hues which the history assumes
when refracted through their various minds. (p. 112)
The poet gazes on lyric love,... and the well-known

features are glorified into those of the Redeemer,
dropping down 'to toil for man, to suffer or to
die.' For to him, poetry, love, and religion, are
but three aspects of one great creative force, not
logic or reason, though he identifies it with the
Logos. (p. 113) This love at first sight is but
one stone of the temple of Lyric Love. The whole
constitutes a complete philosophy, distilled from
Plato, and coming down to us in a succession of
poets, of whom Dante, Petrarch, and Shakespeare
in his sonnets, are the chief. (p. 114) The Greek
chorus represented a whole population; and Mr.
Browning introduces populations--half Rome, and
the other half-Rome.... When philosophical criticism regards the hero of literature simply as the
spokesman of his age, it proposes to writers the
problem of making the characters they invent not
individual and idiosyncratic, but samples of common opinion. (p. 115) Some people think that the
day of novelists has passed its meridian, and that
the sun of journalists is about to rise. For society, they suppose, is growing tired of the exceptional, and is beginning to feel its interest centre
in the common action of mankind. (p. 116) Sen-
sationalism may be the last fitful glare of the novel
of exceptional character and situation, and journal-
ism the first twilight and the model of a school
about to arise. Mr. Browning's poem is cousin-
german to a series of newspaper articles. (pp. 116-
117) Then all classes contribute their comments,
and improve the occasion to enforce their various
social theories, their belief in the corruption of
the aristocracy, their distrust of trial by jury.
(p. 117) Although Mr. Browning makes use of
these expositors of opinion, he does not cease to
accompany their utterances with a running commentary of his own, sometimes expressed, sometimes
understood, forming a perpetual gloss on the text,
and ever making us alive to the relationship in
which the sentiments dramatically expressed, stand
to those of the poet himself. He writes with a
didactic purpose.... But besides the peril of making one's-self a common enemy by calling all
things by their right names, such a way of deliver-
ing his message would be obnoxious to the common
charge against all human testimony and human
speech. He must therefore deliver his message

in the way of art, which 'nowise speaks to men,
only to mankind,' which tells truth obliquely by
painting the picture that shall breed the thought,
and thus both satisfy the imagination and save the
soul. (pp. 117-118) In his more extensive studies,
where the reaction of the characters on each other
had to be exhibited, he has always shown a deficiency in the power of inventing plots. (p. 119)
He seized on his treasure, the old book, gloated
over it, talked of it, investigated the records connected with it, brooded over it for four years, and
told its story over again. (p. 119) Guido is Mr.
Browning's Iago; in him we have his ideal of wickedness. Guido is not a man of strong passions
urged by his nature to vice. He is, on the contrary, an artificial man, one whose hinges turn
not on the pivot of passion but on that of reason.
(p. 121) Mr. Browning tells us miles more about
them than we are told about Hotspur or Cordelia;
yet they come miles behind Hotspur and Cordelia
in definiteness, dramatic energy, and elevation of
individual character. (p. 122) Guido's speech to
his confessors before execution is one of the most
powerful in the poem. But perhaps the most satisfactory on the whole is the monologue of the aged
Pope.... The poet himself speaks behind the
mask. It is not however that the poet becomes Ro-
manized, but the pope becomes tinctured with his
presenter.... In this canto of the poem, consequently, Mr. Browning's whole circle of teaching, feeling and criticism may be most conveniently studied.
He will be found to possess great unity of principle.
(p. 123) Special in verse as Mr. Carlyle's in
prose, his felicitous power of working at once upon
contradictory models, consciously copying Euripides
but producing something even more like Aeschylus
and, in attempts to advance beyond the most advanced of the Greek dramatists, falling back upon
the mythical beginnings of the Greek drama. His
great virtue is that he has an impetus, a rush,
which, to a great extent, hides his contradictory
faults. It carries the reader over pages of 'prose
swell'd to verse, verse loitering into prose,' over
sheets where thoughts lie jumbled together, close
packed and without room to move.... If there
were not positive evidence to the contrary, Mr.
Browning might be considered a careless poet,

bestowing ample pains on amassing his materials,
but little on their organization. But whatever
trouble he may take he evidently lacks the power
to give any great unity to the multifariousness of
his farrago.... But to the intelligence he repays
minute study. He presents a boundless chaos of
accidental knowledge. (pp. 124-125) The difference
is that the burlesque of Beaumont becomes serious
in Mr. Browning.... Yet there is more to admire
than to forgive in Mr. Browning. Like Plato he
is a poet because he is a poetical philosopher,
though it may be a question whether his philosophy
does not tend to strangle his poetry. His powers
may be guessed by the opposition he has encoun-
tered. Smashers clip gold, not copper. But to some
his very power is repulsive. There are still many
wise men, and men of taste, who would have their
teeth drawn or toes amputated rather than read
him. And those who can appreciate him are often
so struck with the multifariousness of his merits
in detail that, without appraising him higher than
he deserves, they are apt in criticising him to
raise expectations which the reading of his poems
will fail to satisfy. (p. 126)]

3.   Mrs. Browning reveals that Browning visited a Roman
artist-jeweler (The Letters of Elizabeth Barrett Browning,
ed. Kenyon [New York, 1897], II, 354-355); Browning writes
in the ninth line of the poem, "(Craftsmen instruct me). "

4.   [Technically, alloy was the resulting solution or mixture
with which Browning first molded the poem: the facts of the
Old Yellow Book were the base metal, gold; the imagination
of the poet provided the copper which made the pure crude
facts malleable and, because harder, suitable to hammering
and the incising of the file. It is interesting that the anonymous author saw clearly wherein Browning's fancy (copper)
made the dead facts (gold) malleable and thus suited to shaping and designing. Mrs. Orr became baffled one step short
of his progress. After she had recognized that soft gold
"must be mixed with alloy to gain the necessary power of
resistance, " she then chose to equate Browning's facts, not
with the soft gold (even the honey of which he wrote), but
with the term hard facts. The anonymous author himself
faltered in his third step--he did not know, or take time to
remember, that a gold ring has only a face of pure gold,
that copper remains in mixture with gold throughout the

interior.]

5. "Gold-copper alloys tarnish on exposure to air owing to oxidation of the copper, and blacken on heating in air from the same cause. This oxidized coating may be removed and the colour of fine gold (not that of the original alloy) produced by plunging [spraying would do the same] the metal into dilute acids or alkaline solutions, the operation being technically known as 'blanching. ' The colour of some alloys may be improved without previous oxidation by dissolving out some copper by acids, a film of pure gold being thus left on the outside which can be burnished. French jewelers use a hot solution of two parts of nitrate of potash, one part of alum, and one part of common salt for this purpose. " (T. K. Rose, The Metallurgy of Gold [London, 1915], p. 35)

6. [See Essay Three for a clarification and reaffirmation of this essential attribute of the alloy metal, that is, the copper of the ring, the imagination of the poet.]

7. The Ring and the Book, ed. Dowden (Oxford Edition, 1912), p. ix.

8. [See Essay Seven for a partial retraction of this charge against the Pope.]

9. [In the writing of this essay I was better informed on ring-making than on poetic inspiration, but it is odd that Robert Langbaum did not know I was sketchily paraphrasing the conclusion of Book I, when he asks if "poetic medium" meant immaterial medium, implies Milton's facts were exalted in nature while Browning's were corrupted, and wonders who was being "lifted" up to very heaven by Browning's art. ("The Importance of Fact, " Victorian Newsletter, No. 17 [Spring 1960], p. 14)]

10. [In keeping with a PMLA requirement of the time, William Riley Parker added the two summary sentences. I would have preferred for the second: The imagination of the poet was the copper which, added to the pure crude facts of gold, made The Ring and the Book one of the important studies of human nature in English literature.]

3.

ROBERT BROWNING: "OUR HUMAN SPEECH"

Reprinted with permission from The Victorian
Newsletter, Number 15 (Spring 1959), pp. 1-9.
Supplementary material is indicated by brackets.

Critical acceptance of The Ring and the Book as a
nineteenth-century poem of significance often includes observations which may be used to challenge the integrity of the
poem and the craftsmanship of its author.   For it is difficult
to consider as significant, though the judgment be offered in
the kindest spirit, a poem whose theme, pervading imagery,
and characters are believed not to be representative of the
poet's intent.   If Browning has said that he did not depart
from the facts of his source, the critics do well to question
the validity of his Ring metaphor, his theme, and his characters.   But the more effective the criticism the less significant the poem should become, and this conclusion many
Browning scholars seem reluctant to draw.   A. K. Cook,
for example, has written:

> The facts of the book were the jeweller's ore; the
> poet's fancy was the jeweller's alloy; his fancy
> mixed with the facts--the poet's poem--was the
> jeweller's ring.   Perhaps the admirable metaphor
> was pressed too hard.   Browning tells us repeatedly
> that just as, when the jeweller's art has been ex-
> ercised upon his ring, he disengages the alloy, so,
> when the poet has fashioned his poem, he will dis-
> engage his fancy from it.   But he does not disen-
> gage it, there is no 'repristination'; unlike the
> jeweller's alloy, the poet's fancy does not 'fly in
> fume,' it cannot (happily) be 'unfastened' from the
> facts.   (Commentary, p. 2)

J. E. Shaw has recorded similar observations:

> It cannot be denied that the personages in Browning's

39

great poem, The Ring and the Book, are of the
poet's own making, and he himself would have been
the first to acknowledge them as his own creatures.
On the other hand, his repeated assertions that, in
mingling his fancy with the material derived from
the Old Yellow Book, he has not misinterpreted the
facts contained in his source, and the insistence
upon the poet's historical fidelity by the editor of
the 'Book' and other critics, have been regarded
with suspicion. Indeed, the question has recently
been raised whether The Ring and the Book is not
a glorious misinterpretation of the Old Yellow
Book.

My own belief is that it is a glorious misinterpretation, but at the same time that the interpreter is
sincere. ("The 'Donna Angelicata' in The Ring and
the Book, " PMLA, XLI [March 1926], 55)

And recently Robert Langbaum has observed: "Another sign
of relativism is that Browning counted it such a virtue for
his poem to be based on 'pure crude fact. '... His truth had
to be taken seriously, which meant in a positivist age that
it had to have the facts behind it, had to emerge from the
facts. "[1] But when Mr. Langbaum comes to the use Browning's characters make of fact, he concludes: "The Pope
does not weigh argument against argument, fact against fact,
but cuts right through the facts to a sympathetic apprehension
of the motives and essential moral qualities behind the deeds.
... All the morally significant characters of the poem cut
through facts in the same way" (p. 141; The Poetry of Experience, pp. 120-121).

Characterizing much of the analysis of The Ring and
the Book, this conflict between historical accuracy and poetic
necessity imposes a limitation on the significance of the
poem that other critics have tried to remove. These critics
believe that Browning was fully conscious of the poetic use
to which he put his raw material, and they have sought by
interpretation of the poet's Ring metaphor to show that the
conflict between fact and fancy may be due to misunderstanding of a complicated figure of speech and to certain ambiguous statements from the poem. No one, however, has elaborated on Browning's dual use of the word truth to suggest
that a second misunderstanding may have added to the confusion into which the Ring metaphor and the interpretation
of the poem have fallen. Yet it can be advanced that Brown-

ing's practice, which entails the use of the word truth on
page after page of the poem with recurrent textual analyses,
is intended as an application of the metaphor as well as a
preparation for the concluding and possibly thematic passage
which begins:

> our human speech is naught,
> Our human testimony false, our fame
> And human estimation words and wind.
>
> (XII. 838-840)

In Book I of the poem Browning seems to use truth
generally in the sense of fact or factual evidence.   At line
141 he begins a brief summary of the narrative of the Old
Yellow Book, with which he concludes: "This is the bookful; thus far take the truth [fact], / The untempered gold
[fact], the fact untampered with, / The mere ring-metal
[fact] ere the ring [poem] be made!" (I. 364-366) Then
the poet asks, "What has hitherto come of it?" (I. 367)
"Was this truth of force? / Able to take its own part as
truth should, / Sufficient, self-sustaining?" (I. 372-374)
"If so, " Browning adds, "into the fire goes my book and
what the loss, since you know the tale [facts] already?"
(I. 374-377) "If not, " he proposes, "may I ask, rather
than relate, who were Guido and Pompilia? What manner
of man and woman were they; and what do you think of this
or that? What do you think of the young, frank, handsome,
courtly Caponsacchi who was the declared lover of Pompilia
and precipitator, through his elopement with her, of the
tragedy? Was his strange course right or wrong or both?
Was the old couple justly slaughtered? Do you know Gaetano,
and can you answer if Guido killed his wife for bearing him
a son?" (I. 377-409) Presumably Browning thought that
these questions could not be adequately answered with factual
evidence from the historical source.   So he continued:

> Well, British Public, ye...
>   will you have your proper laugh
> At the dark question, laugh it! I laugh first.
> Truth [fact] must prevail, the proverb vows; and
>   truth [fact]
> --Here is it all i' the book at last, as first
> There it was all i' the heads and hearts of Rome...
>   Yet a little while,
> The passage of a century or so,
> Decads [sic] thrice five, and here's time paid his tax,
> Oblivion gone home with her harvesting,

And all left smooth again as scythe could shave.
(I. 410-421)

The truth about which Browning has thus far spoken
suggests statement of fact or alleged fact.   To contend that
Browning would doubt the self-sufficiency and force of truth
in a sense other than that of factual truth, or that he would
say that truth in a sense other than that of factual truth was
in a book or the head of a human being, is, it appears to
me, to run counter to the many pronouncements on truth to
be found in his other poetry.   Nor, except in the sense of
fact or alleged fact, does the disappearance of truth after
the "passage of a century or so" seem to conform to Browning's general faith in an ultimate truth.

Concluding that his questions could not be answered
by London folk, though they knew the facts, and that away
from the scene of action the story had long been forgotten,
Browning took his book to Rome to try "truth's [fact's] power
/ On likely people" (I. 423-424).   "Have you met such
names? / Is a tradition extant of such facts?" (I. 424-425)
(Notice that facts and names are readily exchanged for
truths.)   The Romans answer: "Why, you'll waste your
pains--'on names and facts thus old'--and end as wise as
you began, if you search for records; but thanks in the
meantime for the story, long and strong, a pretty piece of
narrative enough.   Do you tell the story straight from the
book?   Or do you vault it through the loose and large, hang-
ing to a hint?   Or is there book at all and aren't you dealing in poetry, make-believe, and the white lies it sounds
like?" (I. 427-456)   The poet replies to the Romans:

                                  Yes and no!
From the book, yes; thence bit by bit I dug
The lingot truth ["pure crude fact"], that memo-
     rable day,
Assayed [analyzed] and knew my piecemeal gain
     was gold ["fact untampered with"], --
Yes; BUT FROM SOMETHING ELSE SURPASSING
     THAT,
SOMETHING OF MINE WHICH, MIXED UP WITH
     THE MASS [FACTS],
Made it bear hammer and be firm to file.
Fancy with fact is just one fact the more;
To-wit, that fancy has informed [formed, animated],
     transpierced [penetrated],
Thridded [threaded] and so thrown fast the facts

                else free,
          As right through ring and ring runs the djereed
          [wooden javelin c. 5 ft. long]
          And binds the loose, one bar without a break.
          I fused my live soul and that inert stuff [facts],
          Before attempting smithcraft, on the night
          After the day when, --truth [fact] thus grasped
                and gained, --
          The book was shut and done with and laid by.
                          (I. 457-472; capital letters added)

        Browning's explanation includes three specific acts:
first, he accumulated the facts of the book; second, he bound
them together as one binds together a series of rings by
placing them on one rod; and third, he brought the facts
back to life by fusing them and his "live soul." To this
point in the explanation of his function as a poet, Browning
has referred to his imaginative contribution as "alloy,"
"fancy," "something else surpassing," "something of mine,"
and "live soul"; in the remainder of Book I he also calls it
"such substance of me interfused," "motions of mine," and
"surplusage of soul." Believing that man, the creature, in
attempting "to grow" repeats God's process in man's due
degree, Browning continues:

          Man...
          Creates, no, but resuscitates, perhaps....
          May so project his surplusage of soul
          In search of body, so add self to self
          By owning what lay ownerless before, --
          So find, so fill full, so appropriate forms--
          That, although nothing which had never life
          Shall get life from him, be, not having been,
          Yet, something dead may get to live again.
                                      (I. 712-729)

        This quotation, I believe, may be accepted as typical
of Browning's thought on poetic creation. Such a conception
is prominently displayed in "Abt Vogler," the famous passages in "Fra Lippo Lippi" are of a similar bent, and,
though less well known, lines 17-117 of Book IX offer the
most complete representation of Browning's attitude on creativity to be found in The Ring and the Book. Many poets
have adopted an imagery comparable to Browning's to illumi-
nate the creative process, and some have expressed it in almost the same language used by Browning. Swinburne, in
the prelude to Tristram of Lyonesse, would "give / Out of

my life to make their dead life live / Some day of mine,
and blow my breath / Between the deep lips of forgotten
death. " And Shakespeare, probably when thinking of his
own dramatic creativeness, leads Prospero to say: "Graves
at my command / Have waked their sleepers, oped, and let
'em forth / By my so potent art. " Since Browning's re-
vivifying force, which he describes as a spirit (I. 776-778)
lighting his eye and letting him have his will with the dead,
is considered by Browning himself to be of value surpassing
that of fact, one may hesitate to accept Mr. Langbaum's re-
emphasis of the belief "that Browning counted it such a virtue for his poem to be based on 'pure crude fact' " (p. 131;
The Poetry of Experience, p. 109). To be sure, as long as
the emphasis is placed on "fact" in "pure crude fact, " the
interpreter has every reason to believe that Browning thought
"it necessary to justify a liberty of interpretation which has
always been granted poets. " But by shifting the emphasis
from "fact" to "pure" and "crude" as the poet so often seems
to direct, one may find himself in agreement with the poet
and in disagreement with those who believe that Browning
pledged absolute fidelity to fact. Emphasis on "pure" and
"crude, " moreover, permits the reader to believe that instead of emerging from the facts, Browning's poem restores
to life the facts long dead and long forgotten.

Without wishing to lessen the prospector's exultation
in finding "gold, " the rare metal with which Browning in a
ring metaphor would naturally compare the facts of the Old
Yellow Book, one may also question Mr. Langbaum's statement that "it is impossible to overemphasize the importance
Browning attached to... 'pure crude fact' " (p. 150; The Poetry
of Experience, p. 132). Browning's insistence upon the figure of "the gold" and his long preoccupation with Pompilia's
plight prove that he valued the facts of the Old Yellow Book
over less compelling facts, but perhaps not, as several critics have thought, [2] for their quality of being precious.
Through qualifying words or contextual development in Book
I, Browning seems to direct an even greater emphasis to the
pristine quality of gold: for example, "slivers of pure [un-
mixed] gold... Virgin, " "Gold as it was... Prime nature, "
"untempered gold, " and "as the ingot... lay gold, (beseech
you, hold that figure fast!). " The parenthetic entreaty
seems to lay stress on a fear by the poet himself that gold
would not be thought of as pristine metal; that Browning's
imaginative contribution, the alloy [metal, copper], [3] would
not be considered more valuable than the pristine facts.
Without violating metaphorical usage, Browning could have

regarded the facts of the old volume as the "pure gold [fact]"
surface of the completed poem; the facts, in turn, would
have been supported beneath by his interpretive copper which
remained hidden in the poem--the gold ring--to give it durability and fixed shape.   This reading conforms to the demands
of ring-making, and in Browning's recorded visits to the shop
of an artificer he may have watched the final act of ring-
making in which a spurt of acid removes all surface copper
and leaves a film of pure gold.   If all the copper is removed,
the gold again becomes soft and resistant to tempering, and
the ring becomes a spongy mass of pure gold less serviceable
or subject to permanent shaping than solid gold. [4]

Other examples of Browning's use of the word truth
to mean "dead truth [fanciless fact]" (I. 696-697, 143-144)
may be selected from the poem.   One of the best is in Book
I, lines 838-881.   As a stone falls on the surface of the
water, so "any fact" (I. 840) falls on the "smooth surface
of things. "   Like an observer who guesses by the splash and
vibrations and who feels after the vanished stone, the world
in Browning's poem crowds the bank of the pool and guesses
at what were figure and substance of the fact by the splash
and "vibration in the general mind, at depth of deed already
out of reach. "   Consequently, Browning says, the world fails
to find truth [fact], that deceptive speck, at the bottom.
Browning's illustration receives its force from the universal
operation of the laws of refraction.   Half-Rome feels after
the vanished truth [fact], but his finger falls wide of the
mark, simply because of this law.   If he is standing directly
over the fact, Browning continues, he reaches in the right
direction, but not far enough.   If he is standing at an angle
from the fact, he not only fails to reach far enough; he also
reaches in the wrong direction.   Thus the world reaches,
swerving back and forth in "over-belief" and in under-belief,
but never far enough and seldom in the right direction for
the truth [fact].   Half-Rome, Other Half-Rome, Tertium
Quid, representing the world's guesses; Guido, Caponsacchi,
Pompilia, the Pope, representing the actors' guesses--each
in turn reaches and misses, though each attempts it "all for
truth's sake, mere truth, nothing else" (I. 881).   Because
Browning started his figure with "any fact, " and used "truth"
and "fact" synonymously throughout the figure, it would seem
that he meant at the end of it, "all for truth's [fact's] sake. "

Browning's method then is to call up voices which, in
speaking, will represent many different points of view.   Half-
Rome's voice expresses the opinion that Guido is more right

than wrong; Other Half-Rome thinks Pompilia less wrong
than right; and Tertium Quid believes a "reasoned statement
of the case, something bred of both," is the intelligent verdict.   Then rises Guido's voice, "ripe for declaring truth
[fact]" (I. 953), because with the Vigil-torture "they were
wont to tease the truth [fact] out of loth witness" (I. 981),
though Religion started up and said, "Henceforth find truth
[fact] by milder means" (I. 1009).   Guido soon reveals that
truth [fact] fails to satisy his more obtuse sense (I. 957ff) and
temporarily chooses to rationalize his defense.   Was his not
a perfect case of causa honoris, and was he not thereby pro-
tected by the unwritten law?

> While life was graspable and gainable
> And bird-like buzzed her wings round Guido's brow
> Not much truth [fact] stiffened out the web of words
> He wove to catch her; when away she flew
> And death came, death's breath rivelled [shrivelled]
>   up the lies,
> Left bare the metal thread, the fibre fine
> Of truth [fact], i' the spinning: the true [factual]
>   words shone last.
>
>   (I. 1275-81)

Following Guido's are the voices of Caponsacchi and Pompilia,
after which the lawyers search out truth [fact] with their "patent truth-extracting [fact-extracting] process" (I. 1114). When
the words of prosecutor and defense lawyer--men who must
rely on the letter of the law--have died away, the voice of
the Pope is heard.   Although sufficient facts have been presented to enable him to condemn Guido, the Pope discloses
his mistrust of facts alone and bases his ultimate judgment
upon the spirit of the law, an application he may make since
he is "called of God."   "From the other world he feels impress at time" (I. 1224) when "he is wont to do God's work
on earth" (I. 1234).   [I now think I was wrong on the Pope;
see Essay Seven.]

    Browning has revealed that in The Ring and the Book
his "business was to explain fact" (Wedgwood Letters, pp.
143-144, 183), but he would have been hard pressed indeed
to find a uniformly acceptable interpretation of the contradictory facts of the Old Yellow Book.   Even J. M. Gest's
legal account of the story, though an historical not a poetical
version, provides matters of opinion which are subject to
dispute.   Quite naturally Browning wanted the individual reader of the poem to believe that the final judgment rests with

the reader.   Nevertheless, Browning frankly admitted that
his characters are idealized (Wedgwood Letters, p. 163),
and that the wickedness of Guido--"that prodigy of evil"--
shall rise to the limit conceivable (Wedgwood Letters, p.
153).   Just as frankly Browning elaborated on a prophetic
guidance which imposes itself on all final decisions.   He
thought of himself as a prophet of Elisha's stature, entitled
to interpret the world anew in the light of divine truth as
revealed through love.   He also thought of himself as a high
priest, giving utterance to the needs and aspirations, the
fears and faith of mankind.   "He dedicated himself, " Stopford
A. Brooke says, "to the picturing of humanity; and he came
to think a Power beyond ours had accepted this dedication,
and directed his work. . . .   He believed that he had certain
God-given qualities which fitted him for this work" (The
Poetry of Browning [New York, 1902], p. 402).   Near the
beginning of the poem Browning claims divine guidance when
he describes the discovery of the Old Yellow Book: "(Mark
the predestination!) when a Hand, / Always above my shoul-
der pushed me" (I. 40-41).   In the old book itself, under
his name, Browning inscribed: "For me the Muse in her
might hath in store her strongest shaft. " On the day he
found the book, the tragic story of Pompilia was enabled to
act itself "over again once more, " because "the life in me
abolishes the death of things, / Deep calling unto deep" (I.
520-521).   And when comparing his own resuscitation of the
characters of the book with Elisha's resuscitation of the
Shunamite's child, he adds, "'Tis a credible feat / With the
right man and way" (I. 771-772).   Browning accepted this
high function as his "due / To God" (I. 1403-04), the dis-
charge of which would "save the soul" (XII. 867).

Browning's belief in his high calling is closely related
to the reason for his intense agnosticism concerning human
knowledge.   The belief that total or final truth is unattainable
in the world was a stronghold of his faith. [5]   In The Ring and
the Book, however, the entire distrust of intellectual knowledge and the complete reliance upon the heart evinced in
Browning's later poems, had not reached an absolute division.
Both Pompilia and the Pope are conscious of the value of
knowledge as well as of its inadequacy to represent the infinite.   The difference between The Ring and the Book and
later poems is that Browning was, in the former, in the
process of scuttling knowledge, but had as yet insisted only
upon the limits of knowledge.   He felt that mankind's use of
knowledge was narrowly limited and that only the artist, with
his keener sensitivity and divine assistance, could make prof-

itable use of knowledge.   Although art too is denied the use
of knowledge in the later poems, in The Ring and the Book
it is engaged in presenting the truth through intellectual as
well as intuitional and inspirational means.   "No dose of
purer truth than man digests, / But truth with falsehood,
milk that feeds him now, / Not strong meat he may get to
bear some day" (I. 830-832; see Hebrews v. 11-14).   Consequently the heart or the soul is the only completely reliable
source of truth for mankind.   As the heart is schooled in
"things pertaining to God, " so will it be weaned gradually
from the "milk of truth. " Not even the Pope, as I read
Browning, had been completely prepared for the "meat of
truth. "[6] In their search for truth [fact] all characters of
the poem missed the one agent which might have revealed
the total truth.   Because they were still relying upon knowledge, looking for facts, they were unable to feel truth.
Browning, no doubt, thought the Pope's judgment the most
satisfactory, and he makes it evident that this satisfaction
was reached through an appeal, finally, to the heart [see
retraction on this "appeal, " Essay Seven].

     Browning's second broad use of the word truth, I
therefore suggest, is based on his distrust of man's splin-
tered and incomplete knowledge, that is, [indemonstrable][7]
fact; on his idealistic attitude toward life; and on his acceptance of a calling as highly held as that of ancient priest
or prophet.   Wherever the particular and the general, the
individual and the universal, are in conflict, Browning seems
to reveal a consistent distrust of the particular and the individual [fact]. [8] Supporting passages from The Ring and the
Book which cling like burrs in the mind are not easily dismissed:

                    --that who trusts
         "To human testimony for a fact
         "Gets this sole fact--himself is proved a fool;
         "Man's speech being false, if but by consequence
         "That only strength is true: while man is weak,
         "And, SINCE TRUTH SEEMS RESERVED FOR
              HEAVEN NOT EARTH,
         "Plagued here by earth's prerogative of lies,
         "Should learn to love and long for what, one day,
         "Approved by life's probation, he may speak.
                    (XII. 601-609; capital letters added)

    What does the world, told truth, but lie the more?
                                        (X. 673)

> Truth rare and real, not transcripts, fact and false.
> (IX. 107)

> Not so! Expect nor question nor reply
> At what we figure as God's judgment-bar!
> None of this vile way by the barren words
> Which, more than any deed, characterize
> Man as made subject to a curse: ...
> But when man walks the garden of this world
> For his own solace, and, unchecked by law,
> Speaks or keeps silence as himself sees fit,
> Without the least incumbency to lie,
> --Why, can he tell you what a rose is like,
> Or how the birds fly, and not slip to false
> Though truth serve better?...
> Therefore these filthy rags of speech, this coil
> Of statement, comment, query and response,
> Tatters all too contaminate for use,
> Having no renewing: HE, THE TRUTH, IS, TOO,
> THE WORD.   We men, in our degree, may know
> There, simply, instantaneously,...
> (X. 347-378; capital letters added)

Browning's recognized dissatisfaction with the lawyers and his unsympathetic treatment of minor characters and speakers may result from the dependence of these individuals upon individual fact, upon their own individual smallness. Truth [indemonstrable fact], on which Browning lavishes unnecessary derision in the above passages, seems subjected to belittlement wherever it appears in the poem. 9 The contrast of truth ["fanciless fact"] with truth [fanciful fact] which seemingly runs throughout The Ring and the Book may find its culmination in:

>   our human speech is naught,
> Our human testimony false, our fame
> And human estimation words and wind.
> Why take the artistic way to prove so much?
> Because, it is the glory and the good of Art,
> That Art remains the one way possible
> Of speaking truth, to mouths like mine at least....
> But Art, --wherein man nowise speaks to men,
> Only to mankind, --Art may tell a truth
> Obliquely, do the thing shall breed the thought,
> Nor wrong the thought, missing the mediate word....
> SO WRITE A BOOK SHALL MEAN BEYOND THE
>   FACTS.
> (XII. 838-866; capital letters added)

   To say that Browning "adds nothing to the truth"
(Langbaum, p. 151; The Poetry of Experience, p. 133) of
the Old Yellow Book seems to leave in doubt or to consider
as nonessential the poet's preconceived plan to "write a book
shall mean beyond the facts. " To believe that Browning repristinated, or thought that he repristinated, himself out of
the poem divulges a rather faulty knowledge of ring-making
and suggests that Browning did not understand the creative
process through which, in The Ring and the Book, he worked
for possibly eight years. With the exception of God's truth,
which is signalized in "He, the Truth, is, too, the Word, "
the word truth in the poem seems always to refer either to
"fact-facts" or to a result accomplished by talents uncommon
to man and attributable to the influx of divine guidance.
Whereas Browning recognizes only a weak relation at best
between man's speech--facts--and God's truth, he underscores heavily the power of certain men to apprehend in
part God's truth. Like Wordsworth, Browning looked upon
a poet as a man "endowed with more lively sensibility, more
enthusiasm and tenderness, who has a greater knowledge of
human nature, and a more comprehensive soul, than are
supposed to be common among mankind. " Here is the way
Browning expresses it:

> Why did the mage say, --feeling as we are wont
> For truth [total or final], and stopping midway
>   short of truth,
> And resting on a lie, --"I raise a ghost"?
> "Because, " he taught adepts, "man makes not man.
> "Yet by a special gift, an art of arts,
> "MORE INSIGHT AND MORE OUTSIGHT AND MUCH
>   MORE
> "WILL TO USE BOTH OF THESE THAN BOAST
>   MY MATES,
> "I can detach from me, commission forth
> "Half of my soul; which in its pilgrimage
> "O'er old unwandered waste ways of the world,
> "MAY CHANCE UPON SOME FRAGMENT OF A
>   WHOLE. "
>   (I. 742-752; capital letters added)

Expressions such as "since truth seems reserved for heaven, "
"He, the Truth, is, too, the Word, " and "some fragment of
a whole" are as familiar to Browning's poetry as the star
image or the monastery folding itself in for a night of rest.
Unequivocal conviction of the instability and fragmentary nature of man-conceived truth seems to have propelled Brown-

ing's loyalty beyond the external truth of fact to an essential truth.

Browning or his character often repeats that this or that is a truth [fact], but Browning, I think, avoids saying that he believes it to be a finally trustworthy fact. His purpose was to present the facts in as many different ways as they could be presented. Through frequent reminder by the poet or the speaker that the statement at hand is a truth [fact], Browning apparently chose to justify whatever distortion the facts suffered while passing through his own mind. He must have realized that however greatly he "wrenched" the facts, they could not be disfigured as much as the witnesses and the lawyers had disfigured them. Presumably an abiding distrust of truth [indemonstrable fact] caused Browning to accentuate so many times a word in conflict with his attitude toward life. One can never stop with the facts, he seems to emphasize, and "save the soul. " The apology[10] in "For how else know we save by worth of word?" (I. 837) becomes more meaningful in this context. During frequent visits to the courtrooms of London Browning observed the way of the courts with fact and evidently developed a warm aversion to the "patent truth [fact]-extracting process. " As the contradictory truths [facts] of all trials come to the surface, Browning could have reasoned with his Ring metaphor in mind, so do the contradictory truths [facts] of The Ring and the Book come to the surface. Although it probably does not matter how many, A. K. Cook says, "Browning squeezed almost every drop of fact or alleged fact that they [the pamphlets] could yield" (Commentary, p. xix). But it is not alone Browning's adaptation of innumerable facts or his practice of adding, changing, or deleting facts which accounts for the broad scope of his presentation. By more than either or both of these acts, the broad scope is gained by Browning's imaginative contribution in the creation of character and in the interpretation of motive, all of which he called "alloy" and, like the ring-maker or the courtroom judge, he may plausibly have considered to be hidden from obvious sight.

Critics have sometimes noticed that Browning did not know all the facts of the Old Yellow Book. Other Half-Rome, for example, says that Pompilia died "in the long white Lazar-house...Saint Anna's" (III. 35-37); and the Pope (X. 1499, 1504) and Bottini (XII. 672, 676) say that she died in the Monastery (of St. Mary Magdalene) of the Convertites. Mr. Cook, in a comment on this situation, writes: "The first

identification was the merest guess, and if Sir Frederick
Treves is right in saying that 'no such house [as a hospital
of Saint Anna] had any existence' (Treves, p. 76) it was not
a happy one" (Commentary, p. 281). Both the insistence on
Browning's mastery of fact and the observation that Browning
did not know all the facts originate, at least in part, with
"I had mastered the contents, knew the whole truth" (I. 117),
words Browning spoke about his first or at most second reading of the Old Yellow Book on the day he found it. Browning
must have meant that, as anyone may read a book and say
he knows it, he had read all of this book and knew it. In
the poem different speakers say whatever they wish, or in
any case one speaker says that Pompilia was not carried to
the hospital of St. Anna and another says that she was carried to St. Anna's. Speakers throughout the poem add, dis-
tort, ignore, "wrench and falsify," all turning the facts to
their own purposes. This characteristically true-to-life conduct is one of the fundamental portrayals of The Ring and the
Book. Although characters sometimes speak for the poet,
save for the first and part of the last, each book of the poem
contains the evidence of persons connected in some way with
the trial, giving evidence as they see it, often crippling it
as witnesses are prone to do.

Used as evidence to substantiate Browning's assertion
that he "had mastered the contents, knew the whole truth,"
a statement Browning made to the Reverend John W. Chadwick has become quite well known. Browning said to him
in answer to the query, "If it did not make him very happy
to have created such a woman as Pompilia": "I assure you
I found her in the book just as she speaks and acts in my
poem" (The Christian Register [January 19, 1888]). At least
two serious objections may be raised against using these
words as evidence that Browning thought and said he was
faithful to the facts of the Old Yellow Book. Dowden best
expresses the first objection: "The truth is that he found
in the book whatever he needed and desired to find. Another
reader of the documents might fail to discover the Pompilia
of Browning" (The Ring and the Book [Oxford Edition, 1912],
p. xii). The second objection rises from a conversation of
Browning's recorded by W. M. Rossetti: "Browning talked
about an article in the Temple Bar, saying that he, as shown
in The Ring and the Book, is an analyst, not a creator of
character. This, [Browning] very truly says, is not applicable; because he has had to create, out of the mass of almost equally balanced evidence, the characters of the book
as he conceives them, and it is only after that process that

the analyzing method can come into play" (Rossetti Papers, p. 401).

With the potential qualities before him, Browning enhanced the character of Pompilia until she became a symbol of virtue in distress, but in no place I can find did he assert that another person must see in his Pompilia the Pompilia of his source. Since so many other readers of the Old Yellow Book have quickly determined that the evidence of the case is almost equally balanced, it would be odd if Browning had not made the same discovery. Near the time Browning finished his poem, Carlyle, who had been reading the old book, concluded that the "real story is plain enough on looking into it; the girl and the handsome young priest were lovers" (Allingham Diary, pp. 127-128). Hodell, at a later date, completed an intensive study of the book with the belief that "no one can read these [Celestino's and his associates' oaths] without an absolute conviction of her saintly purity and patience" (p. 281). In 1920 A. K. Cook published a scholarly commentary on the book and the poem. With reference to the poet's attitude, he wrote that Browning possessed "an assured conviction that the charge of misconduct brought against Caponsacchi and Pompilia was for the most part a deliberately false concoction" (p. 293). To which he added: "In spite of the contradictions which I have noticed [discrepancies in Caponsacchi's and Pompilia's depositions] most readers of the Book will share that conviction." Four years later, after having translated the Old Yellow Book, Judge J. M. Gest stated that "it seems quite clearly established that Pompilia was guilty of adultery with Caponsacchi" (p. 610). The oaths of ten witnesses; the execution of Guido, resulting from a trial of which Judge Gest himself says: "The defense that the homicides were committed ex causa honoris runs throughout all the arguments, and this of course turned on the innocence or guilt of Pompilia, which may naturally be regarded as the central fact of the case" (p. 600); the decision of a court and lawyers in whom Judge Gest reveals the strongest faith; and a definite court vindication of Pompilia's fidelity to her marriage vows--all of these truths [facts][11] are insufficient evidence to convince Judge Gest of Pompilia's innocence.

Convinced of the probability of Pompilia's innocence but also aware of the almost equally balanced evidence of her trial, Browning could hardly have chosen a theme more appropriate than the vanity of human speech or a poetic figure more applicable than the metaphor of the Ring. For as

pristine gold without an alloy metal is soft and unsuited to
tempering, so the contradictory truths [facts] of Browning's
testimony were soft and unsuited to tempering without the
poet's interpretive alloy copper.   To correct their weaknes-
ses in taking fixed and durable shape, Browning's poetic copper is added to give substance to the "pure" and "crude"
facts of his source as metallic copper is added by the ring-
maker to give substance and practical value to the pristine
gold.   Strengthening each other in the analogy of pristine
gold and man's truth [fact], the gold surface of the ring and
the factual surface of the poem are further strengthened by a
courtroom analogy in which lawyers and judges search beneath the superficial surface of verbal witnessing for a composite truth.   Where a pledge to absolute fidelity to fact
leaves Browning with a poem whose theme, pervading imagery, and characters are not representative of his intent, a
distrust of truth [indemonstrable fact] by the poet provides
grounds for the valid portrayal of his Ring metaphor, his
theme, and his characters.   We seem invited to believe that
Browning "appropriated" (I. 726) the contradictory truths
[facts] of the Old Yellow Book in order to "chance upon some
fragment of a whole. "

Notes

1.   Robert Langbaum, "The Ring and the Book: A Relativist
Poem, " PMLA, LXXI (March 1956), 131; also available in
The Poetry of Experience (New York, 1957), pp. 109-110.
[The year this challenging essay appeared, W. O. Raymond
wrote that in the discussion of judgments Langbaum incor-
porated "an element of paradox which makes close reading
necessary to disentangle the threads of his arguments"
("Truth in The Ring and the Book, " VN, No. 10 [Autumn
1956], pp. 12-13).   But it is only recently that Raymond's
purpose for stating an objection has been seriously considered
and enlarged upon.   His chief points are:

> The primary factors which account for the rela-
> tivist form of the poem seem to me, however, to
> be individualistic rather than the reflection of a
> general ethos....   The centrality of its relativist
> structure is apparent in Browning's emphasis on
> his method as being in accord with the nature of
> Art, and the only way in which man can attain his
> highest vision of truth....   The core of the relativ-
> ism of the poem, however, according to Mr. Lang-
> baum, is the perception that 'social and religious

absolutes' are inadequate to lead to the full apprehension of truth.... As Mr. Langbaum comments:
'truth is larger and in advance of the formulations
and institutions of any age.' There is a disequilibrium between truth as a spiritual principle, truth
as God sees it, and the machinery of forms and
dogmas.... When these become outworn, fresh in-
sights into truth must be gained through its source
in the human heart.]

2.   Charles W. Hodell, The Old Yellow Book (Washington,
D. C., 1908), p. 231; The Ring and the Book, ed. Dowden
(Oxford Edition, 1912), p. ix; Cook, Commentary, p. 2;
John Marshall Gest, The Old Yellow Book (Philadelphia,
1927), p. 2.

3.   [metal, copper]: see note 4, Essay Two, for this interpolation.

4.   In a letter of May 19, 1863, Browning says of a mutual
acquaintance, "For he wants the proper alloy which should
stiffen the gold in him & keep him from bumps & bruises"
(Letters of Robert Browning to Miss Isa Blagden [1923], p.
90; McAleer, p. 162). Mrs. Browning suggests that Browning had been instructed in ring-making. (The Letters of
Elizabeth Barrett Browning, ed. Kenyon [1897], II, 354-355),
and Browning confirms it: "(Craftsmen instruct me)" (I. 9).

5.   See especially Browning's "Saul," lines 245-253, and,
though the speaker is the Pope, not Browning, one of the
most effective images in Browning's poetry: X. 1307-27.

6.   The Pope indeed wavered between faith and facts. Examples of his indecision: He read the chroniclers (X. 198ff);
spent the day on the court documents (X. 212ff); suspected
an "acuter wit" than his might sound the documents deeper
and reach through guilt to innocence (X. 261-263); stood on
his integrity (X. 276).

7.   [indemonstrable]: see note 9 for reason for interpolation.

8.   [I am indebted to Norton B. Crowell (The Convex Glass
[Alberquerque, 1968], p. 193) for pointing out that an illustration from Stopford A. Brooke, used here but now removed,
very probably does not mean what I thought it meant. Enter-
ing a debate on Browning's concept of truth eight years after
Essay Three appeared, Crowell perceives that The Victorian

Newsletter symposium turned rapidly to a broad discussion
of truth, if not as was hoped directly to Browning's confusing and chaotic exchange of the word truth for the word fact.
He also understands the Ring metaphor sufficiently to appreciate the accuracy it can provide future researchers on
the poem.   I cannot be ungrateful for his approval of my
interpretation.   Nor can I evade responding to the condemnations he attaches to my work, even though they are scarcely more severe than those applied to DeVane, Raymond, and
others as Crowell strikes through all at Sir Henry Jones.
Because Browning, not Jones, created the problem, it is
essential to remember that few, if any, other major poets
have so unwarily exposed themselves to philosophical challenge.   And it may be necessary, though I hope not, eventually to admit that Browning's chief defense rests in the less
erring sense of his poetic vision as contrasted with his
ratiocinative power.

Unfamiliar with the persistency of the critical opinion
which held Browning so long in bond to fidelity to fact,
Crowell misreads paragraphs of mine and of others which
say almost exactly what he thinks they should say.   As he
does not see that I am opposing critics in their belief that
"a uniformly acceptable interpretation of the contradictory
facts" is possible (p. 189), he does not observe that the
long statement "whenever the particular and the general, the
individual and the universal are in conflict, Browning seems
to reveal a consistent distrust of the particular and the individual" applies only to fact (p. 193).   Of course the facts
involve individual witnesses, but the witnesses are so stunted
as individuals they have nothing to do with Browning's doctrine of individualism.   They are: "somewhere 'twixt the
best and worse, / Where crowd the indifferent product, all
too poor / Makeshift, starved samples of humanity!" (X.
1213-15) Crowell simply must know that Browning condemns
inaction and unconcern more readily than he condemns evil.
When Crowell is amused "to hear Browning charged with the
supposedly anti-intellectual belief that 'total or final truth is
unattainable in this world'" (p. 191), he quotes a key paragraph in which my purpose was to suggest that the poet's
darkest disbelief in knowledge was cast as a shadow from
an early stronghold of faith which gradually became irrational and destructive.   Jones puts it thus for Browning: "While
'love gains God at first leap,'... A radical flaw runs through
our knowing faculty.   Human knowledge is not only incom-
plete--no one can be so foolish as to deny that--but it is,
as regarded by Browning, essentially inadequate to the nature
of fact, and we must 'distrust it, even when it seems de-

monstrable. ' No professed agnostic can condemn the human
intellect more utterly than he does" (Browning As a Philosophical and Religious Teacher [Glasgow, 1899], p. 221). My
argument explains why Donald Smalley says that I have advanced the period of Browning's distrust of knowledge farther
ahead in his career than does Jones.

    Perhaps I should repeat that I still believe the poet
was in the process of scuttling indemonstrable, if not demonstrable, knowledge in The Ring and the Book. Though
the incident of scuttling the Graf Spee was much too vivid
in my 1940 writing, it is now clearer to me that by his indiscriminate, almost defiant exchange of the word truth for
fact, Browning may have been more deeply immersed in distrust of human fact and truth in 1868 than I have suspected.
Yet I hope that he may be freed from many of the demeaning
charges which hinge on his agnostic inclinations. For such
reasons, though Crowell left no record of my qualifications,
it seems needful to recall that I wrote Browning was only
"in the process of" scuttling knowledge and "had as yet insisted only upon the limits of knowledge"; that "both Pompilia
and the Pope are conscious of the value of knowledge as well
as of its inadequacy to represent the infinite"; and that in
his art the poet "is engaged in presenting the truth through
intellectual as well as intuitional and inspirational means"
(VN, No. 15 [Spring 1959], p. 5).]

9. [In republishing Essay Three, which evoked spirited
replies from Donald Smalley and Robert Langbaum, I have
made only the brief substantive changes to which attention
is called. To the following observation of mine both of
these critics strenuously objected, and for the same technical reason:

> Truth [fact], on which Browning lavishes unneces-
> sary derision in the above passages, seems sub-
> jected to belittlement wherever it appears in the
> poem. The contrast of truth ["fanciless fact"] with
> truth [fanciful fact] which seemingly runs through-
> out The Ring and the Book may find its culmination
> in

>   our human speech is naught,
> Our human testimony false, our fame
> And human estimation words and wind.

It does not greatly matter that use of "unnecessary derision"
follows and precedes dozens of quoted lines in which truth

[fact] is as roughly treated by Browning as words allow.   Or
that elsewhere in my essay is offered as clearly, though not
as emphatically, arguments both critics turn against me.
But it should matter that whereas I limit "unnecessary derision" to specifically quoted lines and apply "belittlement" to
the remainder of the poem, these men at once drop all
thought of simply "to disparage or to minimize" and assign
to me a belief that Browning had a contemptuous attitude toward all fact, demonstrable and indemonstrable.   That I am
careful to add in several different ways that "as yet [Brown-
ing] insisted only upon the limits of knowledge" does not
placate them.   In attempting to nullify my effort to weaken
inordinate emphasis on fact by any critic of the poem, they
also impute to me the practice of using arguments which
hang on small details and which exclude the bulk of Browning's other poetry from consideration.   To help correct this
omission, I have tabulated all the lines from The Ring and
the Book in which Browning uses the word truth, and these
may be found at the end of the volume.
        Although Smalley and Langbaum choose to disregard
Browning's dominant and indiscriminate exchange of the word
truth for fact, the ironic and ambiguous twists he imposes
on truth, they reason that I make no attempt to distinguish
between demonstrable and indemonstrable fact.   In spite of
my repetition of "statement of fact or alleged fact, "
"wrenched, disfigured, distorted, falsified fact, " and many
other of Browning's methods of belittling fact, they take no
notice.   Otherwise, neither of them could have thought, "In
Cundiff's view, Browning... [displays] throughout the poem a
scorn of the idea that factual knowledge is of any great
value" (Smalley, "Browning's View of Fact in The Ring and
the Book, " VN, No. 16 [Fall 1959], p. 2; italics added).   Of
the quotations I present to reveal the belittlement to which
Browning subjects truth [fact or alleged fact], I think not one
example concerns demonstrable fact.   This ever-expanding
evidence, moreover, seems to provide the key to Browning's
frequent assertions on the frailty of human testimony as well
as substantial indication that the theme of the poem may be
"the vanity of human speech. "   Of the quotations Smalley
presents to reveal the great store Browning set by his
source material, not one, I think, is concerned with indemonstrable fact.   As one might expect, therefore, Smalley,
like the poet at the moment, delights in the indisputable fact
of an old yellow book, while I delight in the poet's "indisputably fact [indemonstrable and ironic],... / Dwindled into
no bigger than a book. "   While Smalley lingers over "Browning's pleasure, keen as it obviously is, " in the actual sand

that dried the ink and the actual creased sheets folded double for more commodious use, I linger over the many alleged but indemonstrable facts, "(So universal is [the world's] plague of squint.)" What facts, we may pardonably ask, demonstrate or establish that Pompilia actually did or did not flirt with Caponsacchi? That Girolamo, Guido's brother, did or did not attempt to seduce Pompilia? That Pompilia did or did not ink over the letter allegedly written by her to Abate Paolo? Demonstrably the yellow book Browning enjoyed tossing into the air and calling his "four-years'-intimate" is a fact. Undeniably Browning made a tremendous effort "to transcribe the truth [demonstrable fact] of small details from his source. " But as most critics would surely concede, this fact of transcribing demonstrable details is the smallest part of his total accomplishment. Smalley is as far from understanding Browning's complex use of truth as Langbaum, when Langbaum writes, "I do not think [Browning] is saying. . . that 'these questions could not be answered with factual evidence from the historical source, ' for the historical source is all he has to go by" (VN, No. [Spring 1960], p. 14). Langbaum had in mind questions like the above on flirtation and seduction as well as similar questions Browning asks in lines 377-409 of Book I.

The difference between Smalley's conclusion and mine is that I believe Browning knew and said, through the Ring metaphor and his many uses of the word truth, he was explaining, interpreting, idealizing the facts of the Old Yellow Book; Smalley believes that Browning provided us with a glorious misinterpretation, despite the poet's intent to assert he did not misinterpret the facts. Our differing beliefs in elucidation, however, do not any longer lend substance to the poetic anomaly in which Browning was thought to be, or at least asserted he was, a historian in his treatment of fact and a poet in his treatment of truth. Smalley's reading of The Ring and the Book outside the framework of a possibly consistent Ring metaphor may enable him to follow the general contours of interpretations similar to those of A. K. Cook and J. E. Shaw. But if Smalley includes the full significance of Shaw's words, he and I remain much closer together in our insistence upon Browning's probable loyalty to an essential truth. No critic has been more positive in this matter than Shaw: "It cannot be denied that the personages in Browning's great poem, The Ring and the Book, are of the poet's own making and he himself would have been the first to acknowledge them as his own creatures" (p. 55). Recognizing the excellence of what Shaw has to say on the development of Pompilia's character, I am still unable to

accept, because of its internal contradiction and its external
derogation of Browning's talent, his now famous phrase,
"glorious misinterpretation. " Consequently I do not go so
far as to suggest that Browning's poem and characters are
independently his own creation. On the last statement,
Smalley and I seem to be in agreement, but for reasons he
associates with Browning's "special pleadings, " Smalley is
not persuaded by the poet who tells us he "appropriated" (I.
726) the contradictory facts of the Old Yellow Book in order
both to "chance upon some fragment of a whole" and to "calculate / By this [OYB] the lost proportions of a style. "

On the other hand, Langbaum early concedes that "no
one could read both the Old Yellow Book and The Ring and
the Book, and suppose that they were the same. " Even up
to "pure invention" in the characters of the lawyers, he adds,
"Everyone admits that [Browning] did not stick entirely to
the facts. . . . We must infer that he is claiming some li-
cense for interpretation and even for amplification and invention" (p. 12). But Langbaum is dissembling, for facts, regardless of their fragmentary or deceptive nature, must
stand unassailable until he himself chooses to discard them.
Else he could not so readily insist that Cundiff attributes to
Browning "contempt for the facts" and introduction of a
"whole elaborate mechanism of factuality just. . . to set it at
naught as a means of arriving at the truth of the poem" (p.
11). This initial urgency to sustain fact also explains why
Langbaum can incautiously assert, "No poet could head
against the connotation, indeed the denotation of precious-
ness in gold, " when Browning forever reveled in turning
things upside down, as illustrated by soft versus normally
hard facts. To Langbaum, Browning's "So write a book
shall mean beyond the facts" expresses the poet's belief
that "fact is merely an index to the truth which is always
much larger":

> The line does not, however, lessen the importance
> of fact; nor does the passage in which it appears:
> "Our human speech is naught / Our human testi-
> mony false, our fame / And human estimation
> words and wind" (XII. 838-880). The false testi-
> mony and estimation are facts in that they happened;
> and the disparity between truth and the false or in-
> adequate expression of it is at the heart of what I
> have called the poem's relativism. But the reason
> for Browning's excitement over his real life subject
> is this: that without the jumble of true and false,
> good and bad, which are the raw stuff of life, there

would be no meaning, no truth. If fact is important as an index to truth, truth itself cannot be
known except through fact or material conditions.
(p. 13; italics added)

Notice that fact as "merely an index to truth" suddenly becomes so important a fact that "truth itself cannot be known
except through fact or material conditions. " But more to
the point Langbaum cannot first deny the possibility of spiritual truth, as in the above, and then reliably advance that
Browning was trying to give "the truth about the moral and
spiritual world" (p. 16). When he says that "it is only
through the sordid events that Caponsacchi, Pompilia, and
the Pope have been able to discover and exhibit the good in
themselves" (p. 13; italics added), Langbaum is not trying
to understand a Christian poet who believed that human goodness perseveres in spite of the evil surrounding it. God
planted Pompilia where she grows, but Pope Innocent could
glory in her instinctive evasion of the "jumble of good and
evil":

> It was not given Pompilia to know much, ...
> Yet if in purity and patience, if
> In faith held fast despite the plucking fiend, ...
> That saints are known by, --if in right returned
> For wrong, most pardon for worst injury,
> If there be any virtue, any praise [Phillippians iii. 8], --
> Then will this woman-child have proved.
>
> (X. 1020-29)

Even though Langbaum earlier defines truth as the
Pope's separation of good and evil (p. 13), we may still be
coaxed into accepting "only through the sordid events" (pp.
13-14). This turn of thought he would accomplish by referring to a frequently quoted letter in which Browning speaks
of the "incidental evolution of good thereby" in the presence
of enormous wickedness and weakness. But let Browning
speak to Langbaum's and Smalley's understanding of the
Wedgwood Letters (pp. 144-145);

> Fire laid and cauldron set, the obscene ring traced,
> The victim stripped and prostrate: what of God?
> The cleaving of a cloud, a cry, a crash,
> Quenched lay their cauldron, cowered i' the dust
>   the crew,
> As, in a glory of armour like Saint George,
> Out again sprang the young good beauteous priest

Bearing away the lady in his arms,
Saved for a splendid minute and no more.
For, whom i' the path did that priest come upon,
He and the poor lady borne so brave,
--Checking the song of praise in me, had else
Swelled to the full for God's will done on earth.

(L 581-592)

With his immersion in factuality, Langbaum may now and
does attribute to Browning the hypothetical but unsubstantiated
statement, "I shall add nothing to the events, " "for the historical source is all he has to go by" (p. 14).   It does not
in the least concern Langbaum that already he is as thoroughly committed to "interpretation, amplification and invention" as ever were Mrs. Orr, Charles Hodell, and J. E.
Shaw; Langbaum's new purpose, however, is to consign
Browning to "the historian's job of restoring and interpreting
the events. " Why he again repeats that Browning "deliberately distorted the 'live fact' or truth" appears to hinge on his
insistence the poet is, as are all capable historians, an imaginative worker (p. 15).
        Smalley also needs the full force of facts to support
his position, but while Langbaum sacrifices facts to motive
Smalley sacrifices them to special pleading. Not wishing to
surrender the traditional line of criticism on fidelity to fact,
Smalley utilizes a thesis that Browning possessed a "familiar
pattern of thought" which, as demonstrated in his Essay on
Chatterton, enabled him "to present the results on his analysis not as a creative work, ... but as a factual study worthy
of inclusion in a sober quarterly review" (p. 5). Thus the
origin of Smalley's faith in Browning's "powers to penetrate
objective data and get at 'the exact truth'" of the Old Yellow
Book (p. 7; italics added). But in estimating Browning's
talent Smalley immediately disguises the nature of powers
Browning held as highly as priest's and prophet's, and glosses over the free play Browning took with data he rarely
found to be objective to begin with. And if Smalley had
thought seriously on the impossibility of Browning's dealing
with facts in a way different from the way of all poets, he
would have anticipated the weakness of arguments which un-
dermine the greatest literary masterpieces while raising
Browning's work to the level of supraperformance. Nevertheless by imbuing Browning with a uniquely clairvoyant power to see through facts to their truth, Smalley may force the
following well-known report by Rossetti to render opposite
meanings: "This, [Browning] very truly says, is not applicable; because he has had to create, out of the mass of al-

most equally balanced evidence, the characters of the book
as he conceives them. " For his purposes, Smalley interprets the reported conversation to mean that Browning arrived at a satisfactory reading of the contradictory facts of
the Old Yellow Book; for my purposes, to mean that Browning saw no way of arriving at a reliable reading of the truth.
He might instead have indicated that my only reason for quoting Rossetti was to oppose the simplistic "I assure you I
found her in the book just as she speaks and acts in my
poem" John Chadwick has perpetuated.

When therefore, in the presentation of a less equivocal approach to Browning's view of fact, Smalley returns to
his interpretation of my reading of Rossetti, it is not inaccurate to say he ignores the bounds of logical abstracting:

> Cundiff remarks that since numerous other readers
> of the Old Yellow Book have found the evidence
> "almost equally balanced, it would be odd if Brown-
> ing had not made the same discovery. " He argues
> (if I understand him) that Browning therefore be-
> lieved there was no way of arriving at a reliable
> reading of the truth behind the evidence of the Old
> Yellow Book.   But this is to assume that Browning
> viewed the Old Yellow Book and the possibility of
> getting at the essential truth latent in its factual
> data in much the same way as another person
> might view them.   (p. 5)

Then, after explaining that the poem on which Browning
worked four to eight years is too restricted in itself to
reveal what the poet was saying about truth and fact, Smalley turns to Red Cotton Night-Cap Country: a poem in which
Browning undertook to interpret truth from the ambiguous reports of a French suicide scandal "with the sort of confidence" he had earlier exercised on Chatterton's life and suicide.   The briefest answer to such an approach is that
Browning convinced few on Chatterton, and that, in disbeliev-
ing the commonly accepted view Léonce Miranda destroyed
himself out of remorse for unfilial behavior, Browning had
to resort to the fantasy that Miranda's hope in leaping to his
death was "that angels would save him and a miracle would
allow him to keep both his religion and his mistress. "

Smalley's most extended argument for Browning's continued and unreserved respect for facts ten years subsequent
to the writing of The Ring and the Book is founded on a
metaphor from The Two Poets of Croisic which recalls the
Ring metaphor developed some fourteen years before.   His

quotation has a natural appeal, and all might go well, if in
Smalley's example,

> But truth, truth, that's the gold! and all the good
> I find in fancy is, it serves to set
> Gold's inmost glint free, gold which comes up rude
> And rayless from the mine,
>   (1209-12)

Browning was not saying the very opposite of what Smalley
reports him to be saying. Smalley suspects this too in writing "Browning here seems, on first glance at any rate, to
exalt his factual materials at the expense of his own imaginative contribution" (p. 3; italics added). And a nearby stanza
would have told him conclusively that Browning's purpose was
indeed something else:

> Wherefore? Who does not know how these La Roques,
> Voltaires, can say and unsay, praise and blame,
> Prove black white, white black, play at paradox
> And, when they seem to lose it, win the game?
>   (1169-72)

The Ring and the Book itself offers Smalley an excellent explication of the playful and admittedly light ironic touches of
The Two Poets of Croisic:

> This is the bookful; thus far the truth,
> The untempered gold, the fact untampered with, ...
> . . . . Was this truth of force
> Able to take its own part as truth should,
> Sufficient, self-sustaining? Why, if so--
> Yonder's a fire, into it goes my book.
>   (I. 364-375)

In The Two Poets of Croisic, as DeVane tells Smalley,
Browning is burlesquing the "brevity of human fame," and,
we may be sure, is in no way bolstering "a more traditional reading of the Ring metaphor." Nor is the poet, in
this typical derogation of human speech and conduct, belittling his fancy or declaring "a remarkably high value upon
'truth' or the gold ore of objective fact."
     As it seems to Smalley that there are perils in lean-
ing too heavily on a close and particular reading of the Ring
metaphor, it seems to me that through a proper understanding of the metaphor he could avoid the following exaggeration:
"[Cundiff] asserts that Browning... avowed through his Ring

metaphor that he meant to create characters of his own without the intention of keeping faithful to the essential truth of the characters of his source" (p. 3). The one purpose I have clung to in studying the metaphor is to indicate that beneath the gold or symbolically factual surface of the poem, is a mixture of fact and fancy in proportions equivalent to the proportions of gold and copper (ten to twenty per cent copper) in a ring. As I have thought of the facts which appear in lawyers' briefs and witnesses' depositions, I have represented the poem's proportions, under the metaphor, as favoring pristine facts as pristine gold is favored over copper. While in the metaphor I find Browning's own cognizance of broad interpretive and idealizing privileges, Smalley sees an "admirable Ring metaphor [pressed] farther than logic would allow Browning to go" and, if interpreted my way, a denial of Browning's statement to Chadwick and of the poet's generous use of source material. But rather than say that in Cundiff's opinion Browning "was in large measure creating... a new personality for the heroine of his poem" (p. 1), Smalley might have recognized the restrictiveness of my phrase, "enhanced the character of Pompilia." Or better still, he might have forewarned the reader he would later be admitting, "It is undoubtedly true... that Browning... speaks... of 'what one calls, idealization of the characters,' and, as Cundiff also points out effectively, there are indeed passages... capable of being interpreted as evidence that Browning felt free to give his Fancy quite a loose rein in creating portions of his poem" (p. 2). On encountering Langbaum's over-emphasis of fact, Smalley insists: "Browning's is the view of a profoundly creative artist unobsessed with facts in any way that is connoted by 'facts and figures.'" On encountering my statement, "Browning frankly admitted that his characters are idealized," he becomes less insistent: "Browning employs idealization, I think, only in the sense of getting at the essence of character, rather than in the sense of creating character that improves upon reality." So to my "enhanced character" Smalley persists in attributing "new personality"; to my "belittle fact" he attributes "concrete fact"; to my gold [fact] he attributes "'truth' or the gold ore of objective fact" or data; and to my "disparage or minimize" he attributes "contempt, derision, and scorn."]

10. Other lines the interpreter should not overlook: "Whose care is lest men see too much at once. / He made the sign, such God-glimpse must suffice" (I. 595-596); "Indisputably fact,... / Dwindled into no bigger than a book" (I. 665-671); "(Which take at best imperfect cognizance, / Since, how

heart moves brain, and how both move hand, / What mortal
ever in entirety saw?)" (I. 827-829); "(So universal is its
plague of squint)" (I. 879).

11.   By this identical evidence Mrs. Orr was convinced of
Pompilia's Christian gentleness and absolute maiden modesty
(Handbook, p. 87).   Writing in 1927, Mrs. Russell can say
only that Pompilia was "in an equivocal position, ... finally
destroyed by a terrific penalty either wholly undeserved or
partly the meed of her own folly" (One Word More on Browning, p. 121).   J. E. Shaw thinks: "She is not a bad girl
made into a good girl; the testimony of Fra Celestino Angelo,
in the Book, represents her as innocent, modest, and for-
giving, dying like a saint" (p. 68).   A point of view different
from Mr. Shaw's is advanced by Paul E. Beichner; "Fra
Celestino's Affidavit and The Ring and the Book, " Modern
Language Notes, LVIII (May 1943), 335-340.   Mr. Beichner
argues that Celestino's affidavit is inadmissible under the
Seal of Confession.   [Addendum: Langbaum has strongly
disagreed, "since there is no sign, as the author himself
admits, that Browning knew this" (VN, No. 17 [1960], p.
12).   And it could also be argued that Celestino recounted
Pompilia's words without revealing her confession.]

4

INTERPRETATION OF BROWNING'S RING METAPHOR

More than the most competent critics realize, an
analysis of the interpretation of Browning's Ring metaphor
indicates that interpretation of The Ring and the Book is
largely determined by understanding or misunderstanding of
the analogy between ring-making and poem-making. Whether
we prefer it or not, Browning's use of truth is inextricably
interwoven with the meaning of his Ring metaphor. If Robert Langbaum had known in 1956 what he learned by 1960,
and further modified in 1966, there would have been at most
only a restricted controversy over absolutist and relativist
truth in the poem. And if a majority of the critics who
have written about Browning's poem had known the metaphor
better, there is a strong chance that far fewer would have
assumed a central truth, all because a ring naturally suggests a focal center but not because Browning ever once
speaks of a central truth in connection with the Ring metaphor or the poem. Interpreters of the poem may turn the
metaphor to preconceived purposes, and editors of individual
editions may comment on it as the poet's method of making
himself clearer, but in so doing they invariably leave the
meaning less clear and dismiss the metaphor as suddenly
as they resorted to it. With all critics of Browning's long
poem in mind, one may venture to say that in the annals of
criticism few instances exist of greater disregard for factual
information than their disregard for the metallurgy of gold.
So great has been the disinclination of critics to seek information on the technical processes involved in the formation
of a gold ring that a summing up of the resulting difficulties
may encourage others to inspect the technical foundation of
Browning's Ring metaphor.

Excluding critics before 1925 who, like Mrs. Orr and
the others quoted in Essay Two, only speculated on ring-
making, we may start with A. G. Drachmann. Not that
Drachmann himself consulted a technical source on the metallurgy of gold, but he did approach the poet's application of

the Ring metaphor in a professional manner. Unfortunately,
he too thought that with the repristinating acid all alloy metal,
external and internal copper, was removed from the gold
ring. Drachmann's second error was to interpret the gold
of the poem, not as the pure crude facts, but as "the truth
contained in the Old Yellow Book" ("Alloy and Gold, " SP,
XXII [July 1925] 418-424). Basing his observations therefore on the inaccurate belief that all the copper was repristinated from the goldsmith's ring, he concluded that all
of the poet's fancy was removed from the poem subsequent
to the end of Book I, which is also the terminal point of
Browning's fancy to Langbaum, Wasserman, Sullivan, Friedman, and other advocates of Drachmann's thesis. If Drachmann had not believed that all the alloy (copper) vanished
from the artificer's gold ring with the spurt of acid, he
might not have deduced that Browning himself (really his
fancy) vanished from the poem at the end of the first book,
and thus might not have misled others. But it was the
"washing with acid" which motivated Drachmann to disprove
Frances T. Russell's severe charge of willful deception by
Browning, the act of "repristination" which today seems to
take precedence over all other speculations on the poem.

In his reply to Russell, Drachmann consequently postu-
lates that Browning "is writing about the universally acknowledged fact that no speech, however true, can be identical
with the truth itself" (p. 420; italics added). With this
sound premise on the relative value of human truth, he
quotes the important passage:

> Let this old woe step on the stage again!
> Act itself o'er anew for men to judge,
> Not by the very sense and sight indeed--
> (Which take at best imperfect cognizance,
> Since, how heart moves brain, and how both move
>   hand,
> What mortal ever in entirety saw?)
> --No dose of purer truth than man digests,
> But truth with falsehood, milk that feeds him now,
> Not strong meat he may get to bear some day--
> To-wit, by voices we call evidence,
> Uproar in the echo, live fact deadened down,
> Talked over, bruited abroad, whispered away,
> Yet helping us to all we seem to hear:
> For how else know we save by worth of word?
>   (I. 824-837)

And he says these lines may be paraphrased like this:

> "I will let this old tragedy enact itself before you
> once more. I cannot do it as if you were present
> at the actual occurrence (and even then you would
> be able to see only the insignificant part, the mere
> facts, not the important part, the motives); but as
> it is so here in this world that we never get truth
> itself, only hear words that bear some relation to
> it, (in another world we may be able to bear pure
> truth), I will tell you the story not straightforward-
> ly, but through the mouths of a number of persons
> --just as we learn about everything else we know. "
> (p. 420; italics added)

Drachmann then says that the charge of "falsehood" and misinterpretation, his answer to Russell, has nothing to do with
the alloy metal: "No dose of purer truth than man digests /
But truth with falsehood, milk that feeds him now, / Not
strong meat he may get to bear some day. " One of the best
glosses on Browning's truth in the poem, these are words
over which most interpreters of the Ring metaphor continue
to trip or to jump clear of entanglement.   But Drachmann
is, of course, more concerned to tell us that Browning, in
using the word truth, "does not mean facts, ... but the motives, the spiritual truth, that which deals with right and
wrong, not with done and undone. " "In short [with the second of three brief recountings of the tale in Book I], we are
told quite plainly the poet's own idea as to the right and
wrong of the matter" (p. 422).   And, as Drachmann adds,
the second recounting differs from the first bare factual recounting only in that it is told in the order of the events
and "that the moral coherence, the motives, the guilt, has
been made plain by means of the poet's fancy. "   Finally,
according to Drachmann: after Browning's disappearance
with the "wash o' the water, " the poet for a third time re-
counts the bare facts, at the end of which "the ring [Book I]
is formed, and now needs only the decoration" (p. 423).

It is generally believed that Browning briefly tells
the story of Pompilia's life three times in Book I, and that
only the second recounting is a fanciful one.   But, inexpli-
cably, Drachmann transposes lines 824-837 (given above and
on the impossibility of man's reaching the truth itself) in
order with them to introduce the first recounting, when actually these lines immediately follow the third recounting and
introduce the lines in which the speakers of Books II-XI are

presented and described.   In so distorting the whole poem as
well as the first book, he should have been restrained by
knowing Browning himself would have transposed the lines in
question if he had intended what Drachmann advances.   A
serious but inaccurately founded interpretation, it is probable
that Drachmann reveals recognition of the inconsistencies of
his arguments in his noticeably abbreviated remarks near
the end: particularly his reluctance to say in unison "the
ring is formed" in Book I while "the finished ring represents
the poem, " and his reference to "decoration" without another
word.   To be specific on when the ring is formed and when
it is finished, as will be seen later, is to add greater substance to the strongest objections one may raise against the
theory initiated by Drachmann.   Apparently he did not care
to label specifically as "decoration" either the middle ten
books of the poem or the poet's posy, though he saw nothing
strange in calling the totally unimaginative material he leaves
us in Books II-XI "the poem" itself.   But by literally interpreting "I disappeared" as the absolute removal of Browning
himself from the poem, when every allusion to and every
other statement of disappearance in Book I refers to fancy,
Drachmann nonetheless succeeded in stamping large on several current explanations of Browning's ring analogy his own
summary thought:

> The gold of the ingot represents the truth con-
> cealed in the Old Yellow Book, --the truth about
> the motives, about the question of moral worth
> and worthlessness.
>
> The alloy represents the poet's fancy that enabled
> him to live through the whole drama, to connect
> the facts into a coherence, to supply what was
> wanting to make a whole, and thus to grasp the
> inner truth of the persons.
>
> The 'repristination,' the washing with acid, rep-
> resents the fact that Browning in the poem (Books
> II-XI) refrains from speaking in his own person,
> but tells us the facts in ten different ways, leaving
> it to ourselves to find out the truth.   (p. 423).

My own effort to explain the metaphor and to disentangle its application by representative critics occurred in
1948, when it was not the happiest time to be working on
Browning, especially The Ring and the Book.   But all of
that was changed in 1956 by Robert Langbaum's advocacy

of the poet's truth as relativist, a lively essay to which I
replied negatively in 1959 (Essay Three).   In 1961 George
B. Wasserman published a third formal interpretation of the
Ring metaphor which, for ingenuity and quality, was soon
favored by several critics who were weary of and outspoken-
ly unsympathetic toward the everlasting analyses of truth by
absolutist proponents.   Its being a probable outgrowth of
Langbaum's published theory on Browning's truth made Wasserman's interpretation a natural one at the time.   But his
thought all in itself, as applied to Browning's poem, remains
influential and especially courageous in the delving into the
poet's "wax and honey" analogy.   He may, as I hope to show,
be proved inaccurate in his analysis of Browning's double
analogy, but in the whole of his essay he opened up an almost entirely new area for worthy study.   That the technical
errors, first to be pointed out, will alter the eventual significance of Wasserman's theory is problematical, but a re-
vision in the light of probable corrections might save the
Ring metaphor from additional tarnish.

By "impurities in an amalgam" ("The Meaning of
Browning's Ring-Figure, " MLN, LXXVI [May 1961], 420-426)
Wasserman clearly but inexactly means copper, the second
alloy metal on the surface of an unrepristinated gold ring;
but by amalgam, introduced into criticism of the Ring metaphor by himself, Wasserman reveals a serious flaw in his
understanding of metallurgic processes.   Normally an amalgam is the result of an addition of mercury (the more fluid)
to silver, though when added to gold mercury's function is
the same.   So an amalgam is an alloy or union suggesting
the opposite of Browning's addition of copper, which in alloy
with gold makes the softer metal malleable, harder "to bear
hammer and be firm to file. "   Hence in analyzing the poet's
analogy of "wax and honey" Wasserman all but once treats
the wax, in the melting together of wax and honey, as a
softening agent, when in reality it provides the substance
needed to slow the o'erflowing honey, as does Browning's
fancy in making the pure facts "crisper. "   In speaking of
"the softness and richness of 'slivers of pure gold'" he
likewise misses an important aspect of gold which Browning
advises him not to neglect: purity (pristine quality), never
richness, is the aspect consistently accented by the poet.
And when describing "a 'fancy' which fused itself with the
facts, " Wasserman off and on forgets that the poet himself
fused fact and fancy, neither in itself being capable of the
function.

The technical inaccuracies which shade the clarity of
Wasserman's interpretation are possibly not too significant
in themselves, but together they bear more weightily on the
progress of his thought.   From the outset he is persuaded
that Browning as poet, perhaps as monologuist himself in
Books I and XII, is more than one consciousness.   This
means that Robert Browning as a poetic recorder of the
facts exercises an objective ego; as a participant (or monologuist) in Book I exercises a subjective alter ego; and as
poet disappears with the recorded fusion of fact and fancy,
which presumably happens in Book I or before the opening
of Book II (pp. 424-425):

"fancy"	"I" [recorder, poet]
"subjective alter ego"	"objective ego"
"subjective identification"	"objective observation"

It is a most intricate dissection of the poetic mind, and
gives rise naturally to the speculations which Morse Peckham and Mary Rose Sullivan have carried forward.   As may
be illustrated also with these critics, the technical flaws
which have been named become more serious and more numerous as subjectivist and relativist advocates pay less and
less attention to the specified object of their thought.

That Wasserman probably knew Drachmann's pioneer
interpretation of the Ring metaphor and gleaned encouragement from its possible meaning is implicitly stated in Miss
Sullivan's interpretation.   As she expresses it: "A. G. Drachmann... sees the gold as 'the truth about the motives' and
the alloy as the poet's 'fancy, ' but he interprets the repristination as 'the fact that Browning in the poem (Books II-XI)
refrains from speaking in his own person... leaving it to ourselves to find out the truth'" (Browning's Voices in The Ring
and the Book [Toronto, 1969], p. 20).   Yet whereas Drachmann stresses our finding the truth (now admittedly coercive-
ly imposed by Browning), Wasserman is not thematically concerned with the truth.   He is therefore on solid footing,
when insisting that Browning's Ring metaphor must be considered as an organic part of the poetic context; on loose
footing, when restricting "organic part" "to the larger structure of the first book of the poem" (p. 421).   For with the
latter act of precluding organic unity to the total poem the

separation of Book I takes place and predicates the remaining essay, an irregular pattern of thought which first may
be contested by virtue of Wasserman's own insistent logic
on the metaphor.   If Wasserman is demonstrably concerned
over separation of the metaphor from its poetic context by
others, he should even more logically be concerned by his
separation of Book I from the remaining eleven books of the
poem.   Whether Wasserman considers the first book, save
for lines 478-678, to be a nonpoetic introduction (as Drachmann implies) or a monologue spoken by the poet (as Miss
Sullivan states), he and they owe allegiance also to the total
poem, including Book XII which they virtually discard, even
though the poet himself is thought to be the dramatic speaker.

    In three admirably concise sentences Wasserman goes
to the heart of Browning's task as Browning himself very
probably saw it: "Art, then, is a re-presentation of life
or truth through the agency of the incomplete and formless
records which that life has produced.   The poet must recognize the life for which the facts stand, 'calculate... the lost
proportions of the style, ' and attempt to restore that life.
As the jeweler [?] 'binds the loose, one bar without a
break' and engraves the surface of a ring with 'lilied loveliness, ' so the poet must seek the motives of actions, 'the
informing thought, ' at the same time restoring to them the
dramatic elements of narrative" (pp. 422-423).   But then
Wasserman reverts to his plan of isolating Book I by asking,
"What of the repristination of the amalgam mentioned in the
earlier lines?"   And by ignoring the stated purpose of the
analogous spurt of acid, though within twenty-one lines of
type he juxtaposes "And forth the alloy [fancy] unfastened
flies in fume" (I. 25) and "I disappeared" (I. 687), he can
with Cundiff "realize that 'Browning would have us think
that he similarly removed himself from the FACE of the
poem. . . .   He restored to the surface of the poem a pure
narrative of the book, knowing that his fancy had contributed
to the interior structure'" (pp. 423-424).   "Thus interpreted, "
Wasserman continues, "'repristination' is nothing more than
an analogy of the manipulation of point of view, for it is by
assigning the task of narration to various dramatic personae
that Browning is able to 'remove himself from the FACE of
the poem'" (p. 424; italics added).   I have not, however,
dared to complicate the Ring metaphor further by going beyond the symbolic application Browning himself makes of repristination: clearly, he wished to pretend that evidence of
his fancy, not himself, was erased from the factual surface
of his poem.   So Wasserman, who seems to accept my in-

terpretation up to this point, concludes that "Cundiff overlooks a more important distinction implicit in his own interpretation, that between a 'fancy' which fused itself [?]
with the facts of The Old Yellow Book and an 'I' which disappeared from this fusion, a distinction between a subjective
alter ego which identified itself with the life behind the fact
and an objective ego which recorded that life" (p. 424). As
we shall see, there is room for vastly different interpretations of "manipulation of point of view" and "lilied loveliness,"
which supposedly are considered the same by Wasserman and
those who follow him.

At once recognizing the difference between fact and
truth in Browning's poem as a matter of degree, not kind,
Wasserman sets up a mental equation

honey	fact	gold
wax	fancy	experience [copper ?]

in which he sees the softness and richness [purity and pristine quality ?] of honey, fact, and gold; the substance and
durability of wax, fancy, and experience [copper]; and then,
like John Killham, he thinks the poet's analogies unusual, as
they surely are. But the analogies would be less unusual if
Wasserman himself had not complicated Browning's thought
by introducing experience in his equation when the poet specifically equates wax, fancy, and copper, the alloy metal.
Introduction of experience is thus a contestable change and
explains why Wasserman is required to go astray in saying
"a 'fancy' which fused itself with the facts." Browning, the
literary artificer, explicitly says that he fused fancy with
fact (I. 469), indicating that though fancy may play over the
facts ("the extant remains of human experience") of the book,
the poet's experience--his total being--is larger and more
all-inclusive than his fancy alone, and manipulator of both
fancy and fact.

By inference, very probably by documentation, Wasserman's understanding of repristination to be Browning's
analogy for the manipulation of point of view has substantially
contributed to recent subjectivist and relativist treatments of
The Ring and the Book. Appearing five years after Langbaum's essay on the relativistic aspect of Browning's truth,
Wasserman's essay does not overtly express the doctrine
that knowledge, at most subjective and relative, is derived

from one's own consciousness; that we know directly no external object; that there is no objective standard, test, or
measure of truth; and that individual feeling is the standard
by which to judge right and wrong.   But his implied thoughts
do suggest a relationship through which Peckham and Sullivan
have been greatly stimulated, if not actually guided, in their
efforts.   Carried to its logical conclusion, for example,
Wasserman's "At the instant of its birth, the life of fact
begins to die" (p. 422) need not, but almost inevitably does,
entail the exclusion of recognition by Browning of the undeniable, though feeble, dignity of man's thought, experience,
and reserve wisdom.   For this reason, a brief diversion
from Wasserman may not seem altogether inappropriate.

     Well-known and honored for his scholarly explications
and broad syntheses, Morse Peckham has nonetheless misread the author of The Ring and the Book.   In Browning's
early poems, as Peckham states, the poet had his doubts
about many things, truth included.   But long before 1864-
68 old things are passed away, and Browning, in a culminating response to frustrated ambition and his "due to God," is
irrevocably disposed to show that in man's fated striving
only God's truth is worthy of being designated his final goal.
It should not have been so difficult for Peckham to see that
in presenting the truth obliquely, Browning meant just that,
not that truth is subjective and deliberately fabricated.   Using Browning as a kind of subjective alter ego, however,
Peckham advances the belief that to the historical Browning
the object had no determination beyond the will of the subject.   What he does technically in creating a twentieth-century Browning merely removes the poet a step or steps
farther from the facts, and is harmless enough: Is the
Robert Browning of Elizabeth Barrett's Elizabeth Browning's
Robert Browning Robert Browning's Robert Browning?   ("Historiography and The Ring and the Book," Victorian Poetry,
VI [Autumn-Winter 1968], 245-246) But however earnest he may be, Peckham invites suspicion of subverting to
a peculiar purpose a poem as essentially Platonic, a poet
as essentially idealistic, as The Ring and the Book and its
author.   In Browning's search for reality, he at least found
persistent reminders of a divine spark in man as well as of
all kinds of illusions.

     Peckham's belief that Platonism (that is, idealism)
disappeared with the Enlightenment insofar as genuine intel-
lectualism is concerned, may explain why he and several
other critics of Browning see no good reason for Altick's

and Loucks's chapters entitled "Here's Rhetoric and to
Spare!" and "Poke at Them with Scripture." Yet it is not
a particularly novel idea, through a long recital of precedents for the new historiography, to reach the assumption
that Browning might have been a Rankean-type (see Essay
Two, note 2, for a much earlier advocacy) historian in the
writing of The Ring and the Book. The evidence of Platonic
and scriptural influence upon Browning, throughout his poetic
career, is overwhelming; the evidence of Browning's being
one with Ranke remains tenuous in the equation,

$$\text{B...} \quad @ \angle cB @ [(a @ x) + (b @ x) + (c @ x)...] \rangle.$$

Severe lessons in the twentieth century, in all realms of
human activity, are re-teaching us that nothing is made substantive by the mere assertion thereof. So it may be hoped
that it is not untimely in criticism of Browning and The Ring
and the Book to expect reasonably documented proof of pronouncements as radically different as Peckham's:

> Robert Browning, the English poet, was saying the
> same thing in The Ring and the Book. Art is
> "true" because it is a lie and doesn't pretend to
> be anything else. Art cannot redeem the world,
> but it can give the man who looks at the world the
> experience of value. (Beyond the Tragic Vision
> [Braziller, New York, 1962], p. 259).

> Thus Browning indicates that the experience of
> value is but momentary; .. no propositions, no con-
> ceptions, no metaphysical truths, no moral veri-
> ties--nothing can be derived from that experience....
> Value, then, lies not in intuitively perceiving a
> truth or in embodying and incarnating transcenden-
> tal truth in reality, but in breaking through an il-
> lusion. (p. 275)

> Therefore, in the 1860's in The Ring and the Book
> [Browning] concludes, as I have already suggested,
> that truth, historical, scientific, or moral, or
> metaphysical, cannot be known; but that the function
> of art, which makes no claims to truth, which is
> quite frankly a lie, is to so affect the mind of the
> observer that his orientations are shaken up and
> restructured, thus releasing him to do a significant
> act. (p. 275-276)

> Even of Browning as speaker is this true, as his
> continuous redefinitions of the word "truth" imply
> and reveal. Even of the Pope is this true, for in
> deciding whether or not to permit Guido to be exe-
> cuted he redefines himself in historical terms;
> moreover, he is anachronistic about it. His posi-
> tion is that truth wears out, and that Christian
> truth has in fact worn out; but that his role as a
> Pope requires him to sustain it, even though he
> foresees the Enlightenment with uncanny accuracy.
> (Victorian Revolutionaries [Braziller, New York,
> 1970], p. 121)

Such a bold attempt to make of Robert Browning a
moral instrumentalist, ignoring the poet's proclaimed faith
in a truthful and loving God, is unique. It would, I therefore suspect, be pointless to challenge Peckham's reading of
the Pope's monologue, his understanding of Fra Celestino's
purpose in Book XII, or to refer to commonplace thoughts
like "and save the soul beside, " "for God's will done on
earth, " "know there, simply, instantaneously, " and "how
else know save by worth of word?" Nor, apparently, would
it change anything to remind Peckham that in Browning "the
experience of value" and the "significant act" are always
followed and earmarked by their failure to consummate an
idealistic goal. Nonetheless, in that Browning's art tells
the truth obliquely, a shading away from the essential--a
pattern of indirection--is compulsory, all because of man's
restricted perceptivity, not for his preference always to tell
a lie. Innumerable men have borne witness to this rationale
for man's limitations, for his inability to tell the whole truth.
And only by excluding from Browning's thought the profound
motivation for his agnosticism concerning human knowledge
may Peckham hope to transform the poet into an instrumental gadget. For the recorded drive of Browning's life is
that of a poet, consciously performing as sage and prophet,
and in The Ring and the Book paying his due to God through
a Pope eulogized for his representation of truth, through a
Pompilia immortalized for her vision of truth and love,
through a Caponsacchi dedicated to truth and love in a world
beyond, and through a loved one poetized for attainment of
all three absolutes. By substituting the word value for the
word truth in Browning's long poem, Peckham attempts to
eliminate the fruits of the mind, the heart, and the will, the
whole essence of the man. The poet he synthesizes and
calls Browning is a poet I have never read.

Returning to Wasserman--his emphasis on experience
as an important constituent of poetry, on art as an autonomy
equivalent to the life which produces its materials, on the
possibility of Dickensian-like characters performing exclusively on their own, and on the relativity of truth--we still have
reason not to despair.   The famous passage to which it all
points is an old conundrum,   and the troublesome line is
"Fancy with fact is just one fact the more":

> thence bit by bit I dug [from the book]
> The lingot truth, that memorable day,
> Assayed and knew my piecemeal gain was gold, --
> Yes; but from something else surpassing that,
> Something of mine which, mixed up with the mass,
> Made it bear hammer and be firm to file. ·
> FANCY WITH FACT IS JUST ONE FACT THE MORE;
> To-wit, that FANCY has informed, transpierced,
> Thridded and so thrown fast the FACTS else free,...
> I fused my LIVE SOUL and that inert stuff,
> Before attempting smithcraft, on the night
> After the day when, --TRUTH thus grasped and gained, --
> The book was shut and done with and laid by.
>   (I. 458-472; capital letters added)

To me, the line means that any fact turned over in the imagination becomes always a new and somewhat different fact,
and consequently a second fact.   To Wasserman, the line
means that "the fancy, by virtue of its plasticity [substance
and durability would be nearer the poet's meaning], is able
to approximate or realize any vital principle or action.   The
'fancy' allowed Browning to have his will with the facts (I.
778), enabled him to conceive imaginatively and as a formal
unity the life of which, in response to the facts alone, he
had only a vague intuition" (p. 425).   But from here on in
his interpretation Wasserman admittedly begins to reveal his
uncertainty.   Fancy is undoubtedly involved in lines 707-778,
but if line 778 ("Letting me have my will again with these")
is put into its immediate and lengthy context, we see that
Browning was allowed his will with the facts through the in-
termediaries of a special gift.   This gift is like the mage's
gift, an art of arts which would enable Browning to write
his name with Faust's, and encompasses for the poet a belief that he had resuscitative powers of the soul comparable
to Elisha's--all of which Browning here calls not a fancy but
a laughing spirit which touched every part of his body, lighted
his eye, and let him have his will with the facts.   And it
should not be overlooked that this same spirit which pos-

sessed him in Florence at the beginning of the imaginative
process, guided him during the poem's composition in London, the creative point at which Miss Sullivan picks up Wasserman's interpretation.

Assuming therefore, but not accepting, that spirit in
his chosen passage (I. 707-778) means fancy alone, we may
pursue Wasserman's arguments to their conclusions.   From
lines 458-706 of Book I, three fourths of which give the
poet's first subjective recounting of Pompilia's story, Wasserman selects a limited number of lines to establish his
reading of Browning's creative process, chiefly: "I fused
my live soul and that inert stuff / Before attempting smith-
craft" (469-470).   It is regrettable he could give only one
paragraph to lines (458-472) so exceptionally crucial yet so
intractable they have defied confident analysis.   Like his
fellow interpreters he may have become exhausted by Browning's proliferated metaphors and illustrative embellishments.
But it is more likely he thought he had adequately prepared
the way by adoption of a consistent understanding of the two
opening analogies, the wax and honey, the copper and gold.
Thus, momentarily ignoring the ill-chosen "amalgam, " Wasserman can pointedly say that fancy, like wax [and copper],
informs and binds.   He can also recognize that the poet
"fused [his] live soul and the inert stuff, " but then he reverts to patterns stemming from the "amalgam" in order to
draw a distinction between composition and creation which
proves to be most confusing.   To say "the essential poem,
'my fancy with those facts, ' already existed in Browning's
mind as he paced the terrace of Casa Guidi, mulling over
the facts of The Old Yellow Book, " is to place the creation
of the poem before the organization of the facts, and reminds
one of Langbaum's having Browning throw his poem, not the
OYB, into the fire.   Wasserman forgets that the analogous
rings are first tied together by one rod.   Yet "mulling"
leaves the impression of continued planning on the poet's
part and conforms better to the meaning of "my fancy with
those facts" (I. 678), a line which appears near the end of
the full passage, not as implied by Wasserman at the beginning.

Either the allied processes of mixing and fusing (I.
462-469), about which Wasserman writes, say approximately
the same thing or Browning is speaking of two separate acts
only he could distinguish satisfactorily for us.   The meaning
of "mixed up" and "fused, " independently or when analogously
applied to gold and copper, indicates Browning was repeating

himself; "live soul," however, may or may not accord with
fancy. In Essay Three I suggested that Browning first accumulated the facts; second, he bound them together as one
binds rings on a single rod; and third, he brought the facts
back to life by fusing them and his "live soul." To this
understanding I still hold. In the first statement by Browning, fancy seems to have the limited function, on being
mixed with the facts, of holding them together; in the second, "live soul" seems to suggest that Browning, through
the agency of his imagination, restored to life the long dead
persons of the book. And both fancy and live soul seem to
be agencies which, when mixed with the mass of facts by
the poet himself, make the facts respond more properly to
hammer and file, tools again indicative of artistic control.
It is not at all farfetched to predict that future interpreters
will find these lines as intractable, though just as fascinat-
ing, as have their predecessors.

     In his brief treatment of the crucial passage under
discussion (I. 458-472), Wasserman concludes: "To the extent that it was the 'fancy' only which entered the fusion [a
foregone conclusion], Browning, the objective self, had 'disappeared' from the amalgam. The terrace passage vividly
draws this distinction between the ego and the alter ego by
exploiting their respective functions of objective observation
and subjective identification" (p. 425). But why travel so
far around something Browning had made perfectly clear
from the beginning? If one wished simply to establish that
Browning disappeared with the finished poem, not with Book
I, the easiest way would be to quote: "I disappeared; the
book grew all in all;... / Lovers of dead truth [fanciless
fact], did ye fare the worse? / Lovers of live truth [fanci-
ful fact], found ye false my tale?" (I. 687, 696-697) Whether Browning's alleged disappearance occurred at the end of
Book I or at the end of the whole poem is, then, the issue,
and since Miss Sullivan clearly proposes Book I, it will be
well to meet that issue when her recent book is considered.

     If one desires to show how an artist depersonalizes
himself, which seems to be Wasserman's chief purpose, he
may begin by explaining twentieth-century experimentation
with point of view and end with Henry James's central intelligence or any other neatly comprised solution. Whether
others will be detained long by the new phraseology is beside the point. But Browning gave no evidence of wanting
to be unknown as creator of the characters of The Ring and
the Book. In reality, he insisted that the characters were

his creations, the result of his plan to make them as historically convincing as possible within the framework of a created poem.   Of course he distinguished himself from his
fancy which, through his own mental processes nonetheless,
carried him the whole flight from Arezzo to Castelnuovo; in
the brief course (I. 497-660) of describing that flight, moreover, he eight times says he saw, one time knew, the incidents as they developed.   Wasserman's effort to show that
"the poet's fancy is actually not separated from the poem"
is unnecessarily wrought, since earlier he had said, "It is
a commonplace of aesthetics that no element of an artistic
whole can be isolated from that whole, and that any objective
or subjective element which enters into the composition of
an art work remains an immutable part of it" (p. 423).
Evidently an aside, Wasserman's return to an unisolable
fancy is not essential to his last paragraph.   The thrust of
his words is that "in the release of the spiritual fancy from
the corporeal poet, there is something akin to the concept
of 'repristination.'"   That is, with the Ring metaphor Browning wished to suggest depersonalization.   But by positioning
himself solidly in every book of the poem Browning made it
impossible for anyone to say reliably that the poet withdrew
from the poem at any point except in a symbolic way.   For
his own involvement at every stage of the development of
The Ring and the Book, Browning has enunciated his reading
as the one he was inspired to present, his artistic design
as that of telling the truth obliquely, and his desire as that
of chancing upon some fragment of a whole.   If the traditional prologue and epilogue are now rejected, there are still
Browning's directing (introducing) or speaking beyond doubt
in Books I and XII as evidenced by residence, religion, citi-
zenship, formal and informal dedication, providential guidance; and his inability to stay out of Books II through XI as
evidenced by the constant filtering through of RB in character, exposition, and imagery.   It is not surprising, then, to
read finally that Wasserman judges "the jeweler's repristination of the amalgamated ring" to be "only an approximate
analogy of the creative process of the poet."   Or to be told
that "the poet's fancy is actually not separated from the
poem," that whatever repristination there is occurs "before
the poem is written down."   Such an interpretation is, of
course, sharply contrary to the long-standing belief that
Browning on the completion of his poem wished symbolically
--'"T is a figure, a symbol"--to remove his fancy from the
surface facts as the ring-maker in reality drives the surface
copper off in fume with the spurt of acid.   Wasserman's
thinking may be bolder than his conclusions, as Miss Sullivan

tries to prove, but he does say, perhaps a bit indirectly, that Browning repristinated himself out of The Ring and the Book (Books II-XI, which he calls "the poem") somewhere in Book I. He also leaves the impression that repristination does not concern the fancy, but the poet instead. Because Miss Sullivan advances in some detail a similar thesis, it will be helpful to continue with the proposals of both critics, in the light of Drachmann's earlier thoughts.

Not a book from which it is easy to extract the pertinent or dependable matter on poetic artistry, Browning's Voices in "The Ring and the Book" is nevertheless an earnest attempt to make the poem more readable, "less tiring and repetitive." How Miss Sullivan, capable of sensitive perception and cumulative critical effect, could misplace her avowed mission so early and become enmeshed in a thesis as tenuous as "voice and address" will justify what is to be said about Chapters I, VI, VII, and VIII. Deciding that "voices" are more conducive to "truth telling" than convincingly created and vocally adept characters, she explains:

> [Browning] means the breathing of life and voice into the characters of the old yellow book, then, to represent his pure ring of art; the three narrative summaries [of Book I] were necessary to highlight the progressive steps involved in fashioning the ring--first, the preparation of the crude material (finding and studying the written record); second, the moulding of it by mixing in a firmer, more malleable material (his emotional and imaginative re-creating of the scenes leading up to the trial); and third, the purifying of the shaped ring by the withdrawal of the alloy (suppression of his own personality in the dramatization of the events surrounding the trial). (p. 15)

So after rejecting the efficacy of plot, theme, characterization, and imagery to clarify the meaning of the poem, she traces its growth from weak early attempts at technical correctness to glorious accomplishment in dramatic form, and then attributes the success to Browning's voices. Books I and XII are therefore dramatic monologues spoken by the poet; Books II-XI are dramatic monologues spoken by the individuals involved in the trial. The poet's enthusiasm for truth and fact, for instance, does not deter her from believing that Browning deliberately underscores voices as his solution to a difficult organizational problem. Nor does Browning's struggle with man's intellectual and emotional inadequacies keep her from encouraging her reader to think that through a dramatic reproduction of their voices, from which the poet is ostensibly withdrawn, Browning happily brings his historical characters back to life again. As in her determined recapitulation of the characters' speeches--where Miss Sullivan abstracts individuals possessed still of their author's living attributes even more accurately than Altick and Loucks or W. David Shaw (The Dialectical Temper [Ithaca, 1968])--she will not permit Browning's voices to fade even though they are the most reluctant entities of her dramatic cast. If voices say more than his created characters about Browning's skill, voices we should have; if Miss Sullivan's method places an idle step between the characters and their historical prototypes as well as their readers, the best repair is to forget about it.

Limiting her equation of Browning's analogy of ring-making and poem-making to

$$\frac{\text{fact}}{\text{fancy (personality)}} \qquad \frac{\text{gold}}{\text{copper}}$$

Miss Sullivan avoids Wasserman's substitution of experience for copper only to expand the poet's fancy into the equivalent of personality, or of total poet. It is a design, backed not by the poet's logical and sequential presentation but by her selection of poetic lines which always include the word voice. Since this is Miss Sullivan's method, one may first submit her illustrative lines before paralleling them with additional lines for which no explanation is given. For the sequential development of Browning's analogy in Books I and XII must be recalled in order to indicate that the problem of repristination is essentially unrelated to that of making Book I a dramatic monologue, spoken by Browning himself: her way of pulling Book I back into Wasserman's designation of "the poem" (Books II-XI) while retaining the act of repristination as applicable only to the poet himself. Quoting lines Wasserman would have been required to quote, had he not simply assumed Browning was the monologuist in Books I and XII, Miss Sullivan emphasizes THE VOICE SPEAKING in Book I (pp. 3-8). Whether Book I is a voice or a poet or a character speaking or inditing an introduction or argument to a long poem may or may not seem important in an explanation

of the poem and its controlling metaphor. But we are shown
lines by Miss Sullivan which cannot be disavowed without
proper cause.

As the crux of her argument (Chapter I), though she
clearly recognizes the intent as a common poetic manner of
introducing actors, Miss Sullivan isolates the following lines
from Book I: "Here are the voices presently shall sound /
In due succession. " "The printed voice of him lives now as
then. " "First you hear Count Guido's voice. " "Ah, but you
miss the very tone o' the voice. " Why she chooses to overlook "To-wit, by voices we call evidence, " just five lines
above her first quotation and the only other use of voices in
Book I, becomes clearer as we advance. But with the appearance of voice in the whole poem 36 times--8 in Book I,
one in Book XII--and the appearance of voices 6 times--2 in
Book I, none in Book XII--one wonders what Miss Sullivan
might have done with the word true on recalling it appears
116 times in the poem--7 in Book I, 7 in Book XII--or with
the word truth which appears 193 times--29 in Book I, 16 in
Book XII. Even though the word voices does not appear in
Book XII at all, she encounters no obstacle in the disposal
of Book XII, an essential part of The Ring and the Book, by
saying that the last book, a "continuation" of Book I with
some "diminution of speaker [Browning] due to lack of personal reference, " is "obviously somewhat different" in its
being "a summary of events" with two-thirds of the material
mere quotation (pp. 164-168). Her four quotations including
voice or voices from Book I alone are therefore sufficient
to give Miss Sullivan reason for showing that Browning repristinated himself out of the poem from the end of Book I
to the beginning of Book XII, thus turning over the remainder
of the poem to actors whom Browning as a member of the
cast introduces but with whom he has no stated imaginative
alliance.

Many scholars, including Miss Sullivan in her un-
guarded moments, have contested the independence which
poetic or dramatic characters are said to gain from their
creators; they know it is impossible for a poet's imaginative
contribution to be isolated and expelled from his poetry. For
example, Miss Sullivan herself is no more sure of the repristination of Browning than she is sure of the opposite:
on different occasions she says that Browning "is never the
detached, impartial observer" (p. 8), his voices speak out
"without further intervening comment by the poet" (p. 11),
he "is no detached observer, but a passionate partisan of

Pompilia and the priest" (p. 12), he "lets the actors in the
original drama come before us to speak for themselves" (p.
18), he reconstructs "the events of the murder trial in such
a way that his audience will be able to decide for itself who
was telling the truth" (p. 8).   To be sure she is distinguish-
ing between fancy and personality; she is also speaking about
one and the same poet.   But with the purpose of clarifying
Browning's use of repristination, a symbolic form she does
not think too fragile to sustain minute inspection or to be
turned into an actuality for the poet himself, she places
Browning, the first voice, in a sitting-room (p. 3).   His
audience, which is described as plural and obliquely indicated but intimate, includes "physically present" individuals,
all of whom have disliked him up to this moment, and a
"third person" listener which is later designated the poet's
professional conscience.   Much of her argument she invests
in Browning's manner of address: "London folk, British
Public, do you see this square old yellow book?   Examine it
yourselves!   Give it me back!" the last injunction directed
at a listener who has been handed the book.   Rejecting the
remotest chance that these exclamatory words are rhetorical,
Miss Sullivan concludes: "[Browning's] intimate relationship
with his audience is strongly emphasized by the repeated use
of the 'I' subject in juxtaposition with second person references" (p. 4).   For whom, one surely must inquire, did
Browning so elaborately describe the old book, if all of his
listeners could pass it around, even poet-like toss it into
the air?

      If Miss Sullivan's projection of Drachmann's and Was-
serman's unfinished implications and hypotheses were not so
in accord with the direction they seem required to take, one
might not insist that her eagerness to make the poem dramatic outruns her cognizance of arguments as applicable in
one instance (the reader) as in the other (the listener).   Un-
convincing, then, in her initial attempt to establish Browning
as the undeniable monologuist in Book I, Miss Sullivan moves
to the establishment of her reading of the metaphor, which
is that the Ring serves its only purpose in the SECOND summary (I. 478-678).   Her reason is that Browning's primary
purpose in The Ring and the Book is to demonstrate a superior poetic technique (the dramatic monologue) as exemplified in Books II-XI.   "It [the SECOND summary of Book I]
is an imaginative re-creation of the events leading to the
trial... at its conclusion [Browning] announces that the raw
material is now 'wrought into a shapely ring' and waits only
the removal of the alloy to complete it.   Now follows the

THIRD summary... [after] which is the introduction of the
individual voices of the monologues" (p. 14).   Once these
introductions are made and the poet explains "the procedure
by which he withdraws the alloy [himself]," the reader can
turn to the voices of Half-Rome, Other Half-Rome, Tertium
Quid, and the main speakers.   The repristination has thus
been accomplished in Book I.   How a poet as innovative as
Browning, expecting his poem to be read widely and ages
later, could fail to take advantage of every artistic maneuver
practicable with word and metaphor, seems never to have
been considered by Miss Sullivan.   Yet it does not seem
right to isolate an integral component (the repristination) of
a metaphor as broadly drawn as the Ring and give it the
autonomy Browning must have intended the whole metaphor
to have.

        By slighting the title of Browning's poem, and the
titles of the first and last books, Miss Sullivan became
blinded to lines of poetry which simply take precedence over
voices and repristinative acts.   She does not, any more than
Drachmann or Wasserman, perceive, or at least give credence to the plan, that Books I through XII were welded together as unendingly as the arcs of a complete circle or
ring:

                                    so I wrought
        This arc, by furtherance of such alloy,
        And so, by one spirt, take away its trace
        Till, justifiably golden, rounds my ring.

        A ring without a posy, and that ring mine?

        O lyric Love, half angel and half bird...
        Never may I commence my song, my due
        To God who best taught song by gift of thee,
        Except with bent head and beseeching hand--
                    (I. 1386-91, 1403-05; italics added)

"Till [until], justifiably golden, rounds my ring" of Book I
anticipates and meshes precisely with "If the rough ore be
rounded to a ring" of Book XII:

        If the rough ore be rounded to a ring,
        Render all duty which good ring should do,
        And, failing grace, succeed in guardianship, --
        Might mine but lie outside thine, Lyric Love,

> Thy rare gold ring of verse.
>   (XII. 869-873; italics added)

And line 238 of Book XII--"To make the Ring that's all but round and done"--is as tangible a disclaimer of Miss Sullivan's thesis as poet or poem could possibly offer.   Saying the line merely has to do with "references to the letters" is a most doubtful procedure, especially since the thought, now expressed in Book XII, further anticipates the completion of the Ring with the completion of the last book.   In Book I Browning is saying that if the shaping and decorating of all the books of the poem prove masterful, his Ring will round justifiably golden in Book XII.   This reading is also justified by a line in Browning's adjoining invocation to Elizabeth Barrett: "Never may I commence my song, " my poem, before turning to thee.   If we doubt that in Book II, which immediately follows upon the invocation, and in the remaining ten books Browning is to continue developing his poem into a ring, we need remember that the posy, an inscription as on a finished wedding ring, cannot be engraved until after the completion of the whole poem (shaping and decorating), unless all but Book I is to be dedicated to someone other than Browning's departed wife.   Other lines are available to disprove Miss Sullivan's advocacy of Drachmann's and Wasserman's completion of the Ring metaphor in Book I. But all three should have seen the error of their reading in the single key passage which follows the SECOND summary and from which they derive the repristination of the poet: surely they cannot believe that in the scant two hundred lines of the SECOND summary the Old Yellow Book "grew all in all; / The lawyers' pleadings swelled back to their size" (I. 687-688).   There seems to be no acceptable way of showing that Browning's Ring metaphor applies to anything less than the whole poem.   Exclusive of Browning's express statement that the poem is finally rounded out in Book XII (869), the unity and order, indeed the mechanical titles, of The Ring and the Book are sufficient disclaimers of a contrary view, a view nonetheless required by these three critics to establish the SECOND summary of Book I as the poet's only fanciful treatment of Pompilia's story.

Miss Sullivan, like her fellow interpreters, seems always to make the task more difficult than it need be.   After declaring that the poet-speaker must "establish the circumstances under which each of the monologues is to be given, " she explains that he characterizes the voices, spaces and

times the speakers for dramatic effect, and sets the scene
for smaller personal drama which is to arise within the
larger scheme of things.   The advantage, she insists, re-
dounds to the audience which "gets an immediate over-all
['dramatic, rather than narrative'] view of the entire action"
(p. 16).   In her design to turn The Ring and the Book into
a full-fledged drama, one can of course see both Robert
Langbaum (The Poetry of Experience) and Park Honan (Browning's Characters [New Haven, 1961]) in the background; but
where they withdraw from additional speculation, Miss Sullivan pushes ahead.   What she says is undeniably accurate,
but it would be equally undeniable if applied to all other
forms of poetic communication, blessedly unobstructed by
voices and audiences and pointedly directed by the printed
page to readers.   By offering no more than the routine
methods of spoken and printed words to establish her unusual
thesis on Browning's voices, Miss Sullivan seems almost as
far removed from the reality of the poem as she is from the
reality of the Old Yellow Book.   For unexpectedly she observes that "the poet has already passed sentence on Guido,
found him guilty and condemned him to death" (p. 17), a
matter over which Browning had very little historical or
poetic control.

How Miss Sullivan decides "the audience is to be
called upon to make a judgment of each monologue" is best
made clear by her use of motive as expanded from Drachmann to Langbaum and Wasserman.   She does question the
audience's freedom to decide, on briefly recalling that the
poet reveals "his own opinion about which speaker is wrong
and which right. "   But by depending solely upon motive to
provide the full solution, she discerns that although the
THIRD summary outlines "each observer's failure to see
the whole truth, " "closer examination indicates that these
remarks are not omniscient or conclusive observations at
all, but merely hazarded guesses on the poet's part" (p. 16).
What this shows, she then advances, is "that the poet's view
lacks at this point a most significant dimension, a dimension
which can only be provided by the speakers themselves" (p.
17).   Like Robert Langbaum, she is inclined to confuse or
to lump all judgments together, so that we are not able to
consolidate her thoughts on the judgment of truth or to distinguish the thoughts of participant, reader, Browning, and
God.   In other words, one cannot always tell who is making
the judgment or about whom the judgment is being made.
Thus far, then, Miss Sullivan has said that Browning's fancy accounts only for the imaginative treatment of the SECOND

summary: that his _personality_, which embraces imaginative
talent yet surpasses it in creativity, is revealed in Book I
as monologuist and as "resuscitator" of voices which will
completely control Books II-XI.   Now, she sees the observer
[audience ?] as crucially helped by being given the circumstances of each monologue as drama and by being placed in
position to judge each monologuist independently, since the
poet-speaker's judgment was intended only as a stimulant to
encourage each observer to find the whole truth for himself,
from--be it recalled--somewhat mythically restored, self-
contained poetic voices.   Not only should Miss Sullivan have
remembered that the _one_ appearance of _resuscitates_ in the
whole poem is applied specifically to the dead human body,
not the OYB or voices; she should also have been more skeptical of Drachmann's "[Browning] tells us the facts in ten
different ways, leaving it to ourselves to find out the truth. "

      Struck by the frequent appearance of "I" in Book I
and its proof that the poet himself is speaking a dramatic
monologue, Miss Sullivan finds Browning's exultant confidence
the dominant quality of the opening book, "even more notable
than the ring metaphor" (p. 11).   This confidence, which is
placed in the poet's uniquely held talent to retell the facts
so that his "listeners can experience 'the truth'" (p. 8), she
then surprisingly locates as most evident in the Ring metaphor she cannot wait to discard.   Like Wasserman and
Drachmann, she stresses fancy, or poetic function, without
considering the analogous proportions of gold (fact) and copper (fancy) in the alloy itself.   Not knowing that at most
copper (fancy) represents less than one fifth of the alloy
(poem), she enlarges upon fancy, Browning's term, until
the poet's personality, her term, becomes the end-all and
be-all.   From this base she introduces the undeveloped part
of Wasserman's concept, and she constitutes her argument
on the heavy emphasis of the "I" mode of address in Book I
and the removal of the "something" she interprets to mean
Browning himself.   Just as she does not have grounds for
saying "after [Browning] has fused something of himself into
the _design_" (p. 19; italics added), Miss Sullivan does not have
valid reason for thinking Browning refers to himself rather
than his fancy in "Something of mine which, mixed up with
the mass, / Made it bear hammer and be firm to file. /
Fancy with fact is just one fact the more" (I. 462-464).   Her
purpose is to say that the disappearance of Browning's personality "signals the change from narrative to dramatic
form. "   The inaccuracy is that Browning never makes "removal of the alloy" analogous to "withdrawal of the poet's

own detectable personality" (p. 9; italics added). To her
credit, if Miss Sullivan had not been misled by Drachmann
and Wasserman on the significance of the SECOND summary,
her understanding of Browning's personality could be switched
without too much difficulty to Browning's apparent understanding of fancy. The poet's alloy metal (fancy), in conformity
with the artificer's alloy copper, is beyond question dissolved
in the air from the ring's surface and, if not taken symbolically as her related quotations stipulate, denies the poet in
the evanescent act any potential for withdrawal or for any
other future act, such as power to command fully developed
characters right out of the Old Yellow Book. Early in her
interpretation Miss Sullivan confuses the reader by saying
that in the first monologue Browning "finally concludes with
a last reference to" (p. 9) the Ring metaphor. This she
partially corrects later by permitting the Ring to be returned,
albeit downgraded, to "The Book and the Ring," where the
poem ends. But the real dilemma sets in with undue emphasis on the SECOND summary and the departure she,
Drachmann, and Wasserman take from the intractability of
lines 457-472 of Book I, particularly "Fancy with fact is
just one fact the more" and "I fused my live soul and that
inert stuff."

      Thus Miss Sullivan advances to the last stage of her
interpretation, the immolation of the poet: Book I, she repeats, "is concerned with making the poet-speaker dominant,
dynamic," possessed of "a special power to see truth and
make it known" (p. 17). Although he is not omniscient, he
is knowledgeable beyond the ordinary man and able in his
patient probing of individual motive to grasp truth intuitively
and to share it with the less gifted. "The poet could have
chosen merely to narrate his experience--could have stopped,
that is, with the imaginative re-creation of the story [the
SECOND summary of Book I]--but had he gone only this far,
he would not have persuaded us of the rightness of HIS interpretation: his would be simply one more voice added to the
babel of contradictory opinions" (p. 18). Instead of being
left narrative, Book I, which might itself have been only a
prose argument to the poem, solely intended to introduce the
various speeches, is "made a DRAMATIC monologue like
those to follow." "We need to feel the full weight of [Brown-
ing's] presence and personality in order to appreciate the
achievement of his withdrawal, that necessary last step in
the artistic process by which the poet immolates himself in
his creations in order to let other men see what he has seen
so gloriously. In other words, the real hero of The Ring and

the Book is the poet, and to indicate that he is using himself
as a type of the creative artist, Browning presents himself
as a character--the leading character--in the drama by which
old fact becomes new truth" (p. 18). The necessary extension of Wasserman's thesis--Browning was two different poets
or a dual-purposed poet in Book I--is called by Miss Sullivan a "technique [which] makes heavy demands on the reader"
(p. 185). But, in that Browning still had eleven of the
twelve books of the complete poem to write, one may question whether her metaphorical way of immolating Browning
before the composition of Book XII is altogether without design.

Only the unconcerned will fail to symphasize with
Miss Sullivan in the dilemma she creates. Admittedly she
has Browning, Drachmann, Cundiff, and Wasserman to thank
for part of it. Yet it is her misunderstanding of the Ring
metaphor, her unpredictable reading of isolated lines, and,
with Langbaum, her statements spun from a combination of
relativist and absolutist fibers, which intensify the dilemma.
In trying to understand and write about her critical approach,
one cannot avoid leaving loose ends which are almost always
detrimental to her cause. With the acknowledged aid of
Thomas J. Collins' Robert Browning's Moral-Aesthetic Theory,
1833-55 (Lincoln, 1967), she reasons convincingly that in The
Ring and the Book "Browning's moral philosophy, his belief
about what moral choices are required of man, and his aesthetic philosophy, his belief about what artistic choices are
required of the poet, have coalesced in a single dominating
conviction" (p. 209). Judged by my reading of the poem,
however, she emphasizes the wrong aspect of Browning's
truth, especially when she attributes infallibility to "the
poet's intuitive grasp of truth" (p. 212); but even when carried away by Browning's unique talent for finding truth and
calling forth self-motivated characters, she distinctly recognizes the poet's constant reinforcement of "proof of the unreliability of human testimony" and his imposition of ideal
traits on the most independent of the characters. Best of all,
and more helpful than her skillfully abstracted characters,
Miss Sullivan adds dimension to Browning's comprehension
of the nature, function, and method of the artist as exemplified in his exalted concept of the poet's role. Insofar as
I know, she, Drachmann, Wasserman, and I have made the
only extended studies of the Ring metaphor. In Essay Five
it may be seen that if the objections I have raised against
interpretations by the three are valid, their mistakes are
still not as uncomplimentary as the disregard of the poem

by other critics.   Where many critics have determined not
to consider the Ring metaphor at all, the three critics discussed in this essay have striven, with no small success,
to make better sense of The Ring and the Book through
understanding of the Ring metaphor.   In thus performing,
they have focused, even riveted, attention on poetic lines
and striking imagery most of us have perhaps for too long
taken for granted.

5

INTERPRETATION OF BROWNING'S USE OF TRUTH

The ease with which contemporary critics speculate on the theme and design of The Ring and the Book disguises the intensity of the research which was required to break a very long stalemate. Critics before 1941, as witnessed by Hodell, Cook, Shaw, and DeVane, limited their efforts primarily to defense or denial of the poet's "fidelity to fact, " and seemed destined never to be rid of extremists like Frances Russell or Mrs. Orr. Because it now seems acceptable to speak generally in favor of a poet who, among other purposes, attempted to keep faithful to the essential facts of his source, it is to be expected that advocacy of a single major theme by any critic is more likely to alienate numerous other critics who elicit proof of a disconcerting array of possible themes and designs. Nor is the tendency to proliferate themes solely the choice of the critics, since Browning himself assumed that his poem could sustain unlimited metaphorical, philosophical, and ethical ramification. With the change in critical direction our concern therefore, it is appropriate to begin this essay with allusion to B. R. McElderry's germinal study of the poem's structure in 1943 and extended reference to C. Willard Smith's influential work on Browning's star-imagery in 1941. Studying the star-image throughout Browning's poetry, Smith locates its masterful and culminating application in The Ring and the Book, where star-image and accent on truth are inseparably interwoven. Chart·ing Browning's way through the incidents of his source, McElderry demonstrates the meticulous care with which the poet organized and the skill with which he sifted and psychologically unified the bulk of his material. Clearly, in the work of these two scholars, is announced the beginning of a literary curiosity in the poem, its design and theme, which earlier critics had rarely shown and then mostly in a cursory way.

Influenced naturally by the traditional placement of the climax of the poem in the Pope's monologue, McElderry ("The

Narrative Structure of The Ring and the Book, " Research
Studies of the State College of Washington, XI [1943], 193-
233) and Smith (Browning's Star-Imagery [Princeton, 1941])
provide additional good reasons for locating the climax in
the Pope's words. Whereas the structure of the poem bespeaks Browning's intent to McElderry, Smith derives a
theme of universal truth and justice from the star-imagery.
Guided by traditional understandings of Browning's view of
truth, and by implications of structure and universal truth,
I briefly proposed in 1948 (Essay Two) that the theme of
Browning's poem is developed in the poet's recurrent emphasis on the frailty of human truth as contrasted with God's
truth. In 1956 Robert Langbaum ("The Ring and the Book:
A Relativist Poem, " PMLA, LXXI, 131-154), who had found
congenial ground for an opposing view in Drachmann's 1925
interpretation of the Ring metaphor, called The Ring and the
Book a relativist poem but, like Drachmann, did not specify
a climactic focus unless it is to be deduced from the pivotal
position given the Pope's words. In 1959 (Essay Three),
with the chief purpose of suggesting that Browning's theme
is "the vanity of human speech, " I also directed attention to
the inconsistencies of Langbaum's arguments and the improb-
ability of his relativist theory. In 1961 Wasserman indorsed
Langbaum's theory in an interpretation of the Ring metaphor
which, as we have seen, also relies heavily on Drachmann's
spadework. In 1969 Mary Rose Sullivan and John Killham
entered the listings, the former with an endorsement of Langbaum's relativism and an application of the Ring metaphor
which she submits as an extension of thought engendered by
Cundiff and Wasserman, but which indeed is an extension of
Drachmann and Wasserman, a sharp departure from the limits of my interpretation. On the other hand, Killham emphatically rejects Langbaum's relativism and expresses a firm
conviction that Browning was writing about absolute truth.
Whether Killham knew of my work is unclear, but he rather
oddly inclines toward Julia Wedgwood's fascination with the
excess of evil in the poem and consequently places the climax in Guido's last speech. Of course appraisals of other
critics could be added, as some will be in the next essay;
here, tradition and origin of interpretation and conflict of
interpretations seem desirable criteria in a search for Browning's most significant theme in The Ring and the Book.

      In his study of Browning's integration of eight star-
images in Book X, which is substantiated by incisive reference to echoes of earlier images of light in the poem, C.
Willard Smith seems at first to oppose limitation of any

nature on the possibilities of intuitive and rational human
truth.   His Pope appears to have attained the ultimate in
truth.   But then, perhaps as should be expected, Smith observes: "The Pope...is capable of seeing beyond and through
emotional experience to the essential truth and meaning that
the stars proclaim" (p. 207; italics added).   Before his recorded "essential truth" and nearby "flashes of truth the
Pope had learned to read" may be adjusted to parallel allusions to "universal truth," however, Smith merges human
truth (he never used the word fact) with "eternal and heavenly truth" in a manner which prevents our knowing whether he
means factual information, essential information on which intellect and emotion have operated, or some form of universal, immutable truth, such as God's.   So we are forewarned
that at his choice and in conformity with imagistic procedure,
he can return to earlier emphases and say, for example, that
Browning's star-image is structurally restricted "to the function of association with other images of light that, through
their cumulative effect, produce the grand image of 'white
light' thoroughly appropriate to his principal theme, universal truth and justice" (p. 208).   That Smith was also to express the following thought in no way interferes with his imagistic development: "Truth [fact] in its many forms and
interrelationships among men has come into the poet's grasp.
At least he has made every possible effort to convince himself and his British public that he is telling the whole truth"
(p. 194).   The ambiguity serves his declared purpose well,
and we conclude that Smith did not choose to distinguish one
way or another between human truth and divine or universal
truth.

To my knowledge, no one since Mrs. Orr expressed
a similar opinion had put Browning's possible theme in precisely Smith's optimistic terms.   Not initiated to generate
disagreement, his association of star-images with truth nonetheless encourages one to ask whether he means that Browning's theme is offered from the standpoint of human truth,
divine truth, or a combination of both.   Perhaps the closest
indication of his own position may be found in the lines below:

> Browning evidently intended that the truth of his
> story, the correct interpretation of the events of
> his ring of circumstance, should be realized
> through the intuitive insight of Pompilia, and the
> discriminating wisdom of the Pope.   Pompilia's
> "truth" is personal, individual, and uncomplicated
> by any attempt on her part to see herself disinter-

estedly, or to evaluate her particular experience
in its relationship to the general pattern of society.
The Pope, on the other hand, desires to see a
whole truth, and his judgment of Guido is presented as the result of a dispassionate evaluation of
the facts of the tragedy in the light of their effect
upon society as a whole. An estimate of the value
of Pompilia's "truth," therefore, depends entirely
upon one's belief in the innate purity of her soul
and in the possible universality of her character.
The decisions of the Pope, however, are fortified
by the power of great learning, and by the wisdom
of a magnificent devotion to the ways of God.
Youthful Pompilia has never forgotten the intima-
tions of truth and goodness with which she was
born; the aged Pope has attained to a conception
of truth and goodness that fills the hours before
his death with serenity.   (p. 202; italics added)

For Smith's Pompilia, then, "Caponsacchi is truth,
the truth she cannot realize philosophically." But for his
Pope, the image of the star "is a significant element in the
design through which Browning has intended to express 'the
whole truth,' 'the ultimate judgment,' of the characters and
circumstances which composed the tragedy" (p. 205). Smith's
statement permits one to see that he completed his examination of The Ring and the Book believing the poet thought he
had proved the truth of Pompilia's innocence, the reliability
of the Pope's vision of the whole truth, and the justice of
Guido's condemnation. It is not clear what he means by saying the Pope answers the question, "What is truth?" Since
Smith judges Fra Celestino's performance as a means of
persuading his parishioners of the truth enunciated by the
Pope, we may assume he means simply the truth of God.
But of course such a simplification of the sermon does injury
to Celestino's independence of mind, especially in conjunction
with Smith's unaccountable dropping of the Fra's text--"Let
God be true, and every man / A liar"--from a sixty-four-
line quotation of the sermon. If less interested in the imagery than in the poet's treatment of truth, we are thus
thrown back on our own to determine more precisely what
answer the Pope gives for truth, and in what ways universal
truth is specifically the theme of the poem. That another
reader might deduce from Browning's repeated references to
the frailty of human truth an unusual preoccupation with the
untruthful rather than the truthful aspects of fact, does not
find expression in Smith's study though earlier critics almost

altogether took the former approach.

      Assuming that "the intentions of the Pope are to ex-
plain ever more clearly the single, though complex meaning
of universal truth" (p. 212), Smith finds the convex glass a
positive image in contrast to the negativism of the optic
glass in "A Death in the Desert" and the symbols of immensity in Sordello. His Pope firmly believes that "man's intellect is capable of reducing, to a degree compatible with individual faculty, the 'scattered points' of immensity to a
clear vision that properly may be regarded as the 'known
unknown, our God revealed to man'" (p. 213). But Smith
must and forthrightly does add: "While intellect cannot be
expected to reveal the whole truth, the powers of intellect
may be said to instigate the search that only love and adora-
tion can do their best to complete. 'Absolute immensity, '
declares the Pope, is appreciable only by God himself. "
Thus through a comprehensive explanation of the convex glass
image, we are led to observe that the whole truth remains a
distant goal and to continue our analysis while Smith perforce
returns to his imagery: "Browning has concentrated his attention upon the serene personalities of high minded men who,
like the Pope, have seen the vision of eternal Truth" (p. 215).
But not to be forgotten is Smith's earlier statement over which
imagistic demands, as they should, exercise absolute direction: "The poet thus prepares his reader to accept an 'ultimate judgment' that will glow with the authority of universal
justice, transcend all thought of worldly contradiction, break
through the shades of particular time and space to become
one with the decision of the eternal Judge" (p. 210). To be
sure, Smith confuses us least when, on departing momentarily from use of "vision of truth, " he says plainly:
"Through his speaker [the Pope], the poet here ascends to
the expression of his ardent belief in God as the ultimate
source of Truth and Light" (p. 208).

      An analysis along essentially artistic and imagistic
lines, Smith's interpretation refreshingly skirts Browning's
confusing, ironic, often times indiscriminate exchange of
truth for fact and thereby enables him to develop consistently
the message the stars seemed to proclaim. His difficulty
mounts when the star-imagery converges on the white light
of God's truth. Unlike DeVane, who avoids saying Browning's theme is the recognition and preservation of truth,
Smith three times judges the theme of the poem to be "universal truth and justice. " But if in naming the theme of
Book X Smith means simply that Browning was motivated

by its existence to perpetuate a belief in universal truth and
not attempting to define or prove its reality, I have been obtuse.   That the poet was pointing through whatever partial
truth was known to Caponsacchi, Pompilia, the Pope, and
Fra Celestino to God's truth seems defensible on many
grounds (Essay Three).   That Browning and his Pope were
following St. John and St. Paul in their belief that God is
the only truth is sometimes overlooked.   So it is not of little moment to remember that Browning was exploiting a universal norm to demonstrate the unreliability of human speech
and thought, not to prove something his faith made undeniable.
DeVane's broader judgment that Browning's poem is a reading of life does not exclude Smith's choice of theme, but it
does assign to the imagery, as Smith concedes, a less con-
spicuous role.   While DeVane, on whose scholarship Smith
confidently depends, is content to propose that "Browning's
poem, like Milton's, is finally an attempt to justify the ways
of God to man," Smith thinks it is more nearly an attempt
to "reveal Man to men."   And while DeVane would have the
poem "show that everywhere in the world God has set himself to meet evil in mortal combat," Smith would have the
poem be a justification of universal truth and justice.   To
Smith, it seems not to matter that saying Browning wished
to justify the existence of universal truth, or the innocence
of Pompilia, is equivalent to saying Milton wrote his great
poem to prove that Adam and Eve fell from a state of innocence, or that Eve was no more guilty than Adam.   Browning had definite court records roughly approximating to him
the definitive nature of Milton's source; Browning's case
also was prejudged.   So like Milton, he must have reasoned
that the individuals of his source provided a worthy means
through which to poetize a variety of subjects and themes.
As DeVane takes care to note, Browning "cautions us in the
last Book against reading into his story too cheerful a confidence in the chances of virtue in this world."   An acceptance of the "accursed" splintering and fragmentation of man's
truth in relation to a universal or absolute truth in which
Browning and his Pope expressed such positive faith would,
I believe, have simplified Smith's problem and eliminated
his backing and filling on the subject of truth.

        Appearing seven years after Smith's book on the star-
imagery, my first comments on Browning's treatment of
truth are recorded in Essay Two.   Hoping that through either favorable or unfavorable reply a wider interest in the
subject might be generated, I waited eight years before
Robert Langbaum's view opposing absolutist truth in Brown-

ing was published in 1956.   Whether his relativist view was
projected as an antidote to the traditional absolutist view,
only he can say.   My opinion is that a rapidly changing intellectual milieu had most to do with the direction, even
though Langbaum's 1960 rejoinder to my 1959 response to
relativist truth was prompt and defensive.   Since Essay Two
is primarily an interpretation of the Ring metaphor, I, like
Smith, wrote of Browning's use of truth only as it unavoida-
bly pertained to my subject, the Ring metaphor:

> Browning accepts ART as the one possible way of
> speaking truth.   His artistic way is through the
> addition of "fancy" or imagination, which is God-
> given, like the gift of prophet and seer, and pos-
> sessed only by those "called of God. "   Final truth,
> which God alone is capable of revealing, is, for
> Browning, the only goal worth striving toward.
> Mere [human] knowledge, though not rejected in
> the poem, is partially incapacitated because of its
> restricted use and falls before the potency of di-
> vine truth as revealed through love.   Man, with
> his limited love and his dependence upon knowledge
> or fact, is incapable of seeing or knowing the final
> truth.   But, with the assistance of art, which in
> this poem is the art of Browning, mankind may
> feel the partial or diluted truth which proceeds
> from God.   In their search for fact all the char-
> acters of the poem, including the Pope, missed
> the one agent which might have revealed the final
> truth.   Because they were still relying upon knowl-
> edge, looking for facts, they were unable to feel
> truth.

In Essay Three, my second effort to provoke further
study of the Ring metaphor and Browning's use of truth,
Langbaum's relativist theory served as stimulant and point
of departure.   Regretfully his emphasis on the indispensable
quality of Browning's facts became at once the overriding
issue of an ensuing symposium, in which Donald Smalley was
left thinking he stood halfway between an accent on the poet's
contempt for fact by Cundiff and emphasis on the poet's worship of fact by Langbaum.   As may be gained from note 9 of
Essay Three, it was in my failure to distinguish between
demonstrable and indemonstrable fact that Smalley and Langbaum found opportunity once again to defend Browning's attachment to fact.   Whether the symposium, as I believe,
finally dissipated all arguments for Browning's fidelity to

fact and all assertions of Browning's claim to unqualified
faithfulness to fact, is for others to decide. But it soon
became evident that the symposium had clarified little more
on Browning's use of truth than to make opposing positions
more visible. Because Langbaum's essay and its influence
continue to challenge the foundation of Browning's truth as
well as the traditional interpretation of that truth, more serious rebuttal to his questionable method and his misapplication
of crucial passages from the poem appears very much in
order. For purposes of critical distinction, he has been an
advocate of relativist truth in The Ring and the Book, I of
absolutist truth. So it will be necessary to show in the matters with which I disagree that Langbaum's thought patterns
and thought projections are also at stake: for example, when
he calls relativist a poem which, by his later admission, is
to a very great degree not relativist; when he rejects hun-
dreds of lines which derogate man's speech and thought as
insignificant, while expanding for his purpose atmospheric
lines intended merely to reveal the poet's delight in finding
the Old Yellow Book; when he detains the reader so long
over indemonstrable fact and unspecified judgment, while
knowing all the time he will at last settle on subjectively
evaluated motive as the only reliable basis of judgment.

A persuaded relativist insofar as he discusses numerous aspects of The Ring and the Book, Langbaum has had as
much difficulty understanding absolutists as they have had
understanding him. It may seem, as implied by W. O. Raymond (VN, No. 10 [Autumn 1956], pp. 12-13), that Langbaum
wants the better of two sides, but his greatest problem is
the absence of denotative words which would reveal accurately
his thoughts without stimulating contrary ideas so long associated with essential or absolute truth. For instance, he
cannot give expression to his thesis without using talent, insight, intuition, motive, essential moral quality, God's gift,
human heart, all of which for centuries have been directly
associated with a humanly fixed, recognizable, acceptable
form of truth. Nor can he escape, even try successfully to
escape, the many direct and indirect comments on truth the
poet sprinkles throughout the poem to the confusion and consternation of all commentators (see Browning's uses of truth
at the end of the volume). Added to these formidable bar-
riers, Langbaum knows at once that it is eventually required
of all genuine relativists to disown even the validity of the
facts themselves. So at the end of his essay, after stating
that good and evil are not sufficiently interfused in Browning's
poem, that our judgment is initially and perpetually forced by

the poet, and that the poet's partiality prevents the rise of
proper judgment--always, be it noted, out of utmost ambi-
guity--Langbaum raises "the question of whether facts really
can speak for themselves. " "The relativist conditions for
modern conviction, " he thus concludes, "might explain. . . the
almost universal retreat of twentieth-century poets into. . .
illumination made possible through a personal and temporary
rejection of the facts, or rather of the prevailing system of
ideas through which we perceive the facts. " Surely no one
would deny that judgment of the indemonstrable, unverifiable
factual truth of Browning's poem must be relative, but this
concession only magnifies the nineteenth-century poet's insistence upon man's being motivated toward and guided by
desire for a total comprehension, consequently a perfect
judgment which only an infinite mind can be expected to deliver.   Truth [fact] Langbaum very positively espouses, but
it is a personally acceptable, temporary component which,
though it soon loses its luster, is for the nonce less relative
than a more relative counterpart.   Insight and intuition, if
not totally ratiocinative, are entirely self-contained and admit of no reality beyond the confines of self-consciousness.
In the thick of his arguments for relativism, Langbaum says
the Pope sees "that myth, dogma, and the machinery change,
but truth remains, " the truth Euripides anticipated in Christian morality.   Then he forthwith adds that truth "remains
always in advance of the machinery, " "always ahead of the
age. " Despite his ambivalent security in both camps, however, it is almost as if the only valid difference between
relativist and absolutist truth to Langbaum is their attribute
of being either posterior or anterior, with of course the implied exaltation of man's truth and the denial of God's truth.
From human trial and error of the future, Langbaum envis-
ions phenomenal outcroppings of higher and higher forms of
new truth; from past human trial and error, he evokes nothing more than man's mistake in looking to a universal
norm.   In short, as the absolutist is thus carried beyond
comfort by Langbaum, so Langbaum is carried "beyond the
possibility of comfort" by Fra Celestino's textual "God is
true and every man a liar. " Such polarization clearly explains why the direction of Browning's thought is essential
to an understanding of The Ring and the Book.

Because, as Raymond first observed (p. 12), Langbaum's arguments for thinking The Ring and the Book a relativist poem demand the very closest reading, one does well
to reply immediately when he disagrees and to establish
specific cross-references on the paradoxical elements. Even

then, with definitions verboten--even for words so essential
as relativist and truth--certain assumptions must be accepted
and certain concessions granted.   Unspecified points of view,
which may sometimes be either the poet's, the character's,
the essayist's, or the reader's, delay us.   Judgments, often
times undistinguished, frustrate us.   Facts, from which
Browning's truth promises to emerge, are unexpectedly made
meaningless until reinterpreted, while characters, created
for the vital nature of their perspectives, are rendered unreliable by admission of the poet's shaping.   Logicality of
statement does not always follow a sequential line or an ex-
plicable level.   Prevailing uncertainty coerces one into reading ahead and then backtracking, or into continual submission
to Langbaum's will.   But, as we shall see, when Langbaum
insists that the importance of facts cannot be overemphasized,
he does not really mean it; he knows that the fact to be observed must be observed by some eye, and later reveals
his plan by placing a correspondingly absolute emphasis on
the observer.   Indeed, Langbaum might have told us right
off that his uncommonly emphatic accent on 1) fact, to be
followed by an equally emphatic accent on 2) point of view,
was planned as prelude to a comparably emphatic accent on
3) motive, subjectively arrived at.   Such a revelation, however, would have hampered frequent return at Langbaum's
volition to fact, point of view, or motive with paradoxical
emphases and uncertain transitions the reader presently has
less incentive to challenge.

        Whether the truth of Langbaum's fact is any more
than the meaning of fact itself remains indeterminate throughout the essay.   But it will be helpful to begin this study with
two of his quotations on fact:

            These then are the unprecedented conditions of
            The Ring and the Book--not only that the poem
            was to be no mere illustration of an external
            principle [universal truth ?] from which the facts
            would derive meaning, but that the facts themselves,
            all of them, unselected and as they came to hand...
            were to yield the meaning.   (The Poetry of Ex-
            perience, p. 135; italics added)

        The second quotation, made three years later in fur-
ther elucidation of his reason for emphasizing fact, is even
more explicit:

            Without the jumble of true and false, good and

> bad, which are the raw stuff of life, there would
> be no meaning, no truth.   If fact is important as
> an index to truth, truth itself cannot be known ex-
> cept through fact or material conditions.... It is
> only through the sordid events that Caponsacchi,
> Pompilia, and the Pope have been able to discover
> and exhibit the good in themselves. [1]

It was the inflexible stress on fact of the first quotation, the assumption that Browning was composing a social
document, perhaps a novel, rather than poetry, which moved
Donald Smalley to respond: "A sizeable distortion... Browning's pleasure in the Old Yellow Book... does not... suggest
... 'the ordinary Philistine's devotion to his facts and figures'"
(VN, No. 16 [Fall 1959], p. 3).   Notwithstanding, each time
Langbaum recalls Browning's "naive wonder" at tossing the
old book of facts into the air, he reiterates more positively
the poet's confidence in factuality until he reaches: "It is
impossible to overemphasize the importance Browning attached to the crudely and even sordidly realistic quality of
his story" (Poetry of Experience, p. 132).

Thinking The Ring and the Book derives its meaning
from a relativist ethos, Langbaum designates two signs of
relativism: 1) its monologue form "can be justified only on
the relativist assumption that truth cannot be apprehended in
itself but must be 'induced' from particular points of view";
2) its "facts figure as pure gold in the analogy of the ring,
which Browning uses to justify stamping an interpretation
upon the facts" (p. 109; italics added).   At first, then, the
monologue is Browning's way of substituting points of view
for "the objective view of events of traditional drama and
narrative"; later, Langbaum sees need for dropping the act
of "interpretation" in favor of "a projective function" (p. 133).
But if he had explored the Ring metaphor more carefully, he
would have realized that Browning, like the artificer, stamped
both the fancy (copper) and the facts (pristine, not precious,
gold).   Technical knowledge of the Ring metaphor in his
analysis would also have informed Langbaum that in the repristination only the surface alloy metal (fancy) flew off in
fume. [2]   Underneath, in the interior of the ring (the poem),
the fancy or imagination continued by necessity to contribute
as much to the meaning of the facts as the nature of the
facts made resuscitation of the historical characters possible.
Technical information on the crucial stamping would thus
have moderated Langbaum's next statement that Browning's
"truth had to be taken seriously" in a positivist age, "had

to emerge from the facts. "   Then he would not have been
required to confess later the very opposite: "The Pope...
cuts right through the facts to a sympathetic apprehension
of the motives and essential moral qualities behind the deeds"
(pp. 120-121).   "All the morally significant characters of the
poem cut through facts in the same way. "

        Emphasizing early and repeatedly the precious quality
of gold facts to the exclusion of their pristine nature, and
moving abruptly to church and state organizational "formula-
tion that has got too far from the facts" (p. 110), Langbaum
interprets the "difficult question" of the fourth of these climactic lines

                This lesson, that our human speech is naught,
                Our human testimony false, our fame
                And human estimation words and wind.
                Why take the artistic way to prove so much?
                Because, it is the glory and good of Art,
                That Art remains the one way possible
                Of speaking truth, to mouths like mine at least.
                            (XII. 838-844; italics added)

to mean that Browning is saying "the artistic way is best for
criticizing a whole false view of things. "   "Art, then, " he
continues, "is truer than philosophical discourse because it
is closer to the facts,... is more convincing... because, con-
fronting false formulations with facts, it causes us to start
again with the facts and construct the truth for ourselves"
(p. 110).   If this seems an odd beginning in literary criticism, I concur.   But by failure ever to distinguish the poet's
use of the word truth from the word fact, Langbaum is enabled in the above quotation to anticipate a transition from
facts with which we "construct the truth for ourselves" to
"truth's ultimate source is in the individual mind; so that
judgment of truth rests on judgment of character" (p. 130).
Henceforth facts, so important at first, will appear or disappear as need for their presence or absence arises.

        In evident contradiction to his portrayal of facts
themselves "as an index to truth, " Langbaum devotes the
next several paragraphs of his essay, pages 110-113, to
poetic and idealized characterizations which severely test
"the crudely and even sordidly realistic quality" of Browning's source material.   But first he informs us that "the
judgments of The Ring and the Book are by no means 'relative, '" if by relative is meant "no one is either good or

bad but a bit of both, " or "indefinite, " or "matter of opinion"
(p. 110). This unexpected move gives Langbaum a chance
to reaffirm his belief that all the established institutions have
missed the point of Pompilia's absolute goodness (p. 113).
It also leaves us quite unsure of whether by "judgments"
Langbaum is writing about poet's or Pope's, poetic participant's or our own particular judgments of Browning's interpretation of what a character's judgment of another character's act may signify. In the final judgment, made authoritative only by the Pope (p. 112), Langbaum's Pompilia is
nothing short of a saint; his Guido, an incarnation of evil.
"Between the moral poles of Pompilia and Guido, the other
characters are assigned no less definite places. " As Caponsacchi "represents the highest in manliness and courage, "
the Pope "represents the highest moral attainment of human
wisdom. " And if the parents, the pro-Guido and pro-Pompilia speakers, and the lawyers are of indefinite moral position, "the judgment of them is quite definite. " "If the reader has read correctly, [moreover,] his judgments should
coincide with the Pope's and to allow no mistake, Browning
tells the main events of the story in his own voice in Book
I, in such a way as to shape our judgments of the speakers
before we have met them. " "The courts, the lawyers, the
representative of the impartial line of Roman opinion [Altick
and Loucks have convincingly eliminated the impartial line,
pp. 136-150], all have committed the 'relativist' fallacy of
supposing that there must be both right and wrong on each
side. " Even "Caponsacchi complains to the court of their
'relativist' obtuseness. " When Raymond insists that Langbaum stops short of considering "the relativity of Browning's
own judgments" (p. 13), he slights the full revelation of the
above quotations. No one has made clearer Browning's
shaping of character than Langbaum. So at this point his
thesis might better be entitled "An Anti-Relativist Poem. "
Perhaps Raymond was holding too close to another of Langbaum's indications of relativism, that in which he sees the
dramatic monologue as Browning's means of replacing "the
objective view [intent ?] of events of traditional drama and
narrative with point of view. "

    In a proper sense to Langbaum, then, the poem "is
relativist in that the social and religious absolutes are not
the means for understanding the right and wrong" therein.
"Pompilia is misled by all the constituted authorities,...
Nevertheless, in spite of all the wrong external influences,
Pompilia finds the right way because her instinct is right"
(p. 113; italics added). "In the same way, the Pope sees

that Caponsacchi was in position... to follow with passionate
spontaneity his immediate perception of the good. " "Not only are the judgments of The Ring and the Book independent
of official morality, they are for the most part in conflict
with it and in this sense relative to the particular conditions
of the poem and to the motives and quality of the characters"
(p. 114). John Killham has recently challenged Langbaum's
insistence upon making "conflict with official morality" an
argument for relativist intent in The Ring and the Book, and,
as will be seen, the line he draws between social and moral
relativism is sharp and persuasive. But it remains here to
be said that constituted authority, rather than representing
"absolutes, " has far more consistently than have individual
judgments insured that its punishment be relative to the of-
fense. Throughout his essay and as a prime explication,
action by individual parent, bishop, and governor is confused
by Langbaum with constituted family, church, and state authority as unreasonably as officialdom is preempted from a
modicum of morality, with all judgments being induced from
single poetic examples. Yet even here, and possibly because he senses a fallacy in the indictment, he would set
things right by adding, "Browning is not saying that all dis-
contented wives are to be rescued from their husbands, but
just this particular wife from her particular husband. ...
Hence the use of repetition and the dramatic monologue--not
because the judgments are a matter of opinion but because
we must judge what is being said by who is saying it" (pp.
114-115). Nor is Browning saying that all mistreated wives
should not be rescued in the same daring manner! The more
pertinent matter is that Langbaum, after earlier representing
Pompilia and Guido as idealized characters, here reinstates
their factual reality. Of course they will make the best possible case consistent with the facts accessible to them, as
Langbaum concedes, but their crude historical motives, sincerity, and moral qualities cannot escape Browning's refin-
ing sympathy or disgust, which in turn shapes and determines
our sympathy. Earlier, while emphasizing the unavoidable
act of poetic shaping, Langbaum seemed right; forgetting the
poet's involvement, he seems far astray in thinking the dramatic monologue form enables historical characters to reveal
themselves totally as they were.

On page 115 of his essay Langbaum readily grants
that Browning pronounces the judgments of the "world" deficient because of the speakers' personal inadequacies, but
while Browning goes on to call the inadequacies "words and
wind" Langbaum restricts them to "germ of failure" and

"prepossession. " Thus by temporarily holding the fact his
only absolute and thereby defining what the truth shall be,
Langbaum can quote with considerable assurance in his relativist theory two lines from one of the best known passages
in the poem, lines spoken by the poet and naturally subject
to pivotal assignment:

> Over-belief in Guido's right and wrong
> Rather than in Pompilia's wrong and right:
> Who shall say how, who shall say why? 'T is there--
> The instinctive theorizing whence a fact
> Looks to the eye as the eye likes the look.
> Gossip in a public place, a sample-speech.
>   (L 860-865; emphasis added)

Thought, in isolation from the text, to mean various things
by various critics, the emphasized lines have been used as
evidence to earmark Browning a relativist, a pluralist, an
agnostic, a barbarian, and a casuist.   As the heart of Langbaum's argument for relativist truth, the two lines are thus
interpreted: "In recognizing the inevitability of personal distortion, Browning does not mean, as I understand it, that
there is no truth, but that truth depends upon the nature of
the theorizing and ultimately upon the nature of the soul of
which the theorizing is a projection. " Effective in phrasing
and limited in scope, Langbaum's sentence in itself rather
convincingly places Browning among the relativists.   But
when one looks at the six lines here quoted or the poetic
context which runs from line 839 to 881, he discovers that
Browning is lamenting the accursed fetters of theorizing, not
by any rational or poetic means to be found in the poem advocating or approving a relativistic philosophy.   Nor is Langbaum's paradoxical interpretation mended by the thin thread
of "Browning does not mean, as I understand him, that there
is no truth. " Since no one was to say that Browning rejected
truth in the Platonic, or Christian, or traditional human
sense before Langbaum and Peckham, Langbaum must first
account for the two hundred fifteen times Browning uses the
word truth to prove through his own speech or that of Caponsacchi, Pompilia, the Pope, and Celestino his devotion to
genuine truth and demonstrable fact, or through others to
express his anger and consternation at man's reprehensible
disregard of genuine truth and demonstrable fact.   From the
one hundred fourteen times Browning uses the words fact and
facts, Langbaum could select many other isolable lines which
demonstrate the poet's attitude toward personally derived
factual truth, but their contexts are of the same regretful

and condemnatory tenor.   As Langbaum insists, "the nature
of the soul" which does the theorizing is supremely important.
But even the poet's exemplary historical characters, despite
their degree of purity or wisdom, are sufficiently incapacitated in mind and soul to encourage the writing of his poem:
else why should Browning write a book shall mean beyond
the facts and their historical integrity?   Much too often
Browning takes cognizance of man's incapacities, but in The
Ring and the Book he does attempt to balance out his persuasion on false testimony and false speech by granting honest motives and partial truth to his acceptable characters.

        Thus far Langbaum has said that truth must emerge
from the facts, even though the Pope and all the other worthy
characters cut right through the facts to the motives behind
the deeds; that we are to construct the truth for ourselves,
even though the facts themselves are to yield up the meaning; that uncertain facts and individual responses to them
are therefore the only means through which truth is attaina-
ble, even though individual judgments in the poem are by no
means relative and the facts are by no means unreliable;
that truth must be "induced" from particular points of view,
even though the poet clearly helps determine the points of
view by shaping the characters; and that because Art is
closer to the facts, Browning's characters reject the exhausted formulations of society, the official morality, and
exercise an independence of action which is to be judged by
individual motive alone.   Now, after contrasting the inadequate
motives of unworthy characters with the high seriousness of
the Pope (pp. 115-120), Langbaum enunciates an ever-pres-
ent, thus thematic, injunction by the poet to remember that
"By their motives shall ye know them!"   The misleading aspect, however, is that while Langbaum, Peckham, and others
would permit any reader to judge the motives, Browning
thinks that only God can rightly judge motive, as I hope to
establish in Essay Seven.   Judgment by readers of the poem,
as Langbaum concedes, is partly determined by Browning's
manipulations and consequently assumes a far less dominant
role than followers of Langbaum like to give it.   Forewarned
by Drachmann's outlined points and by the inevitability of
Langbaum's social thrust, we may wait impatiently for clarification of words like moral and motive.   But just to believe
that Browning's poem rests on facts of which "the eye likes
the look" and on characters for which "prepossession" sets
the lens is, of course, to commit Browning to a denial of
truth in any sense other than that of "instinctive theorizing. "
"After all, " Langbaum adds to his frequently quoted sentence,

"Browning justifies by the analogy of the ring his own instinctive theorizing of the facts...there is disparity between
the accounts of even such admirable characters as Pompilia
and Caponsacchi" (p. 115). Disposed in moments like this
to fall back on the Ring metaphor for ambiguous confirmation, Langbaum here is compelled to disparage the very gold
facts he thinks Browning counts so <u>precious</u> and of whose
analogous large proportions in the Ring he fails to take note.

Because the poet has "alerted" (p. 116) us to specific
inadequacies of the characters, Langbaum explains, "the pro-
Guido speaker...reveals a prepossession" in his marital status, the pro-Pompilia speaker in his bachelorhood, Tertium
Quid through his evasion of moral judgment altogether, and
the lawyers in the mechanical, professional nature of their
selfish motives. "No less than the lawyers, the representatives of Roman opinion" divulge "self-interested motives
which disqualify them as judges of the <u>moral issue.</u> " "The
point for us...is that the judgments are <u>different</u> because
the men who pronounce them are <u>different</u>" (p. 117; italics
added). As Sir Henry Jones pointed out in his age, so may
we in ours: "Having paid its formal compliments to the
doctrine of the relativity of all knowledge, [positivism] neglects it altogether" (<u>Browning as a Philosophical and Religious
Teacher</u>, p. 264). We cannot fail observing that Langbaum
switches his terminology from "instinctive theorizing" to that
of a moral-social relativism as absolute and positive in its
determination of truth as St. Paul's idealism is absolute and
positive in its determination of God and God's truth. Obviously Langbaum's relativism is shaken neither by imposition
of moral positivism nor establishment of one absolute in order to destroy another. Inordinate potentiality for truth-
finding in the socially-oriented seeker for motive is energeti-
cally pitted against the stock of information men of all ages
have accumulated, in some instances for its repetitive nature
dared call wisdom or truth. Thus Langbaum's case for relativist truth in Browning's poem resolves itself into a discourse on moral and social judgment, by individual consent,
which, with two major qualifications, is the juncture at which
Langbaum's essay begins: "Truth cannot be apprehended in
itself but must be 'induced' from particular points of view,...
there can be sufficient difference among the points of view
to make each repetition interesting and important as a psychological fact" (p. 109). The qualifications are: 1) individual judgment is in advance of truth, institutional judgment
loses its truth in exhausted formulations; 2) truth simply
cannot exist in or out of the welter of contradictions which

depicts both man and what man calls fact.

Different from the unworthy characters Langbaum
analyzes, his Pope is conscious of the responsibility of God's
Vicar and makes the ultimate judgment knowing he may be
unjust to Guido.   Nevertheless he judges confidently by "the
light given him" and solemnly stakes his heavenly salvation
on pure motives.   As Langbaum explains:

> The Pope's confidence in his judgment does not
> rest on the supposition that the truth is directly
> or easily apprehensible; but neither does he sup-
> pose that the truth cannot be found in the "plead-
> ings and counter-pleadings" he has before him:
>
>> Truth, nowhere, lies yet everywhere in these--
>> Not absolutely in a portion, yet
>> Evolvible from the whole: evolved at last
>> Painfully, held tenaciously by me.
>>   (X. 229-232; italics added)
>
> Truth is not in any one argument but can be "in-
> duced" from the particular points of view, the way
> Browning expects us to "induce" it from the ten
> dramatic monologues.   (p. 120)

Many a reader, knowing the Pope beforehand had declared himself fallible, has assumed from the above poetic
quotation that a good and remarkable man evolved a truth,
incompletely but laboriously, on which he was willing to
stake his integrity (275-276), but not his future life.   For
Langbaum, the passage means the truth he promises the
"pleadings" will yield in one line is in another line a truth
which may only be "induced. " Taking note of the Pope's
expressed fallibility alongside "the light given him, " he now
places the Pope's reliance in his own judgment upon talent,
intuition, insight, character, and experience, not upon logical searching out (p. 121).   And if, in the run of his essay,
he had wanted to document these intuitive qualities, he could
have not surpassed use of the following lines, except that
they positively disprove his contention of no external force
or influence for truth insofar as Pope Innocent is concerned:

> Yet my poor spark had for its source, the sun;
> Thither I sent the great looks which compel
> Light from its fount: all that I do and am
> Comes from the truth, or seen or else surmised,

Remembered or divined, as mere man may:
I know just so, nor otherwise. As I know,
I speak, --what should I know, then, and how speak
Were there a wild mistake of eye or brain
As to recorded governance above?
                              (X. 1285-93; italics added)

The critics who are skeptical of or opposed to absolute truth and the poet's unfavorable comparison of human
truth with it, have consistently closed their eyes to the hun-
dreds of lines Browning wrote on the subject. And though
the lines are now affixed in a separate section, it is doubtful their convenience will contribute to a fairer appraisal
of Browning's idealism. Even on being told by Langbaum
that the processes of attainment seem identical, these critics take more comfort from "evolvable truth, " as they interpret it, than from "absolute truth, " toward which Browning conditions the evolving.

But, despite the obvious sincerity with which Langbaum approaches "evolvable truth, " his arguments on motives
are those which are probably farthest from textual justification. As in his comments on judgment, so in his comments
on motives, Langbaum does not always make clear whose
motive is at stake. It is as if he thinks the Pope himself
hears the various monologuists; or if not this, that the Pope's
motive is more important than the motives of the representative witnesses, and that the motives of the readers are
still more important, whereas the Pope must decide by the
motives (if Langbaum's word is retained) of the participants
in the tragic murder. In Essay Seven I try to show the mistake in such an argument is that the Pope, having no doubt
in his judgment of Guido, is talking about something entirely
different, but never with the belief his own motives are pure;
he knows better. We should be reminded often that the Pope
asks in Book I, "Am I not Pope, and presently to die, / And
busied how to render my account" (337-338; italics added),
the "yonder passion" (X. 199) he personally faces in death,
not in Guido's death. Guided by most interpretations of Book
X, especially A. K. Cook's, Langbaum will demand conclusive proof of what I promise, but he will also recognize the
fallacy of the Pope's being confident in a judgment of Guido
which may be a "mistake" (p. 120).

Used more often than any other passage in The Ring
and the Book to divest the poem of absolute or idealized
truth, the Pope's words on "evolvable truth" are, after a

sixty-four-line interlude on the disgraceful March day and
the sagacious Swede, followed by six hundred fifty consecutive lines (X. 338-1004) in which is explained exactly "why
Guido is found reprobate" (X. 399).   Taken in order, the
lines of the immediate context of "evolvable truth" (X. 194-
282)--exclusive of the definitive nature of "figure of fact /
Beside fact's self" (X. 216-217), "not absolutely in a portion, " and pontifical fallibility--may be shown to weaken distinctly any belief that a final truth is evolvable by whatever
the means.   But by the same lines it may also be shown
that the Pope thought he had reached a satisfactory precedent
on which to condemn Guido.   Bold and dramatic, the Pope's
resolution, as expressed in "All's a clear rede [tale] and no
more riddle now" and "there is not any doubt to clear, " is
therefore declared to be as substantial as the mound on
which nearby pine trees are growing.   It is not doubt over
the judgment of Guido which makes the persistent rain so
chilly (X. 286), but doubt over the manner and method of
man's judgment generally.   To miss the Pope's spiritual
wavering at the end of his longest day, to discount the doubt
which escalates his distinction between seed (X. 280) and
fruit (X. 341) of act, is the equivalent of canceling the high
drama of the Pope's return to composure in mind and spirit
by way of a renewed and more confident faith in God and
God's truth.   "Not so!" Pope Innocent exclaims, in rebuttal
to his own disturbing doubt on man's accustomed way of judging:

> Not so! Expect nor question nor reply
> At what we figure as God's judgment-bar!
> None of this vile way by the barren words
> Which, more than any deed, characterize
> Man as made subject to a curse: . . . .
> . . . .
> Therefore these filthy rags of speech, this coil
> Of statement, comment, query and response,
> Tatters all too contaminate for use,
> Have no renewing: He, the Truth, is, too,
> The Word. We men, in our degree, may know
> There, simply, instantaneously, as here
> After long time and amid many lies,
> Whatever we dare think we know indeed
> --That I am I, as He is He, --what else?
>   (X. 347-381; italics added)

From this confirmation of faith in an exalted, ideally existent
truth, and buttressed by an irresistible sense of divine guid-

ance, the Pope can offer his many reasons for the condemnation of Guido.   It has not been explained very well why Langbaum, or any other critic, should persist in rejecting these
least ambiguous of all the Pope's words.   Yet the inescapable
suspicion is that those who ignore the passage have no reason
other than distaste for the Pope's thought.

        For all his effort to get to <u>motives,</u> the importance of
which no one disputes, Langbaum then feels compelled to abstract his truth one step further.   "Thus, " he summarizes,
"truth is psychologized in the sense that the facts do not reveal it. . .   The moral judgments are definite and extreme,
but they depend upon our total apprehension of the characters
themselves.   What we arrive at in the end is not <u>the</u> truth,
but truth as the worthiest characters of the poem <u>see</u> it" (p.
122).   It is not the time to ask again about admitted "shaping" of characters by the poet or how historical judgments
made nearly two hundred years ago can "depend upon our total apprehension. "   As psychologized truth means no less
than personalized truth to Langbaum, so historicized truth
means no more than exhausted institutionalized formulations.
But since on miscarriage of one institutional judgment the
Pope may predicate the end of Christianity's period of triumph, we may ask why the period did not end sixteen hundred
years earlier with St. Paul's identical denunciations.   How
Caponsacchi's admirable conduct may challenge a whole system and precipitate its demise, how a future Pompilia by individual conduct may keep essential Christianity alive through
right instinct, are less important as questions than as proof
of Langbaum's total dependence upon personalized truth.
Their disequilibrium (his, by daring to break the Christian
rules; hers, by keeping them, p.   123) admittedly drive
Caponsacchi and Pompilia in opposite directions, but as
long as their actions vilify institutional truth and exonerate
individual truth, it is preferable to laying any charge of
guilt at man's own feet.   How Euripides anticipated Christian
morality "without benefit of Christian revelation" is also
less significant than how Euripides, Jesus, and other great
teachers reached common moral and ethical beliefs without
benefit of an external principle of any kind.   Taking his cue
solely from the independent actions of Euripides, Pompilia,
and Caponsacchi, Langbaum's Pope "comes to see that the
truth is something other than the machinery by which men
try to understand it. "   "He sees. . . that the machinery changes,
but truth <u>remains</u>--never in equilibrium with the machinery
and sometimes in direct conflict with it" (p.   123; italics added).   It matters little that in a contiguous illustration Lang-

baum reverts to a future displacement of truth: that is, as
psychologically the truth about a man is larger and in advance
of our understanding, so historically truth is larger and in
advance of any institutions or formulations (p. 124).

On moving to "the Pope's dialectical perception of
the developing disequilibrium between truth and machinery"
(p. 134), however, Langbaum can hardly be excused for failing to mention that the Pope's only use of the word machinery involves exclusively the dread spectacle of "sin and sorrow" (X. 1375-81) as the antithesis of individual man's responsibility to love and be loved.   Instead of noticing, for
example, that Browning's use of "machinery" is as effective
as Milton's use of "engine, " Langbaum exploits the word un-
mercifully.   And he much too easily disposes of Fra Celestino's "God is true and every man a liar" in an allusion to
Celestino's "somewhat Antinomian perception of [truth's and
machinery's] eternal opposition. "   Antinomian to whom?
Surely not to the Pope who after saying man's words have
no renewing adds: "He, the Truth, is, too, / The Word. "
Surely not to the poet who again and again proclaims his
misgivings about human testimony, human fame, and human
estimation. And surely not to St. Paul who provides Fra
Celestino the text responsible for his sermonic diatribe.
One does not wonder that Langbaum opens the adjoining paragraph with: "Not only does Browning show the inadequacy of
most people to judge Pompilia, but he sets the action against
a detailed historical background the purpose of which is to
show how far the disequilibrium between truth and machinery
has gone since 1698. " But it would be instructive, in Langbaum's continuing challenge to the church and institutional
life, to learn what happened in the same sentence to "the
inadequacy of most people. "[3] When Guido weasels his way
into the church, it is the fault of the church; when crime
and vice spawn Pompilia, it is the fault of society; when
the Comparini greedily seek to exploit an inheritance, it is
the fault of law; when Guido cynically barters his rank for
Pompilia's dowry, it is the fault of nobility and law; when
Tuscan governor, bishop, and court scandalously side with
Guido, it is the fault of national church and state; when one
convent shamefully sues for Pompilia's estate, it is the fault
of Christendom; and when Guido's peasants plan his murder,
it is the fault of all existing agencies of civilization.   Not
once in Langbaum's social indictments is one individual held
responsible for one infraction.   Yet the misapplied and in-
flammatory word machinery, when returned to "this dread
machinery / Of sin and sorrow" as the Pope's intended use,

identifies a disequilibrium between truth and the individual comparable in its rascality to that Langbaum assigns the establishment. ˎ It is especially difficult to believe he is serious when he writes that "Guido and the Pope make the same historical observations, though for opposite reasons and with opposite judgments" (p. 127). And if he is serious, does he mean more than that a good man in any age, observing the ways of the world, is distressed; a bad man, observing the same world, rejoices?

Not satisfied himself with the foregoing definition of psychologized truth, Langbaum continues, "Psychologically, the right instinct of Pompilia and Caponsacchi is a guarantee that truth maintains itself in the human heart in spite of history, of external change" (p. 128). In the language Browning's Pope and Celestino would be more prone to use, Langbaum is writing about the everlasting conflict between good and evil. But he forgets that as truth maintains itself in the good heart, so is it lost to the evil heart. The corruption which made Guido's crime possible no more destroyed the old order than the virtue of Pompilia washed the world afresh with new truth. Nor does Pompilia find the right way in spite of the age, as Langbaum insists, but because, as Pompilia herself insists, she depended on "the Truth's self: / God will lend credit to my words this time" (VIL 1198-99). Such obviously easy documentation reduces to futility Langbaum's effort to make of Christian truth a truth which is "different from and anterior to any cultural expression of it, " so he may then assert that its renewal must be tested "against truth's source in the human heart" (p. 128). Langbaum can reason as he chooses about the phoenix-like renewal of human truth, but never acceptably about the Platonic and Christian truth with which Browning was imbued, until he recognizes that the truth, according to both doctrines, is provided if not imposed externally and requires something more reliable than man's heart alone for its renewal and continued sustenance. To say "the Pope sacrifices the social order, and even the Christian era, to Christian truth" is to forget that the record of the whole sordid affair was promptly lost for one hundred fifty years. Speculation enlivens all forms of criticism, but it has always been thought the better practice to keep within narrower perspective topics as tangential as those expanded by Langbaum. He completely misses the point that brief references to old and new orders, Molinism, the doctrine of infallibility, and natural theology only incidentally "add to the poem's metaphysical and moral judgment a small further discreditation of reason as an instrument of knowledge and of ethical decision" (Altick and Loucks, p. 335).

Seeing good reason for Browning's introduction of Molinists, Langbaum does particularly well in emphasizing their belief in a direct apprehension of God and their brief significance as a historical entity (p. 129). But there is something impossibly askew in his isolating a two-line reference to the Molinists and making it the "text" of one thousand lines of pontifical exegesis: "Leave them alone...those Molinists! / Who may have other light than we perceive" (I. 315-316). Whereas the Pope is speaking beyond question about the truth of heavenly salvation (X. 1630, 1689), Langbaum thinks it the Pope's way of saying, "Recognized truths shall be sacrificed for unrecognized truths, " not asking, "Shall recognized truths be sacrificed to truth yet unrecognized?"

> Must we deny, --do they, these Molinists,
> At peril of their body and their soul, --
> Recognized truths, obedient to some truth
> Unrecognized yet, but perceptible?--
> Correct the portrait by the living face,
> Man's God, by God's God in the mind of man.
>   (X. 1869-74)

As Langbaum himself points out, we are dealing with the Vicar of God. So it is not adequate to cite a word here and there to prove one thing, when the Pope's discernible religious concerns tell us an entirely different thing. After rationalizing the reasons for his judgments of individual participants in Pompilia's case (X. 399-1238), the Pope is immersed in a second period of meditative doubt which encompasses, not Guido's condemnation, but his own method of judgment, his privilege to judge, and a challenge to his faith in God (X. 1239-84). This "keen dread creeping" he slowly balances out as a "wild mistake of eye or brain" (X. 1292) and overcomes in an affirmation of faith, which nonetheless is conditioned by grappling still with doubt (X. 1302). Then as an appointed representative of God in prayerful contemplation (X. 1308-1850), the Pope insists that though the nature of God's "dread play of operation" is incomprehensible, it is still believable, by reason of love--the atonement--alone. Otherwise, the Pope argues, as he again exemplies by use of individuals and institutions, both good and bad, "this dread machinery / Of sin and sorrow, would confound" him. As sage observer of man, he can neither forget the promptitude

for good nor blink the obduracy to good. Even so, as God's
shepherd, not now as a judge, Pope Innocent is most reluc-
tantly though inevitably forced to ask whether lukewarm acceptance, perhaps blatant disregard, of God's atoning love
and man's moral responsibility is really salvation (X. 1630).
Salvation and faith in God therefore become the controlling
thought and, as I advance in Essay Seven, initiate the appearance of Euripides, a pagan who asks the most disconcerting question a Christian can be asked.   Homiletically,
both the Pope and the poet score high.   For the Pope first
accepts the guilt of all men, then reassesses his own personal salvation before considering the salvation of his flock,
and finally turns his thoughts to individuals who lived before
and beyond Christ's redemptive act.   Unjust disparity in opportunity for salvation thus causes him to challenge the faith
of his contemporaries, not the truth as Langbaum suggests,
and to compare that contemporary faith unfavorably with
early Christian as well as Euripidean faith.   Much has been
written about Guido's possible salvation and possible damnation, and both Caponsacchi and the Pope rather hesitantly
permit him to slide out of existence.   But since Browning
and his Pope did not believe that any man, regardless of
his stain of evil, could be permanently lost to God's grace,
it is revealing, on consideration of Guido's crime and the
degree of current faith, to find the Pope, in the image of
the "cornfield dance of fools" (X. 1838), restricting his condemnatory thought to language more nearly Greek than Christian.   Browning's Pope thinks that ignoble confidence and
cowardly hardihood now make the old heroism impossible.
Perhaps this is why his comparison of the faith exhibited by
Euripides and contemporary worldlings suffers a dramatic
limitation we do not experience, for example, in Body and
Soul debates structured on the premise of eternal damnation.
Knowing, however, that the evidences of current religious
faith were most disheartening, the Pope is moved to ask,
"Who is faithful now?"   Like prophets of the Old Testament
and apostles of the New Testament, he nonetheless already
knew that no one is as faithful as he should be or, better,
should want to be.

        Woven together of complex theological truth, simple
biblical truth, and some interesting Browingesque speculations,
the Pope's thoughts on salvation ("Well, is the thing we see,
salvation?") clearly prepare the way for "I / Put no such
dreadful question to myself" (X. 1631-32), which concludes
the third and most awful period of doubt.   Because God's
Power, Wisdom, and Goodness are the central truth of his

own existence, assuring him a sinful man of personal salvation, the Pope dares not offer judgment where only God
knows the heart and exacts the service (X. 1672-73; spoken
by Euripides).   This we learn as the Pope moves from
thoughts of inexhaustible human trial and error, the possibility that man's faith comes alive and expressive only under
the most adverse conditions.   To overlook the Pope's primary assignment of declaring God's gift of salvation as Langbaum does, however, is still less incomprehensible than his
reversal of the role played by the Pope's experimentalists.
For eight times Langbaum writes unequivocally of the Pope's
foreseeing a promising new age, era, or order to be ushered
in. 4 To be sure, the Pope speculates briefly on the consequences of an Age of Doubt, one in which recognized
truths may give way before yet unrecognized truth, but, as
Browning himself clarifies the passage,

> If he thought doubt would do the next age good,
> 'T is pity he died unapprised what birth
> His reign may boast of, be remembered by--
> Terrible Pope, too, of a kind, --Voltaire.
>   (XIL 775-779)

A thoughtful critic cannot read the Pope's monologue, beginning with line 1851, without observing that the first sixty
lines are preparatory to expression of the Pope's profoundest
misgivings about the future.   Of course some one Pompilia
will "know the right place by foot's feel" in the next century,
not however by accepting Langbaum's evolvement of truth (p.
123) but by steadfastly asking, "Wherefore change?"   (X.
1887) While admitting that Caponsacchi was once directed
discreetly by his heart, the Pope decisively submits that
"chance brought him safe" (X. 1920) only thus far.   And
the Pope prefers, by a great degree, that Caponsacchi be
another Augustine, making the Church the ruling law of his
life, rather than a Loyola, adapting his life to the times.
Biblical scholar that he is, Browning's Pope knows that instinctive evil flourishes like the green bay tree, and he pas-
sionately fears the consequences of a new age of doubt in
contrast to momentary reflection on unrecognized truth a
new age may find.   The second experimentalist (X. 1930),
guided like Caponsacchi the first experimentalist (X. 1909)
by instinct but of an opposite kind, therefore chooses not
the glorious life but one of lowest appetites.   His appearance in the Pope's train of thought moreover gives rise to
a new tribunal higher than God's law, one which is to be

manipulated (regretfully) by the "educated man" (X. 1976-77).
And confirming the Pope's own fearful anticipation, educated
man's educated "junior" (X. 1996) briskly takes "permission
to decide" (X. 1991) in instinctive confrontation with the divine law.   It is contempt of God and His Truth, and of them
alone, that the Pope calls civilization, the return of the Gold-
en Age when Civilization and the Emperor succeed to Christianity and the Pope (X. 2015-30).   Not at all the hopeful
scene Langbaum would have us imagine but, in the name of
truth as Browning expounds it, one in which the natural man
gets a predictable Christian comeuppance in the Pope's im-
patient answer to the youngest experimentalist's threat and
demand for Guido's acquittal:

> I will, Sirs: but a voice other than yours
> Quickens my spirit.   "Quis pro Domino?
> "Who is upon the Lord's side?" asked the Count.
> (X. 2099-2101)

"The moral of the story," then, is not, as Langbaum
would have it, "that the good was vindicated by just the dandy
priest doing what his vows and the laws of Church and State
expressly forbid" (p. 113).   It is rather, in the Pope's words
from which Langbaum also quotes, "a miracle and an act of
God."   Even Molinism in Browning stands more directly for
the primitive faith and the truth once and for all delivered to
the saints than, as Langbaum theorizes, "for an anti-dogmatic,
an empirical and relativist, a psychological and historical approach to religion" (p. 130). [5]   As Langbaum concludes his
essay, therefore, his arguments ring less and less acceptable
to Browning's thought and art and more and more demonstrable of Langbaum's twentieth-century proclivities.   He must
say that "truth's ultimate source is in the individual mind"
(p. 130) if he believes "the poem is not to derive meaning
from any external standard of judgment, but is to be the em-
piric ground giving rise to its own standard of judgment" (p.
131).   Only if he believes that behind Browning's devotion to
facts and figures "stands the positivist's faith that ultimate
truth lies locked up in the facts" (p. 132), may he add, "once
dramatized, imbued with life, the facts can be depended upon
to yield their meaning... [for] the only reason for dramatizing
the story at all is not to impose truth upon it, but to make
the truth accessible" (p. 133).   Consequently, because Langbaum's "poet adds nothing to the truth," he as resuscitator
"is the superlatively effective psychologist and historian, the
arch-empiricist who works toward greater concreteness and
not, as in traditional poetic theory, toward general truths.

His talent lies in the 'surplusage of soul' which enables him
to project himself into the facts, apprehend them sympathetically in other words, and thus apprehend their life" (p. 134).
It is a long essay, with a multitude of interesting side issues.
But, exempting the attack on institutions, Langbaum's focus,
of course, is on a denial of truth in any sense other than that
Browning's poem "establishes a pole for sympathy," so that
the reader also may project himself into the facts, thereby
apprehending their life.   The poet's "meaning," Langbaum
tells us, "comes not from the theoretical interpretation but
from the intensest concreteness."   But because "it can be
argued that Browning does not entirely let the facts speak
for themselves," treat each point of view impartially, allow
judgment to arise out of the utmost ambiguity, Langbaum's
final question is whether facts really can speak for themselves (p. 135).   This he answers by saying that Browning's
"aim... would have to be the aim of any genuinely modern
literature," which is momentary illumination through a personal and temporary rejection of the facts, or at least the
system through which individuals perceive the facts.

        As I have indicated by use of so many quotations from
Langbaum's essay, it would be incorrect to suggest that he
has not recorded all the good and bad things which may be
imputed to the phenomenon truth.   Characterizing the style
and thought, his paradoxes have demanded an analysis far
more extended than normal exposition asks.   But these arguments are all grist to the mill, since Langbaum's design has
been to keep us circling giddily until a fact cannot be told
from any other speck which may fall on the smooth surface
of things.   Motivated by an extraordinary opposition to any
form of organizational conduct, he would have the individual
sole and final arbiter.   It is as if any fragmentary thought
he or any one else including literary characters expresses
becomes forthwith an established fact, albeit subject immediately to denial, contradiction, or displacement, since its
early death carries the seed of new fact, ad infinitum.   His
attitude toward institutionalized truth of the seventeenth century hardly escapes being called symptomatic, since neither
the Pope nor Fra Celestino is any more or less modern in
his condemnation of false practices than are Isaiah, Jeremiah,
and Amos, or the great Greek poets, tragedians, and historians.   On the other hand, his placing Robert Browning's total
reliance upon the truth of the individual, compromised as
that truth endlessly is, is as inconceivable as placing the
poet's reliance on Voltaire.   Since Langbaum rejects the
pristine quality of gold, longer thought simply on the pre-

cious quality of Browning's gold facts might have restricted
the severest reaches of his speculation. More serious
thought on the telling of truth obliquely, that is, of facts
indirectly, might also have lifted him over the temptation
to turn The Ring and the Book into a historical document.
Like Morse Peckham's, Langbaum's attempted adulteration
of Browning's long poetic lament over the sparse dimensions
of man's truth and language, when contrasted with absolute
truth, is a suspiciously calculated move to install the poet
in an age one century later than the one in which he was
molded.

Most interested in reminding us that the meaning of
The Ring and the Book "has to do with the PROCESS by
which the artist sees and shares his vision of truth" (pp.
175-176), Miss Sullivan opens her chapter "To 'Tell a Truth
Obliquely'" in a way which enables us to recall her thoughts
on the Ring metaphor as we learn them on Browning's truth.
Expectedly, she neglects the implications of to "tell a truth
obliquely"--to tell the facts indirectly--and interprets the
poet's comments on his art to mean "that no man can see
the truth in any human event so clearly as the artist" with
his special gift for evolving the truth:

> Limited as he is by his own human knowledge, the
> artist can nevertheless in his role as "resuscitator"
> take long-dead historical personages and restore
> them to life by giving them voice; in the process
> of their subsequent self-revelation, with the poet's
> own voice concealed or "withdrawn, " they expose
> the truth gradually, each voice giving one limited,
> relatively reliable or distorted facet of the whole.
> The reader-audience shares in the poet's final vis-
> ion of the truth by assuming temporarily each
> limited viewpoint, measuring and judging the ex-
> tent of its distortion, and extracting from it what-
> ever expression of fact and opinion is valid, if
> any.   (p. 175; italics added)

That the reader, when inclined to share the poet's vision, is
thus persuaded on balance by the poet's structuring of the
personalities and attitudes of his speakers, is acceptable to
all.   The reason for objection rises when Miss Sullivan adds,
"The difference is that the poet has arrived at his viewpoint
in a unique way:... he has evolved the truth about their moti-
vations" (p. 177).   And though she occasionally takes note of

"human inability to see truth whole" (p. 169) and "the untrustworthiness of human speech ['prejudices, blindness, and
distortions']" (p. 172), she means precisely what she says
about the poet's unique talent for knowing the truth.

If then, as I think, Miss Sullivan is demonstrably confused over Browning's view of truth, her confusion must grow
out of the conflicting statements she adds to an adaptation of
the conflicting interpretations of Smith, Cundiff, and Langbaum.   On even keel at first, she reasons clearly that Browning's purpose for multiple monologuists is "the detection of
relative distortion which each allows" (p. 181) in his revealed motive.   To those opposed to Pompilia, she attributes
a blindness--"broken fragments of truth"--to the girl's goodness.   Each of these, she says, "had condemned himself to
a lifetime of half-truths and distortions" (pp. 184-185).   To
those who favor Pompilia's goodness, she attributes "a greater grasp of the truth, because their motives are purer."
The Pope, Pompilia, Caponsacchi, and Pompilia's Half-
Rome, "each in his own way and on his own level, all reach
toward the truth... Although they comprehend the power of
goodness and the weakness of evil, the truth for each can be
no more than a light shrouded in darkness:...   Their light
remains only a faint reflection of the brilliant white light of
the poet's vision;...   We understand that they see as much
as it is given to man to see without the poet's gift of divine
inspiration" (p. 185; italics added).   Here, with the poet
freed from all canker of partial truth, Miss Sullivan sounds
least like Langbaum, more like Smith and Cundiff respective-
ly in her references to the white light of the poet's vision of
truth and man's limitations as seen in the poet's repetitive
pattern.   Bolder than any of these critics, however, she
thematically equates whatever truth she is writing about with
the capacity of the poet to find all the truth.   Only gradually
does it become evident that her thoughts are as firmly fixed
in personalized truth as Langbaum's are.   The one difference
is her added belief that the meaning of the poem is simply
the process by which Browning sees and shares his vision of
truth.   That she substantiates this process--voices and ad-
dress--by saying it is comparable to the process described
in the Ring metaphor scarcely explains why the reader has
such a hard time in his step-by-step apprehension of truth
(p. 186).   One cannot believe Miss Sullivan could evade in
Smith's pure white light reference to the absolute truth of
God; so it must be her thesis which dictates the strange
transposition of truth to the poet's capacity to find truth.
Of course, this change does not make it easy for her,

without confusing the reader, to indicate how truth is personalized in Browning while Browning is depersonalized in
his nine speakers in order to let the reader share Browning's
vision of truth (p. 196).

"Without the poetic intercession, " Miss Sullivan thinks,
"the glorious truth God provided for man would continue to
lie hidden as it has for two hundred years" (p. 210). Multiple dramatic monologues allow Browning "to demonstrate
the partiality of the individual human perspective and... to
transcend that partiality to evolve a single all-encompassing
truth" (p. 208; italics added). Because Browning has forged
through years of unremitting effort the precise instrument for
making truth apprehensible, he "can now use the dead fact
to teach a universal, a lasting, truth. " With his God-given
skill for penetrating the confusion and contradiction, "he
could not have misread the record; to do so would be to
deny the infallibility of the poet's intuitive grasp of the
truth" (p. 212). Miss Sullivan commits her greatest error
in thinking the poet actually can do "God's work on earth,
making Him apprehensible" and serving as link between time
and eternity. It is, among other things, a confusion of poetic purpose further complicated by suggestion that the poetic
function approximates the incarnation (p. 210, note 21). Yet
she seems unaware that her position makes it awkward later
to say that she agrees with Langbaum and Peckham, who believe Browning is artistically reordering, re-creating, and
dramatizing in order to permit the reader to "do a significant act" in seeing truth (p. 211). Representative of a fairly
large group of impressionistic critics, Miss Sullivan carries
us farther in her imagistic mixture of absolutist and relativist theory than we will to go.

With the inadvertence of enthusiastic critics as well
as of some competent scholars, Miss Sullivan gives Browning's intelligence extremely short shrift. The truth of the
facts of the Old Yellow Book is one issue; the existence of
a universal truth from which man's appraisal of the facts
falls short is another issue. A third, and less likely issue,
is the belief, running from Mrs. Orr to Miss Sullivan, that
Browning's poetic assertion of Delphic powers should be
taken as an accomplished act. Few critics believe any longer that Browning told the whole truth of his facts, much less
the total truth of all. Yet Miss Sullivan's inseparable weld-
ing of poetic claims and poetic performance threatens to re-
habilitate a past confusion in Browning's indiscriminate exchange of the word "truth" for "fact" which, hopefully, was

nearing extinction. Even though she returns to the old problem of fidelity to fact with a compensatory element in
Smith's "vision of truth, " she seems determined to misread
critics both with whom she agrees and disagrees. She thinks
that J. Hillis Miller is writing about the truth of facts in the
Old Yellow Book and the truth of the poet, and that Langbaum
comes to a somewhat similar conclusion (pp. 209-210). Miller is writing of Browning's early acceptance of a universal
norm on truth which he "tediously" reaffirmed the remainder
of his life, of "the transcendence of God and the impossibility
of joining finite and infinite. " Langbaum is speaking of the
absence of a universal norm and Browning's acceptance of
the relativity of all truth [fact].   Nor can there be much
doubt that Miss Sullivan is thinking solely of the truth of
Browning's interpretation, when she disagrees with A. K.
Cook, who accepted Lord Morley's classic assessment: "The
whole poem is a parable of the feeble and half-hopeless struggle which truth has to make against the ways of the world. "

        In thoughts of the impenetrability of the OYB facts to
the ordinary reader and the "flashing forth" of truth to
Browning on his first reading, Miss Sullivan concludes that,
"as the gold and alloy metaphor reminds us, . . . the poet is
not free to compromise or dilute the truth in any way: the
process merely involves a willingness on his part to stoop
to the level of ordinary man, to offer him, 'No dose of purer
truth than man digests, / But truth with falsehood, milk that
feeds him now'" (pp. 212-213).   Of course she is bluffing on
the metaphor, and she appears to offer a solid contradiction
in "not free to compromise" and "stooping. "   But she is not
alone among Browning scholars in shunning the ready biblical
gloss which indicates that Browning, in accordance with his
St. Paul, deplored the need to stoop.   As I have tried to indicate, Miss Sullivan's comprehension of The Ring and the
Book is much more significant than her thesis on voice
and address.   If only she had trusted her "all reach toward
the truth, " revised her "grasping [at] truth, " and permitted
Browning's art "to evolve [toward] the truth, " she would not
be so far from those who think Browning reserved for truth
an awe as great as that of the Breton mariner: "O, God,
Thy Sea is so great and my boat is so small. "

        In a 1969 essay John Killham, who may or may not
have followed Raymond's brief but cogent review (VN, No.
10 [Autumn 1956], pp. 12-13) of Langbaum's essay, explains
why he cannot accept a modern and relativistic interpretation

of The Ring and the Book.   After first calling on Pater,
Wordsworth, Carlyle, and Browning for evidence of their
familiarity with "relativist" thought, he draws a most helpful distinction between social and moral relativism which he
summarizes thus:

> This [moral] relativism is not concerned with
> changing beliefs, attitudes and the like, issuing
> in social arrangements, but relates rather to the
> individual's personal apprehension of the world he
> inhabits.   It is intensely materialistic at bottom,
> and also tends to set the individual above, or in
> opposition to, society, which no longer appears to
> have so obvious a claim to the loyalty of beings
> whose lives are constituted out of experiences
> peculiar to them.   The right of society to make
> laws and to judge and condemn in accordance with
> them may seem questionable.   This sort of moral
> relativism stands in relation to social relativism
> as Anarchy to Culture and it clearly looks forward
> to many features of our own century and its litera-
> ture.   ("Browning's 'Modernity':   The Ring and the
> Book, and Relativism, " The Major Victorian Poets:
> Reconsiderations,   ed. Isobel Armstrong [Lincoln,
> Nebraska, 1969], p. 157)

Even less conciliatory toward a pluralistic interpretation of
The Ring and the Book, Killham bluntly dismisses E. D. H.
Johnson's advocacy of pluralism: "It is the whole point of
the poem that some of the speakers have various reasons,
personal and professional, for quite deliberately juggling with
the 'facts' in decidedly interesting fashion.   To say that each
speaker is sure that he is rendering them veraciously is to
adapt the poem to the theory" (p. 158).   But after absolving
Langbaum, the earliest proponent of relativism, from total
apostasy, Killham subsequently finds Langbaum's position
"not very far from Johnson's idea of pluralism after all. "
This likeness he mainly deduces from Langbaum's well-
known "'truth depends upon the nature of the theorising and
ultimately upon the nature of the soul of which the theorising
is a projection'" and "what we arrive at in the end is not
the truth, but truth as the worthiest characters of the poem
see it. "   In the end, therefore, Killham rests his case
against both Langbaum and Johnson by returning the poem,
as sound scholarship must, to the nineteenth century: "It
stands, in my view, as an elaborate Victorian monument to
the faith that truth does not depend upon human testimony,

but is absolute" (p. 172).

        What Killham does not do, though we have every rea-
son for thinking he could, is to weigh other of his observations with the same caution he displays on relativist truth.
The related observations always appear as firmly held convictions, and their validity is indeed only slightly less fundamental to a clear understanding of the poem than Killham's
attempted resolution of the relativistic-pluralistic implications.
Of course failure to substantiate thoroughly his belief that
Browning did not yield "up the search for absolute truth"
and invite us "to see things as they are" may be attributed
to the limitation of space imposed upon his essay.   Yet
meaning itself of such words as fact and truth, though frequently presupposed by Killham, is more elusive in his essay
than the complicated "man, like a glass ball" (L 1367), an
image lucidly explained by use of the "electric egg" though
oddly interpreted as evil man, not all men.   One may therefore profitably challenge the process through which Killham
reaches some of his persuasions, even if only to illustrate
the difficulty all critics have in penetrating a few ambiguous
yet pivotal terms and words in the poem.   For example, in
a phrase apt for exposing the inescapable overlapping of Ring
metaphor and truth, he reflects: "Its [the metaphor's] re-
quiring us to replace the common phrase 'hard fact' with, as
it were, 'soft fact' is curious, and it does rather suggest
moral relativism, the idea that facts are malleable, and that
each of us is free to impress our own meaning or sense of
truth upon them" (p. 160).   With more precise information
from the poem, with technical information on ring-making,
Killham could have avoided his concession to relativist truth.
Echoing Mrs. Orr, though probably without recalling it, Killham is saying that gold, the softest of all metals, is so hard
when analogously thought of as facts that Browning's imaginative gift should have been applied as a softening agent. Yet
Browning does not once use "soft" or "hard" to describe his
pure crude fact any more than he once uses the word "relative" in connection with truth or fact.   Advocates of relativism, on returning to Mrs. Orr's criticism (Essay One),
may find comfort in her use of human truth, but they will
also find themselves doubly suspicious of a critic who says
the gold of the ring, unquestionably equated by Browning with
his facts, is too soft; the facts of his trial, unquestionably
equated by Browning with the gold of the ring, are too hard.
In different words, if the ring is "overweighted with symbolic
freight, " as Park Honan implies, it is additionally weighed
down by unacceptable opinion for which Browning cannot be

blamed. It is really not so curious, once his Ring metaphor
stipulates the terms, that Browning adopts pristine, not soft,
quality for his facts; in working with pristine gold the artificer is compelled to add the harder copper to give body and
substance to the alloy which he then hammers and shapes into permanent form. It is curious that critics often fail to
account for Browning's poetic malleability in terms of adding
imagination as a hardening or stiffening agent which makes
the pure and crude facts more susceptible of proper shaping
and permanent form. And in so doing, Browning just may
disprove the common belief that he is more culpable in metaphorical choice than his critics in metaphorical acumen.

Almost as unsure as Mrs. Orr on the process an artificer follows in making a gold ring, Killham assumes that
a chemical process takes place in the mixing of gold and
copper (normally ten to twenty per cent copper) for a ring
alloy. But this is not what happens: in the "fusing" or
mixing, gold remains gold, copper copper. Malleability, to
the goldsmith, has only to do with the mass of gold and copper. And malleability, to Browning, has only to do with the
mass of pure crude facts his fancy makes less soft for the
shaping, extending, fashioning, molding into a mosaic the
discrete but related bits of evidence, not with individual
facts which are being altered or, as Killham cannot avoid
admitting, being impressed by the reader's own sense of
truth. Had he known, or known and accepted, the technical
process, Killham might not have felt compelled to offer any
allowance for Johnson's "plasticity of factual reality" or
Langbaum's "relativist ethos." It is with the "fusing" or
mixing of the mass of facts (as identified with gold) that
Browning's imagination (as identified with copper in the alloy)
produced the right degree of malleability, so that the mass
of facts could then be molded into a shape susceptible of
permanent poetic incising and design. Most understandable
in Mrs. Orr, escape by Killham from insecurity in the Ring
metaphor to discussion of "irony" and Browning's inability to
invent "ex nihilo" is not the best way to explain what is "sym-
bolised by the ring" (p. 164).

To take for granted, as Killham does, that "Browning
identifies facts with the truth" (p. 160) is natural enough,
but it is still to evade the need for unravelling Browning's
multiple, sometimes suspiciously tantalizing, application of
the words fact and truth. In unequalled poetic excess Browning fills The Ring and the Book with interchangeable variations on these two words, which to him may mean mere

fact or truth, alleged fact or truth, false fact or truth, demonstrable fact or truth, indemonstrable fact or truth, poetic fact or truth, essential fact or absolute truth.   And as
these variations are played out unremittingly and often indiscriminately in a manner which prevents us from distin-
guishing between simple human fact and an essential or absolute truth, we must also contend with the knowledge that
all is finally dependent upon the individual reader's measure-
ment of the significance of truth to the poem itself.   What
truth, which truth does Browning identify with fact?   What
fact, which fact does he identify with truth?   Perhaps to the
extent we know that the truth of fact is one thing, the truth
of imagination another, we have learned enough except for
Browning's belief in a universal norm for all truth.   Killham's best service was to remind his readers that in the
nineteenth century there were people who joined Browning in
the "faith that truth does not depend upon human testimony,
but is absolute. "   Not based on Browning's "wrangling,
brangling, jangling" over two little words most men would
sooner forget, Killham's essay is strongest against Langbaum
in the placement of Browning's truth in tradition: "It is the
culmination of a tradition reaching back through the Renais-
sance to the foundations of our civilisation;... That this confidence in the accessibility [?] of absolute truth, embodied
in the Christian religion, was undermined in the Victorian
period... is familiar to everyone" (p. 155).   Killham may
mistakenly poke fun at Browning's technical "assaying, " and
fuse the poet's soul with the inert stuff. [6] He may agree
with Miss Sullivan that by "truth" Browning meant he had
found the whole "divine truth, " and indicate with Langbaum
that he holds a dubious attraction for either the poet's "moral explicitness" or his "workable middle style. "   But for
Killham's dealing with the subject as he did, his readers are
well favored.

                              Notes

1.   "The Importance of Fact in The Ring and the Book, " VN,
No. 17 [Spring 1960], p. 13.

2.   Three years later Langbaum accepts the facts of The
Ring and the Book as being alloyed beneath the surface of
the ring, but he fails to see in his definition of "assayed"--
a testing of purity--another argument against his insistence
upon precious gold facts.   ("The Importance of Fact in The
Ring and the Book, " pp. 14, 15)

3. More exercised than Altick and Loucks over the corruption of the Pope's century and its possible analogy with Browning's century, Langbaum also reads most of his charges out of Guido's prejudiced monologues for which the poet must have thought reasonable adjustment would be made.   In addition to his unfavorable use of institutional "formulations" throughout the essay, on pages 122-131 Langbaum uses "machinery" some fourteen times, always in a pejorative sense, and repeats as many as four times each such phrases as "end of Christianity's period of triumph, " "old order has died from within, " "dead machinery still grinds, " "failure of Church and State, " "general corruption of the times, " "domesday's near, " "herald of revolutionary changes to come, " "post-Christian era, " "decay of the old order, " "corruption from top to bottom, " "seeds of regeneration, " "destroying old order, " "social and revolutionary implications, " "age of special privilege over, " and "times are evil. "

4. Exclusive of phrases like "post-Christian era, " "new age" appears on page 123, "new order" on pages 127-129, and "new era" on pages 130-131.

5. For the thought on primitive faith I am in part indebted to William Coyle's excellent essay, "Molinos: 'The Subject of the Day' in The Ring and the Book, " PMLA, LXVII (June 1952), 308-314. He writes, "Although there is little evidence in his references that Browning was altogether certain of the denotation of Molinos' Quietism, he might have been attracted to Protestant implications like justification by faith, rejection of ecclesiastical authority, and abolition of the sacraments" (p. 309).   Since Browning often attended a chapel of the Waldensians in Venice and left other evidence of being a genuine dissenter (Griffin and Minchin, p. 296), it may be that a scholar with Coyle's diligence will tell us yet more about the poet's possible curiosity in the Anabaptists, Primitive Baptists, and other early Protestant groups.   The religious association with Milton cannot be lost in the intense drive of these groups for individual freedom of worship.

6. "I fused my live soul and that inert stuff" (I. 469). Preference for the distinction also hinges on "Such substance of me interfused the gold" (I. 682; italics added) and invites praise of Browning's accurate knowledge of the idiom used by goldsmiths.

6

INTERPRETATION OF BROWNING'S
RING METAPHOR AND TRUTH

The critical uses to which the germinal thought of the previously named studies has been put are manifold. If only through the projections of intervening critics, no one who writes about The Ring and the Book now seems unacquainted with the influential interpretations of Browning's truth and metaphorical ring; even the critics who consider the subject of truth in particular a platitude cannot refrain from accentuating their vexation with those who find pleasure in the continuing quest. Perhaps it is already too late, even uncalled for, to determine precisely what was first said and by whom on Browning's view of truth or any of the other essential interpretations which have gained general approval. But almost always when the development of an essential idea is traced to its scholarly source, it is discovered that variant interpretations are inclined to be impressionistic or at least less applicable than the original broadly drawn understanding. For Browning's long poem, excellent examples are discoverable in the distance contemporary critics stand from Cook's observations on the corruption of the seventeenth-century Church, Coyle's view of the significance of the Molinists, and DeVane's contributions on the struggle between good and evil, the poet's desire to justify the ways of God to man, or the chances of virtue in this world. When something as important as the structure of the poem is involved, however, indirect and tacit references in McElderry's own language and thought are not sufficient to make known to the reader that a necessarily brief digest is different from the outstanding work of McElderry. The same care ought to be taken with Shaw's loosely used "Donna Angelicata" theme and Smith's star-imagery, with the addition of a vivid reminder that whereas Smith's is an imagistic study, the one being undertaken, if it does, converts the references into a very different accounting of what The Ring and the Book says. On two traditional interpretations it is not likely the origins will easily be found, but I believe it was Lord Morley's review which first caught my eye on Browning's interest in absolute truth;[1] on the frailty of human speech and testimony I know that Sir Henry Jones was instrumental in the forming of my belief that The Ring and the Book is probably the watershed between Browning's early confidence in man's intellectual powers and his gradual loss of that confidence. When just the poet's Ring metaphor and truth are thought of, the scholarly work which has too frequently been overlooked in both direct and indirect quotation is Beatrice Corrigan's Curious Annals: New Documents Relating to Browning's Roman Murder Story (Toronto, 1956). No better proof of the quality of her translation and scholarship is needed than a contrast between the accuracy of characters abstracted by Mary Rose Sullivan and by Altick and Loucks. What critics will therefore think of my neglect of the many other studies which impinge on Browning's Ring metaphor and truth, only their rectifying pens will tell. But, excepting the recent essays which carry forward older theses, I have deliberately concentrated on as many germinal and representative ideas as time and judgment allowed.

Convinced that neither skepticism nor relativism plays any part in Browning's multiple points of view, Park Honan interprets the ten dramatic monologues as the poet's means of revealing his ultimate attitude toward the truth ("The Murder Poem for Elizabeth, " VP, VI [Autumn-Winter 1968], 220). He speaks of Browning's visionary apprehension of the truth in Book I, of our confusion over rendering absolute judgment, and of Pope Innocent who "slays Evil's sophistries to preserve Truth" (p. 217). Through the Ring metaphor he sees clearly that Browning's fancy remains fused with the facts, even though he thinks that in Books II-XI the truth is gradually reconstructed in its entirety. But since Honan never reveals what he judges the poet's ultimate attitude to be, never distinguishes the poet's truth from fact, we must assume that he excludes all forms of truth which do not fall within the realm of ascertainable fact and "psychological" significance. Indeed, from its many appearances in the poem, Honan directly interprets truth only as indicative of the limitations of language or of Browning's declining artistic powers. Complimentary in his judgment of Browning's intuitive grasp of mental operations, exploitation of dramatic structure, establishment of convincing backgrounds, and management of imagery and word-choice, Honan admits to Browning's view of historic truth only to denigrate it into irrelevancy. Like Altick and Loucks he detects the influence of Carlyle--transcendental insight--rather than of Ranke--

massive primary documentation. Unlike them, he misses
the significance Browning attached to truth and the more
pronounced influences of St. Paul, St. John, and Plato. But
different from critics of his impressionistic persuasion who,
in despair of Browning's incessant moralizing, play as if the
pattern does not exist, Honan frankly writes: "Lest we miss
this [tedious censure of mere talk] and certain other dignified, didactic pronouncements in 'The Pope,' they are reiter-
ated later by Browning disguised as Fra Celestino, and then
by Browning without a disguise" (p. 225). Agreeing with
those who insist that each age should reinterpret for itself
the literature of the past, that impressionistic residue is
sufficient spur for any artist, Honan is of course exasperated
by Browning's advocacy of Christian and ideal truth. Yet
such archaic nonsense he can describe as the "chillier features" of an otherwise commendable poem and whimsically
filter out when it displeases or runs counter to his reading.
It is a curiosity of literary criticism that men like Honan,
Langbaum, Peckham, Sypher, Miller, and Killham fail to observe that Browning "repeats the most familiar of all arguments" (p. 225) on faith in God with possibly no greater
verve and no less variety than they and Leslie Stephen repeat
arguments for being agnostic. When freed from the avowed
purpose of The Ring and the Book, these critics write im-
pressively on Browning's art and talents; when forced to contend with thematic issues they consider outmoded, they flinch
not the slightest in praising the modernity of a poet whose
antiquated notions are thought profoundly inept.

　　　　Strangely approving Johnson's pluralism while rejecting
Langbaum's and Peckham's relativism and implications of
Rankean methodology, Honan is nevertheless captivated by
Langbaum's misreading of the Pope's monologue and more
positive than all three of these men that the primary purpose
of the poem is to reveal Caponsacchi's unconventional conduct
and Browning's determination to expose the futility of most
traditions and the corruption of most institutions. That
Caponsacchi at a still youthful age dedicated his life to the
Catholic Church, that only the Convertites as failing in faith
is attacked as an institution by the Pope, seem refutation
enough. Yet unavoidable information on religious groups--
as of all other meaningful human groupings--should have told
Honan that condemnation of the daily practices of initiates is
stock in trade, always prelude to injunction to greater loyalty
and faithfulness. To priest, preacher, and rabbi such condemnation has never been construed as rejection of the faith
but as reminder to the flock to hold fast to the doctrine,

thus preserving the group inviolable.   Honan's arguments for
the dying order could not be farther from the meaning of the
poetic text than in the statement: "[The Pope's] doubts
about the ultimate basis and value of Christianity finally lead
him to contend [listen to ?] with the summoned shade of
Euripides, who in lines 1663-1783 points out that souls cannot be judged, that his own pagan teaching is at least as
good as Christ's, and that the modern Church is infested
with corruption and beyond redemption" (p. 224).   How at
the same time Honan can say the Pope's decisiveness "symbolizes the bold, brave readiness to believe that will save
humanity in an age of overwhelming doubt soon to be ushered
in by Voltaire" (p. 225) is fortunately beyond our purview.
But it cannot be overlooked that neither Honan nor Langbaum
gives any thought to countless precedents for speeches like
the Pope's or compares the mildness of denunciation by Pope,
poet, and Celestino with the severity of jeremiads by biblical
and classical spokesmen.   With the exception of the Convertites, a semi-institution, all of the Pope's condemnations and
injunctions are specifically addressed to members of the faith,
individuals who if not condemned are first sharply rebuked,
then implored to quit the cornfield dance of fools for a more
becoming Christian demeanor.   If one has never been present
at one of these religious sessions, even such a one as when
the young Browning was rebuked, I suppose it might be impossible to understand the formula.

Given to comparable exaggeration in his responses to
all the established critical dicta on The Ring and the Book,
Honan becomes doubly suspect in his treatment of Browning's
fascination with the OYB facts, Guido's villainy, and the poet's biography.   That the biographical method is made even
less secure in Honan's insistence upon the poet's unrelieved
grief, open defiance of convention, illusion of Elizabeth's
pristine innocence, and use of mythical and historical cog-
nates seems unquestionable.   Browning's much longer struggle with doubt and faith--also an important aspect of biogra-
phy--and his life-long pursuit of the nature of truth are simply excised.   To write that the Pope talks "so very emphatically and decisively to shadows" (p. 224) is of course to ne-
gate the one absolute truth of Browning's life and faith.   To
him, this observation would have been anathema.   Whatever
our own predilections, Browning and his Pope were as firmly
persuaded as Paul the Apostle that neither things present nor
things to come would be able to separate them from the love
of God.   So to advance that Pope Innocent expressed any
doubts whatsoever about the ultimate basis of Christianity

is to forfeit understanding of his intent and manner in saying,
"I put no such dreadful question to myself" (X. 1631-32), and
of still asking, "Who is faithful now?" (X. 1829) When
thinking of Honan's belief that both Browning and his Pope
make up their minds "in the flick of an eyelash" (p. 223),
it seems almost irrelevant to have to deny there is any evidence that either Browning or the Pope failed to judge normally, even protractedly.   And there can be no excuse for
his saying the Pope's judgments are apocalyptic.   The whole
reason for the Pope's third period of deep meditation is his
will to enunciate the resolution that only God can pronounce
Last Day Judgments.   To Browning's Pope no one is ever-
lastingly damned, and resting in the poem are excellent reasons for believing that Caponsacchi and the Pope accept a
stage between this life and the next not appreciably different
from purgatory itself.   As can be seen in Essay Seven, it
is probable that much misunderstanding of the Pope's monologue may be disspelled in the revelation that Euripides was
properly placed in the poem and properly answered when his
topical question is known.

       In the Norton edition (N 433) of The Ring and the
Book from which Park Honan quotes, editor Wylie Sypher
vaguely anticipates Altick and Loucks in the first reasonable
alliance of arguments for both absolutist and relativist truth
in the poem.   Although he himself believes that truth is
relative, Sypher finds in the poem "a strangely intermediate
kind of moral judgment which appreciates the fact that all
truth [human?] is personal and therefore relative, but also,
seen from enough distance, fixed, unchanging, and divinely
ordained" (p. xvii).   Like others who have no more valid
reason than he for stressing confident and absolute performance in Browning's truth-finding, Sypher thinks that the confidence of the Pope and poet in condemning Guido depended
upon (a vision of ?) "absolute moral standards. "   Thus in
Browning's "moral poles that do not shift" and Browning's
faith in the eternal existence of truth and the good, Sypher
locates a naive notion that truth is hard to reach and reacha-
ble, but dreadfully dull.   Using "a fact / Looks to the eye
as the eye likes the look" and "Truth... / Evolvable, " he
then pushes Langbaum's relativism into modern perspectivism
and deduces that Browning believed a composite truth could
be reached through artistic points of view rather than history.
And if Browning could also have supposed that the observer's
perspective can alter the nature of truth itself, he might have
conceived of a full relativity and demonstrated maturity in
perspectivism.   Instead, Browning continued to believe that

either Pompilia or the Pope could see the genuine contours
of truth, because the truth was there to be seen by the right
person (p. xvi). Deducing that the whole truth resides somewhere (with God only?), Sypher lastly adds, Browning was
naively mistaken in thinking that the truth looks different to
each observer; he should have known that the contours of
reality shift with the angle from which they are seen. Since
all of Sypher's observations are made on a cognitive plane,
it is indifferent to him that his supportive lines from the
poem also document the opposite of his contention. He does
not, any more than other relativists, have word good or bad
for "Not absolutely in a portion, yet / Evolvible from the
whole" (X. 230-231), "Existent somewhere, somehow, as a
whole; / Here, as a whole proportioned to our sense, " "the
whole / Appreciable solely by Thyself, " and "by the little
mind of man, reduced...between Thee and ourselves" (X.
1316-24). Despite his commitment to personalized truth,
however, Sypher unhesitatingly delineates gradations of truth.
Caught in the human angle from which all truth must be
gained, Sypher's Pompilia "sees truth clearly, but not so
fully as Innocent, " although his Pope is confusingly removed
from participation and guided of all things by his wisdom.
That Browning's "immoralists, " driven to take a point of
view, "are not entirely free to make their own truth" is an
eminently reliable judgment; that in conjunction with this
statement Browning can be characterized as believing "truth
is an accurately balanced judgment of the facts" is eminently
puzzling (p. xvii). One finishes Sypher's introduction questioning why Browning's forthrightly recognized advocacy of
"absolute moral standards" and "divinely ordained truth"
ever needed to be construed as immature perspectivism and
incomplete modern relativity, when Sypher himself proves it
cannot be.

Not then an altogether unsympathetic evaluation of
Browning's attitude on truth, Sypher's admission that the
Pope saw truth more comprehensively and sanely than Pompilia confirms the belief that to Browning the truth is seen
only in part by whomever the observer, Pope and poet included. It would have been even more tolerable if Sypher
had said simply that all human response to truth or fact is
personal and relative. This he could not do, since he cannot
accept fact as the point of fixity, man as ever the inconstant,
deceiving or being deceived by an instability Browning himself must have grown weary of enunciating. To Browning,
even a composite factual truth is treacherously gained, not
to speak of a possible essential or absolute truth man's

natural condition is severely strained to imagine or to postulate.   This conclusion, which finds warranty throughout The
Ring and the Book, is effectively supported in Browning's
final choice of both "the mediate word" and "the thought":

Art may tell a truth
Obliquely, do the thing shall breed the thought,
Nor wrong the thought, missing the mediate word.
(XII 859-861)

What else can Browning mean than that art may tell a fact
or facts indirectly, admittedly falling short of the mediate
language but still not wronging the thought?   And "thought,"
three times removed from the fact or facts, two times removed from the compromise position of "the mediate," is
not a word for which Sypher or Miss Sullivan, to take a
more extreme misreading, may substitute "clearly only the
poet can claim infallibility in judging the affairs of men" (p.
136 n).   Nor, in this connection, does Browning ever speak
of his evolving "a single truth out of many different fallible
interpretations" (Sullivan, p. 174).   If one is a literalist, he
denies the possibility of Browning's above assertion; if he is
a subjectivist, he sees the oblique truth as an intended lie;
if he is a relativist, he places the value of the temporary
truth or fact in the eye or ear of the beholder; if he is a
perspectivist, he transforms the fact or truth; and if he is
an absolutist, he counts the incomplete fact or truth as evidence of a whole or total truth, though it remains always
beyond his human grasp.   Slanting from the facts of the Old
Yellow Book, subjective selection of the facts, favorable or
unfavorable description of the facts, neglect of or addition
to the facts--all these artistic means seem permissible under
Browning's broad canopy of telling the facts of his source
material.   The poet openly disregards any need to apologize
for falling short of "the mediate word," the intermediate or
compromise position, trusting instead that his words and the
thoughts to which they give rise will not be judged a distortion.   Inborn potential for telling absolute truth was never a
talent to which Browning laid claim; he did speak of a poetic
fancy which enabled him to have his way with the characters
and to chance upon some fragment of a whole (L 778, 752).
If I read these lines correctly, it may then be said that
Browning does not "transform" the facts (p. viii), as Sypher
advances; does not change the facts until they become unrecog-
nizable, as Frances Russell argues; does not alter the facts
in their very nature, as would the perspectivist; does not
leave the facts to be valued by instinctive theorizing alone,

as Langbaum suggests. It is only after the normal processes
of thought that Browning resorts to intuitive guidance, and
much of this activity is no more than the result of rational
compartmentalizing and synthesizing. Once the fact or truth
enters into existence, to Browning it is indestructible yet
computed in its entirety only by God. Where Browning may
exceed the privilege of discussing man's limitations and the absolute nature of truth is in the impression he leaves of getting
possibly closer to the absolute truth than others of his species.

In a move to reconcile the differences between advocates of absolutist and relativist truth as found in The Ring
and the Book, Altick and Loucks probably come closest to
an acceptable compromise:

> The premise of the poem, stated perhaps over-
> simply, is Browning's belief that truth and good
> are, if not synonymous, correlative, as are their
> opposites, falsehood and evil; and that while man's
> truth (most especially, in problems of morality) is
> relative, God's truth is absolute.... The insepa-
> rability of these correlatives, and the doubtful wil-
> lingness and capacity of finite human beings to
> recognize the truth and live according to God's
> law, form the poem's grand subject. (p. 21)

Putting their statement differently, Altick and Loucks then
grant Browning three major topics: "the limitations of human apprehension; the dramatic struggle between good and
evil; and the justification of the Christian faith and of the
inclusion of doubt in God's scheme of human existence."
Whether they apply their compromise consistently is an entirely different matter; but they get into deep trouble right
off with Barton Friedman, a relativist, when they subject
man's apprehension to any limitation and subordinate man's
conduct to God's law ("The Perils of Paraphrase," The
Browning Newsletter, No. 1 [Waco, 1968] pp. 35-43). Nonetheless both absolutists and relativists may find scores of
opportunities to agree or disagree with Altick and Loucks in
expressions such as these: "so did Browning discover in
the records of a sordid murder case a transcendental truth"
(p. 26); "Pure truth, unequivocally expressed, betrays its
purpose" (p. 28); "Wishing to approach absolute truth, he
spent most of his space illustrating relativism" (p. 29);
"Browning's intention is to adopt many points of view, and,
through an intuitive merging of all the separate, limited

facets, to achieve a truth that is greater than their simple
sum" (pp. 34-35); "the coalescence of partial truths into a
transcendent Truth" (p. 37); "Browning displays the principal
reasons why men ordinarily are incapable of discerning, much
less of expressing, the whole truth about any episode of human experience" (p. 39; italics added); "who abjure selfish
interests in their search for truth" (p. 40); "ordinary mortals
who must apprehend divine truth through experience rather
than through the intellect" (p. 56); "as the way to such a
degree of spiritual truth as is accessible to human beings"
(p. 58); "hence, as her monologue concludes this movement
of the poem, the ultimate truth is still to seek" (p. 59);
"[The Pope] claims no special access to truth by virtue of
his office, but his humble awareness that the whole truth is
withheld from men enables him fully to discern whatever portion is vouchsafed from heaven" (p. 68); "the indirectness of
Browning's art has fashioned a circle of transcendent, universal truth" (p. 75); and "With respect to the discovery of
the hard core of truth which Browning posits in Book 1" (p.
79).

          Almost everything which can be said about the absolute
nature of truth is said in Altick's and Louck's first seventy-
nine pages, and though relativist truth may seem less favored,
one additional statement in particular promises a comparable
number of pages will be devoted to the relativist position before the book closes: "In the relativistic sphere of human
existence, no man is vouchsafed a direct vision of the truth.
One can skirt around it, or drive toward it, but none of the
speakers may apprehend truth in its utter purity and whole-
ness.... The Pope and Celestino, though denied direct con-
tact with incandescent truth, at least see into its heart from
a short distance" (p. 80). The point is well taken, for then
follows sufficiently elaborate and telling arguments to justify
the relativist's strongest stand. For example, Altick and
Loucks reservedly say later the Pope knows that "in handing
down judgment on Guido he may err," and that "whatever decision he renders will be secured by intuition and lifelong moral practice" (p. 329; italics added). But then they add:
"The idea of infallibility seems to be introduced expressly in
order that its ensuing discreditation can give further scope
to the familiar principles that man is a creature born to error and that all human knowledge is relative. The Pope's
awareness of these facts, however, does not prevent his de-
livering an absolute judgment on the Franceschini case.
Where moral imperatives are involved, to hesitate or hedge
is to be craven" (pp. 329-330; italics added). This paradox,

this introduction of personalized truth only one page before
their quotation of the long passage beginning "whether a fact,
/ Absolute, abstract, independent truth, / Historic, not reduced to suit man's mind, -- / Or only truth reverberate,
changed, made pass / A spectrum into mind, the narrow
eye" (X. 1388-91), poses the threat of absolute relativism
unless, as may be hoped, by "absolute" Altick and Loucks
mean merely a resolute judgment which, as with all men,
is not freed entirely from lingering uncertainty.

     Supported by Browning's many biblical glosses and
his use of papal infallibility, higher criticism, and natural
theology as implicit ways for further discrediting errant man
and his relative knowledge, Altick and Loucks ingeniously
suppose that the Pope accomplishes for Books II-IV what the
Fourth Gospel does for the Synoptic Gospels (p. 332). This
they do for the good cause of establishing the Pope as interpreter and philosopher rather than narrator and historian.
But in showing it was of little moment to the Pope whether
the stories of the Bible were literal history or myth--hence
to Browning of the denial of St. John's authorship--they over-
ly strain the limits of unusually important poetic lines (pp.
330-335). Five times the Pope cryptically employs the word
"tale" (X. 1348-1409), but each repetition makes it clearer
that he refers, not to the doubts of others to come, but to
the tale of how God so loved the world that he gave his only
begotten son. Loving the tale with his heart and pronouncing
it sound with his mind, Pope Innocent may be expected to
end with thoughts of what Christians and Christian institutions
have done or not done "for Christ's sake. " And he does
just that, before finally confirming his subject in the words
"seventeen-hundredth year since God died for man" (X. 1535).
Need one still reply that Browning's Pope cared a very great
deal about whether "the biblical stories are literal history or
myth" (p. 330) or that "the scripture yields no parallel" (p.
331) concerns treatment only of Pompilia, not of Browning's
attitude toward nineteenth-century "evidences of Christianity";
the unparalleled act is "the kiss turns bite" (X. 1509) of the
Monastery called of Convertites. Alone, the interpretive slip
is relatively insignificant despite the aid it would otherwise
give to Altick's and Loucks's strange insistence upon "justification of the Christian faith" as one of the three broad topics in Browning's poem, but it does lead significantly into
an interpretation which demonstrates these two critics were
also misled by Langbaum into thinking tangential matters are
essential matters.

More familiar with the content of the Pope's monologue
than Langbaum, Altick and Loucks unwittingly impair their interpretation by permitting Pope Innocent to anticipate the substance of a speech Guido had not yet made (pp. 347-361).
The practice first allows them to compare, almost run together, the Pope's thought on the future with Guido's thought
on the present, Guido's evaluation of the present with the
Pope's evaluation of the future.   Second, it enables them to
exploit Langbaum's arguments for the deserving death of an
old order and the hopeful birth of a new order (p. 357).   Yet
one cannot find in the Pope's language hope for a better future day, and Altick and Loucks, even when they forget Celestino's words in their ultimate summation, must straddle
arguments they half accept and half reject.   By juxtaposing
Guido's grotesque reduction of life to pagan hedonism and the
Pope's "tribunal now / Higher than God's, " they may write about
a subject which is implied if not stated in both monologues,
even if they fail to see that the new tribunal eliminates
churchmen they mistakenly impugn (p. 347).   But they drift
far afield (even attributing thoughts of Tertium Quid to the
Pope) in drawing out of Guido's judgment of life in 1698
meaning for the Pope's fear of a new age of doubt.   In a
singularly unsubstantiated way, Altick and Loucks now have
better grounds than Langbaum for advancing propositions not
to be found in The Ring and the Book.   How may one be expected to respond to the illogicality of "Guido himself may
die, but the fact that his type exists at all, not to say flourishes, is enough to cast the future of Christian society into
the gravest doubt"?   (p. 354)   Up to the end of Pope Innocent's soliloquy, Guido had not rejected Christianity openly;
indeed he was counting on its saving his life.   Now one mur-
derer, one rationalist, one stray from the fold can cast
doubt on the survival of a religious order which had with-
stood successfully almost seventeen hundred years of such
inescapable buffeting.   May we so unequivocally condemn all
Denmark because Hamlet found something unsavory at court?
Or all fourteenth-century England because Chaucer knew of
false priests?   If so, does a single disagreement with Altick
and Loucks imperil the very existence of world criticism?
When these two men ask whether an accurate forecast of the
future may be read in the generation of Guido (p. 354), the
answer must be in the negative, especially since what they
tell us of his generation comes largely from Guido's own
lying lips.

Of course the Pope deplores man's failure to rise
above the common level; so did the founder of his faith, so

does his living successor.   But universal (p. 355) inertia is
hardly exhibited in the few individuals who comprise the
Franceschini case.   The Pope's challenge to greater faithfulness by the few was exactly that, not a cry to rise to the
latest renewal or an answer to willful rejection of divine
grace.   "The sheer perversity of the human addiction to
falsehood" (pp. 355-356) which overrides man's yearning for
truth does severely agitate and test the Pope.   And here, it
seems to me, Altick and Loucks have reached the high point
of their interpretation, an accomplishment full worthy of the
hope with which their book went forth.   But the matter which
"chills" (terrifies, X. 1547) the Pope's heart, as I hope to
show in Essay Seven, goes one step beyond their excellent
documentation on truth and falsehood, finding its origin in
the Pope's related and startling question, "Is such effect
proportionate to cause?" (X. 1536)   It is this conclusion in
Browning's life, as well as in his Pope's thought, which required him to introduce doubt as a condition of faith.   Altick
and Loucks nevertheless confuse us on "the supreme truth"
as they earlier confused us on intuition.   How they could
first tell us the Pope "claims no special access to truth"
(p. 68), that "nowhere in the poem is it suggested that any
speech quoted is a product of divine inspiration" (p. 123),
and then tell us "the divinely bestowed gift of insight the
Pope possesses is intuitive, not rational" (p. 330), is left
baldly contradictory.   Now they suggest, after emphasizing
man's addiction to falsehood, that "the supreme truth has
been made known and its pricelessness declared in Scripture"
(p. 356).   But this is to falsify the words of both Browning
and the Pope, unless Altick and Loucks mean that the truth
of God's love has been revealed through the scripture.   Both
poet and Pope make it known that the truth about which they
speak is reserved for another time and place; so do our authors, elsewhere in their book.   Contrary to a rather common belief--best exemplified by Miss Sullivan--that the poet
and the Pope are in possession of the truth, the evidence
most frequently used to establish the belief bespeaks the opposite.   In "No dose of purer truth than man digests, / But
truth with falsehood, milk that feeds him now" (I. 830-831),
Browning is paraphrasing a Pauline doctrine to show the necessity for diluted speech and testimony, not asserting that
he or any other human source can provide the whole truth.

Altick and Loucks quote Celestino's "despairing words"
(p. 356) on human truth and, like DeVane, warn readers
against expecting too hopeful an assessment of man's pros-
pects in Browning's poetry.   Yet five pages later they con-

clude their study on an entirely different note.   What final
opinion is the reader to draw from, first, "the dark atmos-
phere of the poem's close... forbids our reading the poem op-
timistically"; second, "to resuscitate such a shining instance
of sacrificial love and to give it immediate meaning to an
age desperately in need of such examples and all too unwilling
or unable to discover them is, in Browning's view, a poetic
mission of the noblest order" (p. 361).   Or to take one other
example, first, "nor do the incidental events reported in
Book 12 contain any suggestion that a new birth of Christian
spirit is about to occur in the wake of Guido's execution";
second, "In human affairs the pervasive curse of doubt can
be countered only by the vigorous response of a soul inspired
by Christian teaching. "   It is almost as if Browning knew
precisely what he wanted to do, but since he did the opposite
he succeeded in accomplishing the former.   The Pope no more
"welcomes the signs of a coming age of questioning" than he
makes an absolute judgment of Guido; nor do the Molinists
"threaten to 'shake / This torpor of assurance from our
creed, / Re-introduce the doubt discarded'" any more than
Caponsacchi "says in effect, 'I know the right place by foot's
feel, / I took it and tread firm there.'"   Only Altick and
Loucks and Langbaum can explain why they so obviously shy
away from the crucial remainder of the second line, "Wherefore change?" (X. 1887)   In the important passage under discussion, Molinists are introduced for two brief lines, 1869-
70, and have the same significance as Pompilia's question
which is forcefully accented by the Pope, "Wherefore change?"
Closer reading of the poem and fuller understanding of the
teachings of Molinos indicate that the rebellious sect was not
progressive, radical, and renovative, but regressive, fundamental, and traditional, unwilling primarily to accept an in-
termediary and consequently opposed by the Jesuits in their
defense of the confessional.   Without contesting the analogies
Browning could hardly have avoided making between his age
and that of the Pope, or Browning's way of making Pope Innocent more believable in a living milieu, we do better to follow Altick's and Loucks's initial advice and consider the
Pope's soliloquy a philosophical and metaphysical pronounce-
ment.   What they have added to the discussion of truth and
said originally about the character of Tertium Quid and the
natural-law, the natural-man (pp. 335-340) are much more
important to criticism of The Ring and the Book than their
continuation of Langbaum's social criticism.

        Barton R. Friedman has good reasons for his unfavor-
able review of Browning's Roman Murder Story, not the least

of which is the preemptiveness of the authors.   But even if
the textual problems are more complicated than Altick and
Loucks allow, Browning a more complex artist than they
grant, Friedman is less than accurate in condemning the
book and characterizing the study as a "paraphrase" (Browning Newsletter, No. 1, pp. 35-43).   By a fortuitous stroke,
their book is a much needed and not unreasonably represented
compilation of research, almost all of which antidates their
scholarly interests.   Of course the basic research with which
we have largely dealt in Essays Four and Five remains the
more important work and one without which most other criticism of The Ring and the Book would be decidedly poorer.
But to digest the mass of criticism Altick and Loucks present, add enlightening comments of their own, and make it
all readily available in a most readable style is commendable
beyond Friedman's appraisal.   In fairness to Friedman's own
creative scholarship, he also sets too high a standard for his
treatment of Browning's metaphorical usage ("To Tell the Sun
from the Druid Fire: Imagery of Good and Evil in The Ring
and the Book, " Studies in English Literature, VI [Autumn
1966], 693-708).   Predating both Miss Sullivan and Altick
and Loucks, Friedman expounds a thesis which, if not altogether his, is a considerable refinement over DeVane's and
Smith's.   He believes that "the alloy [copper] of The Ring
and the Book--that something of the poet's self which molds
the artless facts into artful form--shows through in Browning's imagery.   The unwinding tale of Guido's treachery,
Caponsacchi's heroism, and Pompilia's murder is under-
scored by a metaphorical substructure which strips the
Franceschinis of their humanity, exposing them as savage
and demonic fiends" (p. 694).   And he convincingly demonstrates that the imagery does form "a substructure of constant truth beneath the variant interpretations of Browning's
speakers" (p. 704), that is, if he means "constant [poetic]
truth. " Otherwise, he too has been misled by Langbaum,
and the early warning occurs in a note (p. 694) in which he
writes, "I do not subscribe to the general thesis of [Cundiff's
1959] article. " He nonetheless adopts enough of the observations on the poet's view of truth to elicit curiosity in his
reason for differing.

Conversant with possibly all the actively discussed
positions on the poem, Friedman uses the imagery as a base
and speculates on the theme and total purpose of Browning's
poem.   He concludes with DeVane and others that the poet
utilizes "the stuff of The Old Yellow Book to depict the cosmic struggle between good and evil, and to prefigure the ul-

timate triumph of good over evil in the universe" (p. 694).
Later in his essay Browning's "chief concern" becomes a
design to justify the ways of God to man, but here "his imagery suggests a witches' mass; it symbolizes the evil under-
lying Guido's every action, and leads to the abrupt, the crucial question: 'what of God?'" (I. 582) Yet when he adds
that "in one sense, of course, this question poses the central
issue of The Ring and the Book" (p. 695), one begins to wonder whether Friedman would rebel, if Altick and Loucks
were to reply, "[Browning believed] that truth and good are,
if not synonymous, correlative, as are their opposites, falsehood and evil. " For Friedman has already said: "Browning
does not deny the existence of an eternal Truth--as if opposed to temporal truths. He doubts most men's ability, however, to grasp that Truth" (p. 693 n; italics added). With
the exclusion of "eternal" from the first clause, the thought
therein expressed could be drawn from the Langbaum statement on which I earlier concentrated and, in its negative
form, appears to be a relativist red-herring. But though
Friedman says pointedly he does not subscribe to advocacy
of an absolute truth from which man at best falls short, his
essay would disprove the point if he did not also ally his
thought with Langbaum's relativistic thought. Indeed, Friedman may not grasp all the implications of relativism, since
he writes, "These partial, and sometimes less than partial,
glimpses of truth are what lead Mr. Langbaum to call The
Ring and the Book a relativist poem" (pp. 701-702). The
difficulty is that Friedman, like Langbaum and Sullivan,
wants the better of two opposing arguments and is willing
to set up the paradox in order to preserve personalized truth.

     Of Friedman's satisfactory penetration into the mul-
tiple meanings Browning gives the word truth, I therefore
have serious doubts. That he probably goes astray most in
following Langbaum is nowhere better illustrated than in his
consideration of the central question of judgment in the poem:
"For most of the poet's speakers hinge their views of the
murder on their ideas of what is natural. This issue is first
raised by Half-Rome...And it is then treated by others of
Browning's searchers after truth, finally to be settled by the
Pope--whose verdict accords with the poet's and therefore
with God's" (p. 698). By many critics it is now thought a
feeble stroke to ameliorate the boldness of this Langbaum
deduction (p. 112) by adding that Browning makes the reader
the ultimate judge, when everybody is cognizant of the poet's
coercive will. It is a misreading of Browning's guidance to
believe he wanted our judgment to coincide finally with the

Pope's, or to forget that the poet's monumental effort to create an artistic work was made to offer his "due to God" and "to save the soul." When Pope Innocent, a member of the cast and thus subject to all the restrictions thereof, steps on the stage and starts his soliloquy, he too falls prey to "What mortal ever in entirety saw?" By his words and his conduct, on "weighing what went before," the Pope confesses to a human deficiency in intellect and intuitive insight. But of greater significance to the question of judgment, the Pope cannot be Browning's mouthpiece if, as Browning distinctly says, it is the purpose of the total poem to demonstrate that Art, Browning's art here of course, remains the one way possible of speaking truth. Are we to discard as inessential to this purpose the other eleven books of The Ring and the Book? Historically Innocent XII pronounced the ultimate formal judgment on Guido, but poetically he is limited to the "voices we call evidence." Even his judgment of Guido's guilt, through which he admits a keener wit may yet reach to innocence, is made before he enters the poem. Hence, Friedman cannot justifiably say that "in the end...the Pope grasps the total truth" (p. 704), unless he foregoes his earlier acceptance of an eternal truth, the limiting power of the poet's imagery to reach toward truth, and anything else one iota short of an absolute "Truth... evolvable." When Pope Innocent's voice rises in Book X, it expectedly echoes what Browning must have thought to be the most nearly satisfactory defense of Pompilia and Caponsacchi by his characters. But, as Friedman so lucidly argues for the imagery alone, Browning's judgment (which may or may not be ours but is certainly never supposed to be God's in more than a hopeful approximation of the whole truth) lies in the totality of his poem--its imagery, narration and description, characterization and action, nuances and modulation of language, all of which are imposed on the reader by the poet's most studied persuasion.

We understand and accept as fitting what Friedman in quoting DeVane means by calling the Pope "the other hero of the poem" (p. 701), but the statement is fraught with probable error. First--although a necessary participant--the Pope is better thought of as God's representative, thus duty-bound first and foremost to proclaim God's kingdom and to explain the way there. To designate the physically inactive Pope a hero is moreover to reject the eternal truth of which only God could be aware, for with the absolute skill attributed to the Pope, Friedman's truth needs no eternal progenitor or accountant. Second--especially if the theme of the poem may

be the ultimate triumph of good over evil, the justification of
God's ways to man, the defense of truth and the exposure of
the human condition--the Pope cannot save "truth just in time
by his condemnation of the sophistries of evil" (p. 701), unless we count "saved for a splendid minute" a satisfying fi-
nale.   Under divine aegis and by virtue of its eternal essence,
the truth about which Browning poetizes needs least of all the
feeble support of mortal man, which sadly encompasses the
superior moral worth of "a great guardian of the fold" (I.
648).   Friedman has to know there is an irreconcilable condition between his human characters who are "searchers after
truth, " attaining only "partial glimpses, " and his human at-
tainers of the whole truth--the poet and the Pope.   Where he
and the other relativists come up shortest is in their unsympathetic understanding of Christian and Greek idealism.   Otherwise, they could not think the poet had any "confidence in
the ultimate triumph of good over evil in the world" (p. 706;
italics added).   One time Friedman adopts Smith's "vision of
truth, " but elsewhere truth is truth pure and simple, not
"constant [factual] truth, " "the whole [poetic] truth, " or an
[imagistic] truth.   Familiar with doubts to which most men
never invitingly open their minds, Browning, except in poetically clear-cut projections such as Pompilia's, could never
have staked his faith on mortal underpinnings.   Far less
blinded by human frailty than the poet's other characters (always excepting Pompilia and Caponsacchi), Browning's Pope
is also one whose temporal and intuitive vision is "modified
/ According to [his] eye's scope, power of range / Before
and after. "   And the great good old Pope, we may suspect,
would have liked to be first in the poem to tell us this.

        Even Pompilia and Caponsacchi are led by the poet to
surmise their possible election as instruments of divine will,
but the truth of themselves and of their transcendental experience remains a poetic flight and an intellectual mystery.
Friedman believes these partial glimpses of whomever the
character justify Langbaum's calling the poem a relativist
poem (p. 702), but the glimpses merely demonstrate that
man's approach to fact or truth is relative.   Nowhere does
Browning make these glimpses more vividly regrettable than
in his lamented "instinctive theorizing" and the Pope's accent
on the limitations of evolvable truth.   Evolvable, yes, to the
extent of the Pope's resolute positiveness, but limited by his
immediate "suppose it so" that he was wrong.   As most critics reason and Friedman concurs, the Pope is very likely intended to embody "the highest moral attainment of human wisdom [a word hardly admissible by a relativist], " a wisdom

which deservedly should be bathed in light (Smith), but the
unqualified arguments of the Pope himself on the frailty of
human speech and thought limit his wisdom to an atom width
in deference to the truth of God.   To be sure it is not Friedman alone who overlooks in his selection of poetic quotations
explicit substantiation of this measureless discrepancy between
man's truth and absolute truth: "As mere man may: / I
know just so, nor otherwise" (1289-90).   Though inadvertent-
ly, Friedman himself reminds his reader that the Pope's
understanding is a spark, poetically intended to convey admirable human avoidance of selfishness and conscientious
search for human objectivity (pp. 704-705).   Yet in that he
also adopts a disconsolate tone over the corruption of "the
world of The Ring and the Book" in which only Caponsacchi,
the Pope, and Celestino can tell the sun from a Druid fire,
thus granting the Pope a vision of Caponsacchi and Pompilia
leading that world into a new order (pp. 707, 701), we can
conclude that Friedman does not distinguish Browning's facts
from Browning's view of truth.   There is no room for absolute truth in new order following new order endlessly in
search of new truth.   Yet much of the disappointment in not
finding Browning's idealistic truth in Friedman's essay van-
ishes with remembrance of the seminal work he projects on
the function of the poet's imagery.   When he tells us "the
result [of Browning's imagery] is that the utterances of his
characters often strike notes their speakers do not hear" (p.
704), Friedman reminds us of comparable and indisputable
information McElderry drew from the structure of the poem.[2]

Isobel Armstrong would make the structure of The
Ring and the Book meaningful by seeing the poem as "a poem
about itself" ("The Uses of Prolixity, " The Major Victorian
Poets, pp. 177-197).   In the course of so doing, she alludes
to "The Word" with reference to the betrayal of language
when she must know it symbolizes God, and the "whole" of
the Pope's documentary evidence when she must know that
in the allusion the Pope has three times limited its application to absolute immensity "Appreciable solely by" God.
She can no more justify the adding of "of God" to "Pompilia
...sees her conscience as the 'clear voice' of God" than the
juxtaposing of "I stand on my integrity" and "I know just so,
nor otherwise. As I know, / I speak" (pp. 182-183).   Pompilia's "angel" is a very lively Caponsacchi, and the Pope's
"integrity" has to do with human facts, his "I know" with
spiritual persuasion, the two thoughts being spaced a thousand
lines apart.   Moreover, she discusses Killham's advocacy of
Guido's second monologue as if it were the unquestioned cli-

max of the poem, whereas "the summit of so long ago" (L
1332), one of Killham's two weak supports, is the poetic
"country in the clouds" to which Browning's fancy lifts his
reader.   Yet we should not want to surrender Miss Armstrong's phraseology as directed against relativism, even as
she continues to multiply discrepancies and substitute New-
man's thoughts for Browning's.   On the relativism she op-
poses, she writes:

> The poem, in fact, is not to be seen as a modern-
> ist poem, as an amorphous gathering of points of
> view and of endless moral possibilities.   The rela-
> tivist view, besides being unable to provide an ade-
> quate solution to the form of the poem ["relativism
> provides the reverse of an organizing principle"],
> makes the problem of Browning's tactless didacti-
> cism even more embarrassing because the end of
> the poem is so clearly stated at its beginning, a
> procedure which violates the aims of a relativist
> art.   (p. 178)

Of course Browning himself said the poem did not come to
a real ending (XII. 1), but the relativist who chances to overlook this line may find greater support in comments in which
Miss Armstrong seems openly to favor his position: "The
reader of these monologues is forced to rely on his own
centre [Newman's language], on the authority of a delicate
sense of moral 'feel' in order to evaluate them" (p. 182).
"And so the poem returns to its starting point, reasserting
the value of self-authorised insight, the truth 'within ourselves,' which has been so heavily qualified in the convolutions of the monologue" (p. 195).   By this dichotomy she
avoids an "aestheticised" response to morality; in compensa-
tion, however, she must sacrifice all resistance to the guidance of Cook and Langbaum on "institutions in decay" (p.
184), "collapse of institutional morality" and "disintegration
of these dead forms" (p. 192).   Nor, in all of this, does
her final appeal to the Ring metaphor seem to buttress her
case: "The ring of the title... is the autonomy of the created
life of the poem smelted from history" (p. 196).

     If the reader who wishes to know something more
about The Ring and the Book is left to Miss Armstrong's
direction, he will be led to think that the central problem
of the poem is "the status of an evaluation--even if it is
the right one--based on the moral 'feel' of a situation, and
the infinite regression involved in the evaluation of that evalu-

ation" (p. 183).   If he recalls passingly well what he has
just read, however, he should not be dismayed.   For a page
earlier she adumbrates the thought more clearly: "The Ring
and the Book is arranged in convolutions of repetition... so
that something can be discovered as well about the processes
of judgment itself, and the nature of judgment is one of the
things the poem is about" (p. 182; italics added).   Like Miss
Armstrong, her reader may be "moved through a process of
growth or of discovery" which is "done by means of a spiral
of repetition" (p. 179), one which enables him "to achieve a
fuller imaginative grasp of the nature of the moral questions
Browning explores so that we end by knowing in a richer way
what we already know" (p. 180; italics added).   But had Miss
Armstrong really seen that the poem is about itself, not herself or any other reader as Killham so cogently argues in
the essay which precedes hers; had she recalled that she
knew all the judgments were predetermined and thus encouraged no further evaluation of the evidence of the trial, she
might have been shocked at the nearness she came to Browning's probable central problem.   This last statement I hope
to give proper reason for in Essay Seven, when Miss Armstrong's thought on the nature and processes of judgment is
reintroduced.

Most of Norton B. Crowell's arguments against my
understanding of Browning's view of truth are met in Essay
Three, note 9, a modified rejoinder to Smalley to which
Crowell had access ("Robert Browning: 'Indisputably Fact,'"
VN, No. 17 [Spring 1960], pp. 6-10).   Crowell's primary
failure of tracing out and documenting thoughts he attributes
to the poet, however, provides an opportunity to demonstrate
with a key poetic passage why he, Miss Sullivan, and others
continue to misunderstand Browning's truth.   Because the
poet himself rarely helps us as much as he definitely should
in his complex use of the word truth, closer attention seems
essential when any gloss he provides may with certainty be
found and utilized.   Probably neglected most often for their
lack of elegance, if not figurative coherence, the three emphasized lines that follow receive enough attention from Crowell,
Miss Sullivan, and a few others to reveal these critics have not
searched out or come to fathom the importance of Hebrews
iv and v to Browning's theory of truth:

>   Let this old woe step on the stage again!
>   Act itself o'er anew for men to judge,
>   Not by the very sense and sight indeed--
>   (Which take at best imperfect cognizance,

Since, how heart moves brain, and how both move
  hand,
What mortal ever in entirety saw?)
--No dose of purer truth than man digests,
But truth with falsehood, milk that feeds him now,
Not strong meat he may get to bear some day--
                                    (I. 824-832; emphasis added)

For when for the time ye ought to be teachers, ye
have need that one teach you again which be the
first principles of the oracles of God; and are become such as have need of milk, and not of strong
meat.   For every one that useth milk is unskilled
in the word of righteousness; for he is a babe.
But strong meat belongeth to them that are of full
age, even those who by reason of use have their
senses exercised to discern both good and evil.
                                    (Hebrews v. 12-14; emphasis added)

Believing that God's truth is the only absolute truth, Browning, like his Pope, nonetheless often used the single word
truth to signify spiritual truth, on the one hand, and the same
single word to signify both fact and alleged fact, on the other.
But if the biblical paraphrase given in lines 830-832 of Book
I is not gratuitously introduced by the poet, it must be intended to emphasize spiritual truth, to deprecate human truth.
That is, when Browning's poetic thought is interpreted in the
light of Hebrews iv and v, individual men and women better
understand things "hard to be uttered" (v. 11) as the schooling
of the heart advances in "things pertaining to God" (v. 1).   As
Browning lifts "heart" (I. 824) from "the word of God...is a
discerner of the thoughts and intents of the heart" (iv. 12), so
he lifts his figure of the milk-and-meat of truth from the
biblical quotation given above.   The point is not alone, as
Crowell would have it, that the human intellect is downgraded
by my saying the heart is "the only reliable source of truth"
to Browning (The Convex Glass, p. 191), but also that the
heart, sometimes the poet's symbol for man's total response,
shows too little sign of progressing toward discernment of
good and evil, toward equating righteousness with the word
of God.   When Crowell does not see that the human intellect
is downgraded, as by Pope Innocent's accent on the "marvel
of a soul like" Pompilia's, it is the Triple Soul he advocates
which gets in the way.   A thesis that Browning attempted to
place equal emphasis on mind, body, and spirit in his early
poetry is not unacceptable, but Crowell's refusal or inability
to observe that Browning gradually lessens his reliance on

mind (knowledge)--not to speak of body--in order to preserve
his optimism, that agnosticism concerning knowledge is in-
cipient in some of the poet's earliest eulogies to love ("Saul,"
for example), indicates too often his reading in Browning
and Henry Jones has been sporadic.

Among the essays to which I have not referred, yet
cannot pass by, are two very good commentaries on Browning's poem, a third which misses its announced purpose
through subtle religious polemics, and Langbaum's subsequent
though less well-known reactions to Browning's truth.   By
several standards E. D. H. Johnson's "Robert Browning's
Pluralistic Universe: A Reading of The Ring and the Book,"
University of Toronto Quarterly, XXXI (1961), 20-41, is
probably the best written as well as the most tantalizing recent study of the poem.   Known to be wrong in technical details (including the fusion of gold and copper), suspiciously
forced in alliance of Browning's and William James's thought,
and weakened by Altick's and Loucks's establishment of Tertium Quid as anything but an objective character, Johnson's
study looks through the surface matters over which critics
continue to disagree and attempts to penetrate Browning's
thought processes.   No one, on reading the essay thought-
fully, can return to the Browning he knew with quite the
same confidence of understanding, a welcome adjustment
Johnson no doubt worked for.   Clarence Tracy's introduction
to Browning's Mind and Art (Edinburgh and London, 1969) is
most interesting for its attempt, though unsuccessful, to reconcile divergent critical stances of enduring separation. His
way, for example, is to slight the "unfortunate ring-analogy,"
dismiss the philosophical and religious articles in favor of
reasonableness and imaginative insight, leave unsubstantiated
Browning's supposed belief he came "as close to the truth
as it is possible for a mortal to come, " and attribute the
poet's omniscience to a shaft of light "sent down to him from
heaven. "   But what he says on the distance Browning required between poet and poetic speaker, a crucial contemporary issue, is much more persuasive and what he gleans
from the poet's use of "evolvable" is pleasant speculation.
In "Adaptation from the Past, Creation for the Present: A
Study of Browning's 'The Pope,'" SP, LXV (July 1968), 702-
722, Charles T. Phipps, S. J. , begins a promising study
scholars have noticeably neglected.   Halfway through, however, he drops his verbal guard and exposes a strong anti-
pathy to Browning's attitude toward the Catholic Church.   Insofar as I know issues of contemporary criticism on Robert
Browning, this development seems the most deplorable.

Surely Phipps is not exceeding his prerogative in the face of
professional criticism which has been blatant in its exposure
of Browning's supposed opposition to Catholic and Christian
practices. It does not help, even if we recall that at an
earlier date Boyd Litzinger revived the old quarrel in probably as ardent a desire to make Browning anti-Catholic as
Langbaum sought to make Browning anti-institution in general.
I hope to leave some evidence in Essay Seven which will encourage Phipps to close his Langbaum, open his Browning,
and reconstitute an essay in which he does not first condemn
Browning's Pope, then inconsistently praise him and The Ring
and the Book as the poet's crowning achievement. In "Browning and the Question of Myth, " The Modern Spirit (New York,
1970), pp. 76-100, but first published in PMLA, LXXXI (December 1966), 575-584, Robert Langbaum distinguishes
Browning's poetry from modern poetry more sharply than
he did ten years before. He also expresses the belief that
the whole point of the poem "was to pull out of a forgotten
and sordid old Roman murder case the Christian scheme of
sin and redemption" (p. 82). Thus through its failures in
ambivalence and explicit morality, The Ring and the Book
does not quite come off. As a result, Langbaum thinks,
we feel "that we are getting not absolute truth, but Browning's notions about absolute truth. " It is the best dramatic
monologues, he adds, which give "us truth as simply a relative manifestation that points somehow to the absolute. "
That is, to him now, "the relative is an index to the absolute... the relative is our way of apprehending the absolute"
(p. 81). With these brief quotations we are enabled to follow
Langbaum's course as he advances with the perspectivism
and instrumentalism of Sypher and Peckham, the subjectivism
and "tactless didacticism" of Armstrong, and the emphasis
on sin and redemption to which Altick and Loucks were so
peculiarly attracted. Langbaum's greatest regret seems to
be that the poet who sketched out what came to be the dominant modern theory of association of disparate elements in
the reader's mind, fell short of accomplishing a recognizable
"epiphany" (p. 87). In not making "his fragmentary glimpses
of life symbolic of the whole, of an absolute vision, " Browning denied himself use of the modern mythical method--the
breakthrough "to a final clarity of vision"--and chance to be
"one of the great poets of English literature" (p. 94). Langbaum's earlier, oftener implicit personalized truth has thus
become explicitly the only absolute truth.

Having dealt with the origin and development of conflicting opinions on Browning's Ring Metaphor and truth, I

come briefly to broader opinions of "a central truth, " "a
circle or ring of truth, " and Chesterton's related "many-
sided truth" toward which readers and critics alike exhibit
almost unanimous agreement. Critics who see Browning's
truth as being beyond man's attainment are inclined to think
less about a circle of truth or a central truth, but excep-
tions among them are to be found in approaches as diverse
as those of J. Hillis Miller, Henry Jones, and W. O. Raymond. Without attempting a tabulation, therefore, I would
guess that scarcely more than one in twenty critics fails to
reveal his apprehension of the Ring metaphor in confident
acceptance of a factual circle or ring, the center of which
automatically suggests a central truth Browning wanted made
known through The Ring and the Book. It was almost inevitable that Mrs. Orr, who had not made a meticulous study
of Book I, would reach conclusions on Browning's truth for
which he had not stipulated an expressed premise. Unfamiliar with the process of ring-making and thus denied symbolic
aid in Book I Browning seems to implant from firsthand
knowledge, she could write intelligently of "a circle of evidence" which resulted in "one central truth, " even though
the poet himself never once refers to a circle of evidence
or a central truth in this connection. Bottinius speaks of
"the main central truth" of a picture, the Pope of his circle
of experience and of God as "the central truth"; but Browning refrains from using any denotations or connotations
which would give overt encouragement to thoughts of a central truth or circle of evidence to be derived from his organization of the facts or alleged facts of the Old Yellow
Book. By implication from the gold ring made of facts and
fancy, indeed yes; by verbal expression, no. And this metallurgical consistency on Browning's part seems to call for
strong emphasis on the pristine quality of gold, the softness
of facts, and the rounding of the ring (the poem) in the
twelfth book, not the rounding out of the truth.

So despite the permanency DeVane gave to Mrs. Orr's
"central truth": "His wife's simple gold ring possibly suggested the circle of monologues somewhere in the midst of
which lay the central truth" (p. 325); despite the virtually
perfect association "ring" bears with central truth, it seems
advisable to be guided by Browning's own explanation of his
creative process. If, to illustrate, Moby-Dick were to be
interpreted without reference to his whiteness, the great
story would suffer a devastating blow. "Ring" to Mrs. Orr
suggested a circle, and from that circle she reasonably but
somewhat romantically elicited a central truth. But if she

had not been first to popularize the meaning she thought
Browning gave the gold ring, later critics would have deduced the same errors.   It simply has not been sufficient
for Browning's facts to be made analogous to gold, the softest of all metals, and in usage consequently to demand that
we consider them soft, not hard.   And even when this demand is acceded to, imposition of a chemical reaction in the
fusing or mixing of gold and copper--a reaction which does
not occur--continues to baffle and cause critics to think the
Ring metaphor ill-chosen.   Naturally, then, Mrs. Orr in the
late 1880's, like Killham in the late 1960's ("Browning's
Modernity, " p. 160), thought first of hard facts and no doubt
would have resisted being told that Browning never speaks of
the facts of his poem as being hard.   Instead, Browning reasoned in conformity with his figure of speech, often applying
to his facts the adjectives soft (by analogy), pure, crude,
dead (sometimes live), but never hard.   He specifically refers to his imaginative contribution as the alloy metal (copper) which makes the base metal gold (his facts) malleable,
that is, harder and more subject to proper hammer-and-file
treatment.   The mistake Mrs. Orr made (if it may be called
one) is therefore as natural as that of Langbaum, whose irri-
tation in 1960 with my emphasis on pristine gold prevented
him from determining that Browning never applies the adjec-
tive precious to gold ("The Importance of Fact, " VN, No. 17
[Spring 1960], p. 12).

To be sure, the facts of the Old Yellow Book were
important to Browning ("For how else know we save by worth
of word?"), but they probably should be seen as the pure
and crude material--in the metallurgical analogy making up
eighty to ninety per cent of the alloy--over which Browning's
fancy exercised informing and artistic control.   Barbara Mel-
chiori's search for uses of the word gold in the body of
Browning's poetry helps confirm the variety of meanings
gold assumed in the poet's mind and the rarity of his focus
on the popularly accepted meaning of precious (Browning's
Poetry of Reticence [New York, 1968].   And a closer reading of Mrs. Orr's influential quotation assists in establishing
the untrustworthiness of other critical knots she has tied:
for example, with Browning's "pure crude fact / Secreted
from man's life when hearts beat hard" (I. 35-36, 86-87, a
whole line repetition) in mind, she wrote nonetheless of hard
fact being "secreted from the fluid being of men and women"
(see full quotation in Essay Two; italics added).   Ring, circle, circlet, oval, rondure, ripple, round, encircle, revolv-
ing, glass ball, and arc--all of these words, by the poet's

use or analogy, may suggest to any reader or critic a circle
of facts, the center of which represents truth, but it is
doubtful that Browning should be held culpable for a natural
or impressionistic misreading of an analogy over which he,
if consistent, creatively reserved the right of emphasis and
direction. Even circular composition (Raymond), circular
imagery (Friedman), and circular seasons (Phipps) should be
suspected, since they fit equally well Tennyson's In Memori-
am and all other lengthy poems.   If we must give direction
to Browning's truth, we probably should describe it as as-
cending from man's truest yet still weak use of fact, through
poetic or inspired truth, toward absolute truth, God's truth;
descending toward absence of any inkling of truth.   We may
quarrel with Browning for not being more lucid; we do art
an injustice, however, when we turn the poet's expressed intentions into something else.   Whether or not Browning deliberately implied his concern over the frailty of language in
the very conveyance of his thoughts through an analogy with
a gold ring, few examples from literature are as well suited
to demonstrate how far from his probable intentions the poet's metaphorical language can remove his reader.

Notes

1.   Morley, who knew Browning in the "high perfection of
social intercourse," also recollects: "A sense of the struggle that truth has to make against slackness of mind, difficulty of vision, and the strange devious ways of the world,
moved some of us with strong feeling for a new poem of
Browning's in four volumes, a parable of that struggle in a
tragic legend.   Say what we will of The Ring and the Book,
its dubious aesthetic, its strain on language and even gram-
mar, the absence from a good half of its pages of music, its
impossible length, yet its intellectual moral is lighted up with
an intensity of dramatic force that is hardly to be surpassed
in literature.   'Half Rome, the Other Half Rome, the Tertium
Quid,' show us how ill truth sifts itself, to how many it never comes at all, how blurred, confused, next door to false
it is figured even to those who seize the hem of the garment.
Apart from the mixed power and tenderness, the diabolic personalities and the angelic, this is what made the supreme
value of the book, and pointed with profound imaginative power and subtlety a moral of which men can never hear too
much.   My extraction of this prose from poetry of such extraordinary strength was indeed the exchange of gold for copper, but it caught the attention, not always the approval, of

other critics, and it gave some pleasure to Browning himself"
(Recollections [New York, 1917], I, 371, 132-133).

2.   Praise of Friedman's understanding of Browning's metaphorical usage is not intended to detract from the comparable
good work of Altick and Loucks or of Miss Sullivan, who surpasses all three in illustrating that usage.   Required in the
abstracting of individual books of the poem to read more
closely than they, she most effectively ties foregoing and
current images together in the Pope's thoughts on life as
a garden (X. 1031-47):

> This one passage gathers up all the major motifs
> of the Pope's soliloquy: his role of gardener (pa-
> pal responsibility) in the growing dusk of a long
> day (his age and approaching death), rejoicing at
> the blaze of the one flower which longs for the
> sun (Pompilia's recognition [acceptance ?] of truth)
> when all hope is dimmed by the 'nothingness of
> man' (discouragement at human frailties) and the
> sense of his own inadequacy (his one blossom, the
> rose he gathers for God, is, after all, not one he
> chose and imbedded in the warm sunlight, but a
> mere 'chance-sown cleft-nursed seed').   The single
> new idea introduced here into the soliloquy, of
> Pompilia as rose, immediately recalls the domi-
> nant flower imagery of her earliest defender, Other
> Half-Rome, who saw her as an abandoned blossom
> growing into beauty amid alien surroundings.   The
> Pope's figure gains significance from its association
> with these earlier memorable comparisons as well
> as from his own strongly developed cluster of im-
> ages having to do with seeds and nurtured plants,
> and it prepares the way for another link with Other
> Half-Rome: the view of Pompilia as saint.   Her
> first defender had called her that, always associat-
> ing her name with religious terms--miracle, soul,
> angels, and the like.   Now the Pope hails her as
> 'Armed and crowned' (1011) in heaven like Michael;
> without sword or shield, she earned her crown and
> now her soul, 'earth's flower / She holds up to
> the softened gaze of God!' (1018-19) (Browning's
> Voices, pp. 128-131; quotation, p. 131)

On the other hand, when Miss Sullivan wishes to describe
the future Pope Innocent is ushering in, she also surpasses
these critics in gloomy foreboding: "As the [Pope's] mono-

logue proceeds, the references to greyness, age, and finality
gradually fuse into one dominant image of night, the darkness
of which comes to represent for him the receding tide of
faith and the growing spirit of doubt and scepticism he feels
engulfing the world" (p. 126).

7.

POPE INNOCENT AND GOD'S TRUTH

Because Browning scholarship is turning more and
more to the Pope's monologue for interpretation of The Ring
and the Book, some critics and teachers of the poet will
understand beforehand why Essay Seven was written. Yet
as few of these individuals as of their opposites who are
justly weary of abstracts will believe, before being persuaded twice over, that A. K. Cook did not leave the invulnera-
ble position for social criticism and for attack on the Catholic Church many present-day critics assume. A similar assertion may also be made with reference to the belief which
critics generally hold on the poetic function of Pope Innocent
and the nature of his judgment of Guido. Only a closer re-
reading of the Pope's thought may convince both sympathetic
and unsympathetic critics that we are dealing with a Pope almost entirely different from the one which has been be-
queathed to us.

The essential thought of the first two recognizable
parts of the Pope's monologue can be grasped within the individual parts or in their combination. He is a man of God
speaking in God's name (163), he bears his sorrow as all
conscientious and humble popes do (200), and he maintains
his thought almost altogether on the next world, thus on the
eternal salvation of souls in this world (155). But the third
part--lines 1239-2135--is so dependent upon the foregoing
development that one cannot hope for clarity without constant
reminder of what is motiviating, what is guiding the Pope's
meditations. Even then, one is required to look more steadily at his broad experience and education than at his ancient
self, more steadily at his papal preoccupations than at his
papal occupation. Asked to "confirm or quash" (27) the trial of Guido, the Pope has devoted almost a full day to the
legal documents and decided to confirm the sentence of death
(208, 233, 260-267, 337, 346, 868, 1257). His only purpose,
then, in reading papal history and in rationalizing his confirmation of the legal sentence (actually, denial of clerical

158

privilege). is to justify to himself his stewardship ("due /
Labour and sorrow") to God ("what gain or loss") (166. 19).
Hence a move away from the dullness of another witness to
Guido's guilt or innocence is as probable as it is welcome,
a return to an art which is most famous for catching souls
in extreme crises. Cook and many others have not seen
this. Miss Sullivan did and ignored it. Friedman and
Phipps did and misinterpreted it. And Isobel Armstrong,
who speaks of the second part of the monologue as a review
and a recapitulation, misses its ultimate significance only
because she is entirely bent on the reader and his point of
view.

　　　　Whatever the Pope's doubts and questionings, they are
the outgrowth of an irrevocable (209) decision made before
the monologue opens, not a means of reaching that decision.
Having performed his duty as best he could, the Pope is now
not concerned with the proof of Guido's guilt or the justness
of Guido's sentence; for him Guido is "convicted of such
crime as law / Wipes not away save with a worldling's
blood" (446-447). His present thought rises from the act
of judging Guido, the errors of judgment he as a man is
subject to, and the extent to which human judgment may go,
even if one is appointed to be God's representative, not "divinely commissioned" or "by God's own choice, " as Cook,
Sullivan, and others say. Interesting and debatable passages
on evolvable truth, irresolution, and barren words [processes
of attaining truth] are of course integral to part one, all of
Book X, and the whole poem, but they should not be permitted to interfere with the course the Pope's insistent thought
is to take. Regardless of what Pope Innocent may hear others say, to him, it is not the fruit (341, 347) but the seed
of act (272) which "God holds appraising in His hollow palm."
So contrary to most recorded interpretations of Book X, the
Pope does not expect to be judged by his last act:

> Why, then I stand already in God's face
> And hear "Since by its fruit a tree is judged,
> "Show me thy fruit, the latest act of thine!
> "For in the last is summed the first and all, --
> "What thy life last put heart and soul into,
> "There shall I taste thy product. " I must plead
> This condemnation of a man to-day.
>
> Not so! Expect nor question nor reply
> At what we figure as God's judgment-bar!
> None of this vile way by the barren words

> Which, <u>more than any deed</u>, characterize
> Man as made subject to a curse.
>   (340-351; italics added)

Witness Browning's transitional "Not so!" which repudiates
the preceding six lines and introduces with its new paragraph
a review (279) of a judgment already completed on the motives, impulses, connivances, plans, instigations, and
schemes of the accused, only incidentally on Guido's last
act (which is the same as his first) or on the good will of
his judge.   When the Pope so positively repudiates man's
normal method of judging as God's method also, we have
imperative reason for following most closely his rational
and metaphysical thought on the <u>act</u> of judgment itself.   Especially since to the Pope, as <u>God</u> has endowed him with
judging faculty, "there is not any doubt to clear," even if
in after-time "some acuter wit" reaches through guilt to
Guido's innocence (233, 239-267).   Pope Innocent is confidently aware "it is the <u>seed</u> of act" which counts with God:

> It is because I need to breathe awhile,
> Rest, as the human right allows, <u>review</u>
> <u>Intent</u> the little seeds of act, my tree, --
> The <u>thought</u>, which, clothed in <u>deed</u>, I give the world.
>   (278-281; italics added)

In part two (399-1238), through a long justification to
himself of his recent decision, the Pope establishes a complete familiarity with the factual information of Guido's case,
and in deriving Guido's revenge as comploted of "Craft,
greed and violence" (733) demonstrates an enviable skill at
courtroom summation.   Neither his intellectual (168, 1244)
nor emotional prowess can be discounted or disallowed, if
any word he speaks or thought he utters is to be granted
substance.   He believes that "Mind is not matter nor from
matter, but / Above," and he enjoins all to "leave matter
then, proceed with mind!" (1353-54)   As an inquisitive and
dispassionate observer of the world he promises Antonio
Pignatelli (383) a fair review of Guido's case, but as a faithful servant of God he will not forget that "Man is born nowise to content himself, / But please God" (435-436; see
also 1821).   To himself, despite the evidence of emotion his
righteous indigation imparts, the Pope does not exceed the
bounds of Christian persuasion when, because of Guido's cul-
minate scheming, he discerns "Power in the air for evil as
for good, / Promptings from heaven and hell," and then rejoices in "how Christ prevailed / And Satan fell like light-

ning!" (622-672)   Ending part two with his severest charge
directed at ambiguous creatures who "elude the choice of
tints, " the Pope returns to the <u>act</u> of judging, a terrible act
incumbent no less on all men th<u>an</u> on himself, since "life's
business" is the choice between good and evil.   Because all
question of his meaning is eliminated by the transitional "So
do I see"--

>   Go!
> Never again elude the choice of tints!
> White shall not neutralize the black, nor good
> Compensate bad in man, absolve him so:
> Life's business being just the terrible choice.
>
> <u>So do I see</u>, pronounce on all and some
> Grouped for my judgment now, --profess no doubt
>   (1234-40; italics added)
>
> <u>But strong meat belongeth to them that are of full</u>
> <u>age, even those who by reason of use have their</u>
> <u>senses exercised to discern both good and evil.</u>
> <u>Hebrews v. 14</u>

--we seem to have no alternative but to conclude that the
Pope's intellectually and emotionally fused thoughts may be
made intelligible only when enlightened by Christian morality,
which is idealistic and understood to be unattainable by man.
In part two, as in part one, many of Browning's personal
convictions are introduced to expand or illustrate the Pope's
meditations: illusion of evil, trial by temptation, doctrine
of election and of elective affinity, martyr-maid and soldier-
champion, man's insensitivity to evil, God's intervention for
good and permissiveness for evil.   For instance, after re-
nouncing "this vile way by the barren words" as proper
method for God's judgment, a method more reprehensible
than even Guido's murderous deed (350), the Pope concen-
trates on the consistency of Guido's premeditated wickedness
(591) in planning the marriage (532, 570).   First, he sees
Pompilia goaded inescapably into suicide or a disastrous
flight by Guido.   When these calculations failed--as if by
divine intervention (641-642)--Guido instituted the "love-in-
trigue" (647) with falsified letters.   Since the letters were
intended to precipitate the flight, the Pope next sees "That
strange temptation permitted" (658), even to the sin of passion which might have resulted from the prolonged compan-
ionship of a priest and a married woman.   With Caponsacchi
and Pompilia in the service of God (685), however, and

Guido in the service of Satan, the "plucking fiend" (904,
1024), the battle again went against Guido. Even when sin
had its way in Pompilia's death, Pope Innocent implies it
was by God's permission and for an eternal not momentary
cause (1421-29). But it would be extremely difficult to show
that any of these poetic convictions or dramatic patterns,
even when they sometimes reappear, are other than tangential to the Pope's overriding involvement with the act of judging.

At the opening (1239) of part three Pope Innocent for
the second time professes "no doubt" (1240, 233) in the de-
cree he had dared to make. The defendants "all and some"
had received just legal treatment in the main (706), and
Guido's punishment was incontestable by the prevailing legal
and moral standards which were applied to the evidence (446-
447).

> Through hard labour and good will,
> And habitude that gives a blind man sight
> At the practised finger-ends of him, I do
> Discern, and dare decree in consequence,
> Whatever prove the peril of mistake.
> Whence, then, this quite new quick cold thrill, --
>   cloud-like,
> This keen dread creeping from a quarter scarce
> Suspected in the skies I nightly scan?
>
> (1248-55; italics added)

That the Pope is now thinking beyond Guido's deserved death
seems clear; that the "keen dread creeping" is instigated by
Satan, whose forces have invaded God's own domain, also
seems clear; and that the severity of the temptation, striking
as it does at the object of the Pope's accustomed nightly
scanning, concerns doubt in God is substantiated by the questioning voice: What if in your confidence (1260) to judge between good and evil, a confidence which is totally dependent
upon God, you should one night find God missing in your sky?
Is "Thy inch of inkling" incapable of "the doubt"? (1265-84)
The subject of the Pope's controlling thought is further confirmed by "Shall I dare try the doubt now, or not dare?"
(1307; italics added) which with its context joins together the
two paragraphs, one ending "nor once face the doubt / I' the
sphere above thee, darkness to be felt?" (1283-84; italics
added) and the other beginning "O Thou, --as represented
here to me." And if one turns to line 1855, the point at
which the long meditation develops whispers of "times to

come," he will find "Re-introduce the doubt discarded, bring
/ That formidable danger back, we drove / Long ago to the
distance and the dark?" (italics added) It is impossible to
locate in lines 1239-1307 any evidence that the Pope is speaking of doubt in Guido's guilt, or of doubt in any aspect of
the life around him, particularly the worth of the Church over
which he presides or the competence of its institutional function. There is considerable evidence that he, like other men,
has been challenged to test his faith in a supreme power, and
that he tenaciously holds with Browning it is only grappling
with doubt "whereby souls grow strong" (1302, 1307).

I do not agree with A. K. Cook's unChristian way of
thinking that Browning, at such a profoundly disquieting moment, would relish an attack on the Catholic Church; the
"rare dignity and elevation" Cook simultaneously attributes
to the Pope's soliloquy is incompatible with the outlook of
sectarian opposition, whether it be Cook's or Browning's.
Long before the writing of The Ring and the Book Browning
had stated his preference of means for communing with God,
but, as A. C. Pigou noted, Christ's visit to St. Peter's on
Christmas-Eve was every bit as warm and extended as his
visit to the little Chapel in London. Beyond all pertinent
and imagined future research on the poem, therefore, Cook's
scattered conclusions first require consolidation, and we do
well to begin with the Pope's challenge to a doubt in God
and Cook's related note:

> [1253-1909.] The 'quick cold thrill' which the Pope
> suddenly feels (1253) and the voice which 'derides'
> him (1265) lead him into the long theological dis-
> quisitions of which I have spoken in the Introduc-
> tion to the Book. It will be observed that in the
> course of these disquisitions (1308-1909) he reverts
> for awhile to his main concern in 1440-1630.

Too promptly in his introduction to the Pope's monologue,
Cook, who also admirably defends the Pope's intelligence
and good will as well as his verisimilitude, is launched on
a personal errand which, if successful, would damn Browning's poem as a mere Protestant polemic. For he writes,
"A deriding voice lures the Pope from the straight path into
long discussions on the ultimate basis of Christianity, the
probable effects upon religion of an age of doubt, the ethics
and theology of Euripides" (p. 199; italics added). First
given to the kind of interpretation here offered, Cook could
never have guessed at how broadly and excessively Langbaum,

Friedman, Sullivan, Altick and Loucks, Honan, Tracy, Armstrong, and others would elaborate on his introductory words and related notes to the tenth book of The Ring and the Book. Two quotations from Cook's introduction may be taken as irrefutable proof, since both have frequently been paraphrased:

> A critic is on firm ground when he maintains that the Pope is represented rightly, and at just the right moment, as visited by blank misgivings and obstinate questionings about the whole ecclesiastical system which is bound up with Catholic theology. His investigation of the Guido-Pompilia tragedy has shown him that he moves in a world in which the ideal of that system is worlds away from realization, and it is most natural that a poignant apprehension that its foundations may be insecure should 'rap and knock and enter in his soul [from "Bishop Blougram's Apology"]'. (pp. 200-201; emphasis added)

> One stark staring fact has, however, confronted him throughout, a fact most injurious to papal authority and to the pyramid of which it is the apex. The representatives of the Church have been discredited by his investigations..., whereas the nobility and the heroism that have been brought to light have sprung from simple human virtue in characters either practically outside the Church's influence or unspoilt in spite of it. All this leads to the raising of the speculative question, Is the Christian revelation necessary for virtue or for the knowledge of God, does it not seem even to hamper? and to the doubt whether it might not be well that the Pope's world should be rudely shaken from its 'torpor of assurance'. (p. 202; emphasis added)

By this quality of logic, it would be no less reasonable to argue that since the Pope as often excoriates individual Christians and the mass of mankind,[1] he thereby defends representatives of the Church for the human vices they have been influenced to sophisticate. A more thoroughly incorrect reading than Cook's would be difficult to contrive. One may go to the poetry alone to disprove what he says, but Cook's pivotal error is much more quickly spotted in accurately and inaccurately presented information he fails to consolidate.

> See this habitual creed exemplified
> Most in the last deliberate act; as last,
> So, very sum and substance of the soul
> Of him that planned and leaves one perfect piece,
> The sin brought under jurisdiction now,
> Even the marriage of the man: this act
> I sever from his life as sample, show
> For Guido's self, intend to test him by.
>
> (521-528; emphasis added)

Cook's note to these lines reads: "The Pope intends to judge
Guido's life by taking his 'last deliberate act' as a sample of
it, just as in 340-45 above he conceives of God as judging
his life by his 'latest act', by what his life 'last put heart
and soul into', i. e. by his condemnation of Guido. " But,
contrary to Cook, the Pope says he is taking "the marriage"
(see 532, 570) as "sample" of Guido's "habitual creed" and
in "340-45 above"--

> Why, then I stand already in God's face
> And hear "Since by its fruit a tree is judged,
> "Show me thy fruit, the latest act of thine!
> "For in the last is summed the first and all, --
> "What thy life last put heart and soul into,
> "There shall I taste thy product, " I must plead
> This condemnation of a man to-day.
>
> (340-346)

--the Pope imagines how others conceive of God's judging him
by his latest act. With pause, however, he takes dramatic
exception, "Not so!" And if we have not nodded on the preceding page we know the Pope's way of looking to God for
judgment, which in Guido's "habitual creed" proves to be the
same by motive or performance (511-531), is through the
seed of act:

> For I am ware it is the seed of act,
> God holds appraising in His hollow palm,
> Not act grown great thence on the world below,
> Leafage and branchage, vulgar eyes admire.
> Therefore I stand on my integrity,
> Nor fear at all: and if I hesitate,
> It is because I need to breathe awhile,
> Rest, as the human right allows, review
> Intent the little seeds of act, my tree, --
> The thought, which, clothed in deed, I give the world.
>
> (272-281; italics added)

In response to the method of God's judgment as conceived here by the Pope, Cook saw not only that it was the
seed of act but also that it was the "seed," as the inward
product (1670), Euripides was to paraphrase from St. Paul
(Romans ii. 28-29).   Cook's note to the last quoted lines,
272-281, runs: "Contrast 341-5. --The doctrine that it is
'the seed of act' that God 'appraises' is constantly enforced
by Browning; the 'vulgar' judge by 'act', he says, 'it is the
outward product men appraise' (below, 1673 seqq.). " Yet,
despite this close, careful reading of separate verses on the
same subject, Cook does not come to know the Pope's meaning in "Not so! Expect nor question nor reply" (347), a substantive transition and the beginning of one of the most ardent-
ly spoken passages in the soliloquy.   It moreover appears
that this same failure to comprehend the purpose of Pope Innocent's emphatic "Not so, " with its elaborate rationale (347-
398), accounts for the wayward interpretations contemporary
critics derive from Cook, largely through Langbaum.   Browning's knowledge of the New Testament told him of its two
methods of judgment--1) seed of act, inward work, dictate
of heart; 2) fruit of act, outward work, dictate of mind--
and in placing his Pope on the side of motive rather than
deed, inward rather than outward work, Browning allowed
his sympathy to fall on the simplicity of Jesus' trust in the
heart rather than on the more methodized teaching of John
and Paul, though all three teachers resort to the fruit of the
tree, the branch of the vine, and the seed of act.   That
such a distinction between seed and fruit of act is necessary
for apprehension of the third part (1239-2135) of Book X,
Browning would have assumed in his readers.   Still, he left
telltale signs of the distinction between motive and deed all
the way to the appearance of Euripides.   To know the Pope
is not delaying sentence because he is fearful he may un-
justly condemn Guido is to clear away all complaints against
and excuses for the Pope's uncertain and manifest theological
"divagation" (Cook, p. 199); all need for the Pope to pronounce sentence on Guido before speaking "some 800 lines"
from which he reaps only tentative conclusions; and all ill-
founded praise Cook and others bestow on Euripides' "appeal"
without considering that if Euripides remains unanswered, if
the masses of doctrinal matters "land [the Pope] exactly at
the point from which he set out" (p. 199), these many lines
are literary excrescences unworthy of genuine critical praise
or analysis.   If, as Cook advances, Pope Innocent gets back
on his main concern only in lines 1440-1630 (not really the
sentencing Cook longs for, but the review he mistakenly
thinks the actual judgment), his monologue is so wretchedly

flawed that not the most sympathetic attachment to Browning could muster dignified excuse. If, as with Cook, Langbaum and others are right in their social interpretation of the Pope's soliloquy, they are also right in believing much of Book X is utterly superfluous.

Thus far we have seen that through emphatic paragraph change and focus on a character who had judged Guido by and expected himself to be judged by the seed of act, Browning predetermines our direction. Beginning with line 399 (part two) the Pope explains that "Guido is found reprobate" (see Romans i. 28) because he believed consistently "in just the vile of life" (512); it was therefore his "habitual creed." In line 347 the Pope repudiates the popular notion that he, at death, would be required by God to "Show me thy fruit, the latest act of thine," as he prepares to review a decision he had based on motive, scheme, plan, impulse, connivance--all seeds of act. In line 1239 he makes unequivocal his position of being a judge between good and evil: "So do I see," "Never again elude the choice of tints! / White shall not neutralize the black, nor good / Compensate bad in man" (1235-37). And in lines 1285-1306 the Pope reveals he is solely interested in defending and reasserting his faith in God, a point made doubly clear by the ending of the paragraph, "Shall I dare try the doubt now, or not dare?" Two times (1283, 1307) in part three Pope Innocent speaks of "the doubt" and each time it is indicative of the temptation through which he is passing and of the temptation men are to face when future days "Re-introduce the doubt discarded" (1855; emphasis added). At the second reference to "the doubt" the Pope begins the prayer "O Thou, --as represented" (1308) which is wholly directed to the subject of faith and doubt in God, not to the subject of institutional inefficiency. Through it all--prayer and meditation--are woven immemorial strands from the essence of Christian teaching and recommended practices. We may thus confidently predict that for Pope Innocent "still faith stands" (1374) before hearing him ask, "How do the Christians deport them, keep / Their robes of white unspotted by the world?" (1452-53), "these who thus battle for the faith" (1487). Quite expectedly the Christians do not perform very well, for they are being compared by the Pope with an ideal,[2] not with the irresponsible pattern of conduct which divided Roman opinion on Guido's guilt. Even to the last resource (1492)--but not including the Church which is a spiritual entity--the Convertites in their worldly act offered an example of Christian failure for which "scripture yields no parallel" (1525). All have sinned, however,

including Caponsacchi, the "God-abandoned" young rustics,
the sad middle group, and the Pope himself, who is nonetheless "Heart-sick at having all his world to blame" (1008).
If Pope Innocent expects to be judged solely by his "little
seeds of act, " he must grant the same hope to the governor,
the archbishop, the Convertites, and the apparently selfish
churchmen he had impetuously judged by their fruit of act.
He cannot forget his own good intentions which have gone
astray; nor can he forget the "tale of Thee" his heart loves
and his reason pronounces sound.   It is a serious misunderstanding of Christianity, as Browning saw it and projected it
in his Pope, not to recognize that Christ founded a religion
which looked to the kingdom of God only in another world.

        As Pope Innocent dares "try the doubt" and surveys
(1239-1422) the reasons for his faith and belief in God, in
God's absolute nature and his incomprehensible choice of
"This one earth... / For stage and scene of Thy transcendent act" (1336-46), he manages every hurdle (1374) but that
erected by the conduct of man.   Along the way he gives elaborate expression to Browning's familiar arguments that life is
a probation waged against sin and sorrow, that striving means
"as good as reach the goal" (1438), and that weakness in
faith may be its greatest strength, particularly since by exercise the moral quality grows and by love self-sacrificing
is born and nurtured:

> The moral sense grows but by exercise.
> 'T is even as man grew probatively
> Initiated in Godship, set to make
> A fairer moral world than this he finds,
> Guess now what shall be known hereafter.
>
> (1415-19)

But it is distinctly the Pope's object to reconsider the causes
for possible doubt in God and he finds the only terrifying possibility in man himself, God's creature whose spotted record
has occupied the Pope's whole day.   It is not therefore a
satisfactory solution to say, as Cook does, that lines 1253-
1909 are extraneous with the exception of 1440-1630 which
revert to the main concern of sentencing (p. 218).   Neither
Cook ("it likes me") nor Stopford Brooke ("it likes me not")
understood what Browning's Pope was doing, but if Cook had
not misplaced the Pope's confidence in an institutional authority to which Cook himself objected, he might have found
it lodged in God instead.   These "some 800 lines, " which
Cook labels "a manifest 'divagation, '" get the Pope exactly

where he wants to go, must go, and Browning, regretfully, closer in 1868 to intellectual agnosticism than generous critics have been willing to place him.

The "quite new quick cold thrill" resulted from a self-imposed challenge to the Pope's confidence in following God's guidance between good and evil. His own faith re-examined and affirmed (1285-1429), it thus becomes the weak and unconcerned faith of other men which touches Pope Innocent with terror (1441), not because disbelievers and skeptics abound, but because Christians themselves so readily turn their backs on God's truth, sinning and not fearing:

> Neither does this astonish at the end,
> That whereas I can so receive and trust,
> Other men, made with hearts and souls the same,
> Reject and disbelieve, --subordinate
> The future to the present, --sin, nor fear.
> (1430-34; italics added)

Even the Christians in their panoply, their loins girt about with God's truth, are "Slunk into corners, " as Langbaum so dramatically upstages them, but only when judged by the fruit of act. Even "the faithful few, " whom the Pope would be expected to take from the immediate criminal affair as example, make little effort to keep their "robes of white unspotted by the world. " But those critics who bypass the Pope's idealistic demands in his condemnation of apparently overt sinful acts are unfamiliar with Christian apologetics:

> How can I but speak what truth speaks low,
> "Or better than the best, or nothing serves!
> "What boots deed, I can cap and cover straight
> "With such another doughtiness to match,
> "Done at an instinct of the natural man?"
> Immolate body, sacrifice soul too, --
> Do not these publicans the same? Outstrip!
> Or else stop race you boast runs neck and neck,
> You with the wings, they with the feet, --for shame!
> (1579-87; italics added)

If the exalted archbishop, the barefoot monk, and the uniquely dedicated Convertites "are the Christians not the worldlings, not / The sceptics, who thus battle for the faith" (1486-87), then on this particular performance "Christ must give up his gains. " Fruit of act therefore is not only less reliable than seed of act as a method of judging; it is also the strong-

est reason the Pope unfolds for doubt in God's guidance between good and evil:

> Can it be this is end and outcome, all
> I take with me to show as stewardship's fruit,
> The best yield of the latest time, this year
> The seventeen-hundredth since God died for man?
> Is such effect proportionate to cause?
>
> > (1532-36; italics added)

Of course the "effect" is not proportionate to the "cause."
Can the "cause," then, God himself, be faulted? Pope Innocent has traveled a most circuitous route, but he is now
back to his reason for preferring the seed of act to its fruit,
the effort by which faith grows strongly, and to the challenge
by a deriding voice to the basis of his confidence in judging
between good and evil.   Yet, "And still the terror" (1537)
increases as the Pope, who stubbornly believes that man is
faced with the necessity of choosing (free will), agonizes
over the visible refusal of Christians--not just the individuals
involved in the murder episode--to battle evil as courageously
as did men of old or as promptly now as Caponsacchi.   It is
this, the Christian's outward refusal to respond to or defend
the good--his only observable sign of faith--which terrifies
the Pope (1547).   While Christian conduct should supersede
the noblest acts of the natural man, it appears to fall behind:

> This terrifies me, thus compelled perceive,
> Whatever love and faith we looked should spring
> At advent of the authoritative star,
> Which yet lie sluggish, curdled at the source, --
> These have leapt forth profusely in old time,
> These still respond with promptitude to-day,
> At challenge of--what unacknowledged powers
> O' the air, what uncommissioned meteors, warmth
> By law, and light by rule should supersede?
>
> > (1547-55; italics added)

Cook interprets "the authoritative star" of this knotty passage
to be "the Church" and is thereby enabled to repeat charges
of its corruption.   I think it refers to Christ, first, because a pope created as sympathetically as Browning's would
not be permitted to destroy himself in grotesque parody; second, use of "in old time" (1551) very probably anticipates
the appearance of Euripides "out of the old time" (1668) and
"warmth / By law, and light by rule" (1554-55) suggest the
warm light a new law of love brought into the world (see

also 436, 1818).   Whereas the Pope is thinking of "man"
(1541) generically, Cook applies the passage to "churchmen,
who know its worth, join the worldlings and sceptics in dis-
regarding it and pursuing worldly aims; it was, for instance,
for mere worldly reasons that the Bishop of Arezzo virtually
abandoned the faith by his treatment of Pompilia.   It may be
said, perhaps, that the Church enfeebled the bishop by cod-
dling him" (p. 223).   Only at the very end of his long note
does Cook feel constrained to add, "The Pope's dismay [is]
at finding that love and faith 'lie sluggish' at the call of the
Church" (italics added). A "call" which may come from Christ
instead, this tardy qualification by Cook is like his "The
Pope's world should be rudely shaken from its 'torpor of assurance'" (p. 202), which misinterprets the Pope's "This torpor of
assurance from our creed" (1854; italics added).   What seems
indisputable, however, is the Pope's inability to find Christian
fruit of act commensurate with God's creative act (see below),
much less commensurate with the atonement.   Can this creature
man, judged by the outward acts of his life, then suggest other
than an imperfect creator, if creator at all?

> And is this little all that was to be?
> Where is the gloriously-decisive change,
> Metamorphosis the immeasurable
> Of human clay to divine gold, we looked
> Should, in some poor sort, justify its [the cruci-
>   fixion's] price?
> Had an adept of the mere Rosy Cross
> Spent his life to consummate the Great Work,
> Would not we start to see the stuff it touched
> Yield not a grain more than the vulgar got
> By the old smelting-process years ago?
> If this were sad to see in just the sage
> Who should profess so much, perform no more,
> What is it when suspected in that Power
> Who undertook to make and made the world,
> Devised and did effect man, body and soul,
> Ordained salvation for them both, and yet...
> Well, is the thing we see salvation?
>   (1614-30; italics added)

For what if some were without faith?   shall their
want of faith make of none effect the faithfulness
of God?   God forbid: yea, let God be true, but
every man a liar.   Romans iii. 3-4

But if our unrighteousness commend the righteous-

> ness of God, what shall we say?   Is God unrighteous
> who taketh vengeance?   Romans iii. 5

> For if the truth of God hath more abounded through
> my lie unto his glory; why yet am I also judged as
> a sinner?   Romans iii. 7

Judged by the intellect and "the thing we see" alone, neither
man nor God makes any lasting sense, "ordained salvation"
notwithstanding.   Trusting, therefore, in the seed of act he
cannot judge in other men--an extrapolation he makes from
his own good intent--and in perfect love in God he cannot
know but may idealistically extrapolate from his own known
limited love, Pope Innocent, "Within whose circle of experience burns / The central truth, Power, Wisdom, Goodness, --
God" (1633-34), cannot be moved from his reason for God.
Nor can Pope Innocent question the efficacy of God's ordained
salvation when he believes both that God will judge the heart,
give full recompense for the inward thought, and that

> There is beside the works [power and wisdom], a
>   tale of Thee
> In the world's mouth, which I find credible:
> I love it with my heart: unsatisfied,
> I try it with my reason, nor discept
> From any point I probe and pronounce sound.
>   (1348-54)

As long as day succeeds the deepest night, for the Pope,
"The light that did burn, will burn!"   As clouds obscure the
sun, man's "outward" life obscures his faith and love which,
though weak, are increasing as "The divine instance of self-
sacrifice / That never ends and aye begins for man" (1640-
58):

> What but the weakness in a faith supplies
> The incentive to humanity, no strength
> Absolute, irresistible, comports?
> How can man love but what he yearns to help?
>   (1649-52)

Having thus left to God the judgment of individuals
Cook, Langbaum, and others are right in believing the Pope
condemned for their fruit of act, wrong in believing he dared
condemn for their seeds of act, Pope Innocent turns to mankind who walk outside his confident but circumscribed world
(1661).   And considering Browning's devotion to and defense

of Euripides, it is unlikely he could have found a better literary, possibly a better ethical, verification of the Pope's persuasion that only God can judge the heart:

> "The inward work and worth
> "Of any mind, what other mind may judge
> "Save God who only knows the thing He made,
> "The veritable service He exacts?
> "It is the outward product men appraise. "
> (1670-74; italics added)

> For he is not a Jew, which is one outwardly;
> neither is that circumcision, which is outward in
> the flesh: but he is a Jew, which is one inwardly;
> and circumcision is that of the heart, in the spirit,
> and not in the letter; whose praise is not of men,
> but of God.   Romans ii. 28-29

To advance that line 272--"For I am ware it is the seed of
act, / God hold appraising in His hollow palm"--introduces
the theme of the Pope's monologue, as I have, and that fourteen hundred lines of his soliloquy prove that theme to be
the act of judging may invite the retort, "Mere coincidence
or circumstantial evidence. " But anyone prepared to read
the first three chapters of Romans will find the thought of
St. Paul so thoroughly employed that some half of the
biblical verses may be collated in thought and diction
with verses by the Pope and Euripides. That the biblical
chapters, in turn, are devoted to the subject of judgment
is also beyond dispute. The long-misinterpreted question
Euripides asks Pope Innocent may be abstracted thus: "I
was born; therefore I lived under conditions whereby the
salvation (1689) affirmed in thy creed was impossible. Yet,
born to perish like the brutes and to live without divine promise, I adopted virtue, waived all reward, and for truth's sake
alone taught the world what my heart taught me. Pope Innocent, who art to answer me, dost thou dare pretend to punish
me (1781) who pricked a sure path across the bog wherein I
find your teachers of truth wallowing in the wide daytime?"
(1683-1790) It may not be the best question Euripides could
have asked. But it was a perennial nineteenth-century religious question and worthy, Browning thought, of the Pope's
meditation as embodied in the antique bard. Cook speculates
on the Pope's failure to answer Euripides (p. 227) without
comprehending that the Pope, who has been thinking aloud all
this time, uses the individualized thought of Euripides to climax his own conclusions on the act of judging. If one insists

upon a more obvious argument, however, the Pope had already answered the question Euripides asks; he did not believe pagans would be excluded from God's grace. Even
more appropriately, the Pope allows Euripides himself to
answer that his faith still rests on the inward work and is
sustained without fear. That is why the Pope, on dismissing
Euripides, starts thinking about future human judgment which
shall be based, not on the heart and the inward work, but on
the mind and the outward work. It is as though the Pope is
saying for Browning that as faith reached its high-water mark
after the tenebrific days Euripides knew, the days of faith
after Pope Innocent will recede rapidly into an era as ungodly
as the olden times. Clearly the most satisfactory answer
Browning could muster for the purpose of his Pope was the
answer St. Paul wrote to the Romans, and this answer Browning gave knowing that Paul too had confessed his indebtedness
"both to the Greek, and to the Barbarians" (Romans i. 14),
"for there is no difference between the Jew and the Greek"
(Romans x. 12).

> For when Gentiles which have no law do by nature
> the things of the law, these, having no law, are a
> law unto themselves; in that they shew the work of
> the law written in their hearts, their conscience
> bearing witness therewith, and their thoughts one
> with another accusing or else excusing them; in the
> day when God shall judge secrets of man.   Romans
> ii. 14-16

It is revealing on the continuity of Browning's religious thought that he found so much to his purpose in three
chapters of biblical expression. It is even more revealing
on his artistic method that he chose the last two verses of
chapter two to open Euripides' speech and then moved back-
ward fourteen verses to the above quotation which epitomizes
the Pope's as well as St. Paul's thought on judgment, forward
two verses to the text of Fra Celestino's sermon, which deals
with the unfaithfulness of man, the faithfulness of God, the un-
truthfulness of man, the truthfulness of God:

> For what if some were without faith? shall their
> want of faith make of none effect the faithfulness
> of God? God forbid: yea, let God be true, but
> every man a liar. Romans iii. 3-4

Other borrowings by Browning from Romans are equally dis-
tinguishable. Not retaining God in his knowledge, Guido is

permitted the same reprobate mind (i. 28; X. 399), and the
Pope's rational man, the experimentalist, is drawn from
Paul's unnatural men, "who hold the truth in unrighteousness
(i. 18; X. 1941). Pope Innocent's attribution of strength and
intelligence to God is related to Paul's visible evidences of
God (i. 20; X. 1363) as his establishment of a future reign of
Godless culture is related to Paul's "changed the glory of
the uncorruptible God into an image made like to corruptible
man" (i. 23; X. 2017-35). Repeatedly faith, heart, good,
righteousness, judgment, and truth are referred to by Pope
and Apostle, and the concern of each is unmistakably riveted
on those faithless ones "who changed the truth of God into a
lie, and worshipped and served the creature more than the
Creator (i. 25; X. 673). It is the belief of Pope Innocent and
St. Paul that "the just shall live by faith" (i. 17; X. 1649);
that, like Abraham, their faith shall be counted unto them
for righteousness (iv. 3; X. 1653-54); and that by the deeds
(works, iii. 27) of the law no flesh shall be justified in God's
sight (iii. 20), since all men openly sin against the law of
his truth (iii. 9-12). Both the Pope and Paul conclude that
"a man is justified by faith without the deeds of the law" (iii.
28), and they make it their bounden duty to proclaim that
salvation is through God's grace alone. When the Pope
speaks of men who "sin, nor fear" (1434), he derives his
thought from Paul's "not only do the same, but have pleasure
in them" (i. 32) as directly as he derives his "Conjecture of
the worker by the work" (1362) from Paul's "the things that
are made" (i. 20). In serving as a "teacher of truth," Euripides simply reasserts in Paul's language what Pope Innocent
has been expounding on the same subject all along. Each
man sees a terrifying rejection of eternal salvation in the
disbelief, dishonor, and discredit men accord to God's truth:
for St. Paul, those "who hold the truth in unrighteousness";
for Pope Innocent, those when "told the truth, but lie the
more. " In formulating Euripides' speech, then, Browning
transposed the closing "inwardly" and "outwardly" (ii. 28-29)
of Pauline thought into the opening thought of the Greek's
speech, lifted the whole notion of judging the act by the in-
tent--a judgment only God can make according to both Paul
and Euripides--and, in a typical Browningesque inversion,
permitted Euripides to answer his own question as Paul answered the Romans: "For when the Gentiles which have no
law do by nature the things of the law, these, having no law,
are a law unto themselves. " Nor is Browning's Euripides
restricted to knowledge of Romans i-iii. The extraordinary
parallel between Greek and Judeo-Christian thought is also
dependent on Paul's speech before Felix and Drusilla. While

it is reported in The Acts that "he [Paul] reasoned of righteousness, temperance, and judgment to come" (xxiv. 25),
Euripides reasoned of "How much of temperance and righteousness, / Judgment to come" (1719-20). A. K. Cook to
the contrary, we have every incentive for believing Browning's Pope spoke truly "in God's name!"

        Whether one can find arguments as obvious for Brown-
ing's selection of Euripides as for his choice of Pauline
thought on judgment is extremely doubtful. Yet from the
traditional associations of Browning and Euripides as well
as from possibly some new associations, we are encouraged
not to discontinue the search. While reading the introduction
to Euripides, A Collection of Critical Essays, ed. Erich
Segal (Prentice-Hall, 1968), one is tempted to assert that
with moderate allowance Browning's name might almost be
exchanged for Euripides'. And, in several of the essays,
one finds strong corroboration of Browning's assessment of
Euripides by a group of respected modern scholars. Their
particular emphases on Euripides as an "irrationalist," as
an "innovator, experimentalist, antitraditional 'immoralist'
and stage-sophist" strike close to language applicable to
Browning, even to language Browning might in some instances
have preferred that his own critics use. To add that Euripides
was ahead of his time, that he was psychologically astute and
introduced shockingly new forms and dramatic themes, is to provide an even broader basis for comparison. Indeed one is left
thinking that the determination with which Browning fastened on
to Euripides confirms a proudly held, personally rationalized,
affinity for the Greek dramatist. Yet as much caution should be
exercised on our appraisal of Euripides as on our being ready
to accept the comparison before balancing out the differences.

        Segal, who utilizes some of the thoughts of the other
essayists as well as his own, stresses the early departure
of Euripides from traditional dramaturgy; his portrayal of
unmitigated misery; his unending paradoxes--life-in-death,
joy-in-sorrow, verbal and visual; his salvation in the nick of
time, deus ex machina; and his perplexing problem of what
is real, what illusory, in an unstable amphitheater of nature
and tradition. He also recognizes in Euripides the many
contradictory characters and situations, the constant evoking
of bold questions and extraordinary ambiguities, and reminds
us that in antiquity Euripides was called "the philosopher of
the stage" and linked with men like Protagoras who called all
in doubt. Segal's observation is that the world of Euripides

was filled with awesome things, but man was not one of them.
He is especially conscious of an ultimate irony in the beginning of Greek drama with the suffering of Dionysus, in the
culmination with a play which presents the suffering of humanity for Dionysus.   Blinded by doubt, torn by conflicting
inner forces, Euripidean characters are master least of their
own actions.   As Segal expresses it, "Homer's epic heroes
no longer had a dwelling in the Greek theater. "   In place of
these, Euripides brought to the stage bourgeois people in
bourgeois surroundings, thus at once destroying the dependable palace and man's control over his own mind.   And if
Segal had been comparing Browning and Euripides, he might
also have drawn additional characteristics from the other
essayists: for example, the personal sense of defeat and
disappointment; the tendency toward fantasy and romance;
the pathos which may degenerate too easily into sentimentality;
the signs of haste, verbosity, and careless or inconsequen-
tial passages; the effort to get too much into a single plot,
character, or situation; the possible preference of women
over men; the fusion and contrast of comic and tragic effects;[3] the creation of melodrama; the daring implausibilities
and the complexity of ideas; and the long-winded speeches.
It is an artistic miracle that with all these faults and inno-
vations the simplicity of Euripidean dialogue is capable of
rising to the sublime.   And it appears less and less a coincidence that Browning, at his best, labored against or en-
dured most of the faults, at his worst, may have found con-
solation in his great forerunner's discernible shortcomings.

      William Arrowsmith, who would establish Euripides
as a dramatist thinking constructively about his immediate
world, insists that Euripides' emphasis was upon ideas rather than character, intellectual stimulation rather than aesthetics.   Moral satisfaction in his plays was not intended to
come easily if at all, and any number of unsolved problems
created discomfort in order to influence social behavior.
Hence the universe created by Euripides would often be susceptible of irrationality or incomprehension.   To "incomprehension" the chorus of the Hippolytus gives typical expression:
"The care of God for us is a great thing, if a man believe
it at heart:... / So I have a secret hope / of someone, a
God, who is wise and plans; / but my hopes grow dim when
I see / the deeds of men and their destinies.   / For fortune
always veers and the currents of life are shifting, / shifting,
forever changing course. "   To "irrationality" Talthybius in
the Hecuba gives more certain expression: "That you look
on men and care?   Or do we, holding that the gods exist, /

deceive ourselves with unsubstantial dreams / and lies,
while random careless chance and change / alone control
the world?" And in the Alcestis both statements seem firmly countered by "God finds a way for what none foresaw,"
for which Browning might have had a ready substitute in
"God moves in a mysterious way." Perhaps unnoticed by
the more optimistic Browning, it is, as Arrowsmith says,
the chance of these thoughts by Euripides to be eliminated
in the movement of the play, but it would be strange if
Browning had missed also the possibility of rejection by
Euripides of an ordered universe, personal responsibility,
and divine providence. No doubt the similarity Browning
thought he had found between Euripides and St. Paul (Paul
quotes Euripides in I Corinthians xv. 33) influenced his loyalty, but that twenty-four hundred years before Browning Euripides had reached a conclusion Browning interpreted as being
also his own was probably the weightier influence. That
conclusion, to which Browning came early and never departed, was that man's wisdom is foolishness in the eyes of God.
Certainly, Browning could never have established an alliance
with Euripides on his confusing fatalism, or his impassable
gulfs in life--young and old, man and god, women and men--
attributed to a malevolent fate. But the striking differences,
if Browning was fully aware of them, did not prevent him
from thinking, as G. M. A. Grube asserts, "that Euripides
the atheist... is a myth" (p. 47).

    If Arrowsmith is correct in believing that "Euripides'
crucial dramatic device is the juxtaposition and contrast of
logos (theory) and ergon (fact)," then the strongest opposition
in the dramatic form would naturally occur between theory
and fact, as Euripides reasoned, between "the Word" and
fact, as Browning very probably translated the Greek logos
and ergon. For it would not have been easy for Browning,
indoctrinated as he was by the philosophical elements of St.
John's Gospel, to see logos as "theory" and the opposite of
truth [fact]. Euripides, Arrowsmith states, "everywhere insists upon scrupulous and detailed recreation of the complexity of reality and the difficulty of moral judgment" (p. 24).
Or, as Thomas G. Rosenmeyer understands the Bacchae,
Browning may have been caught by the manner in which
"Euripides exploits the Dionysiac revels to produce a dramatic action which helps the spectators to consider the mystery and the precariousness of their existence" (p. 151).
That is, with the compelling belief the Bacchae is a forerunner of the Platonic dialogues, Rosenmeyer sees "a poet's
attempt to give shape... to a complex of uncertainties and

puzzles which do not lend themselves to discursive treatment. "
Consequently, Rosenmeyer later says, "the ancient conven-
tions of tragedy stipulate that the dramatic nucleus be es-
sayed from a spectrum of approaches.... In the end the
various perspectives coalesce into one and invite a unified
though never simple audience response" (p. 153). Whereas
fragmentation of character in Euripides becomes a major
concern to Arrowsmith, the question of whether man is a
ravaging beast or "a gentler thing" concerns Rosenmeyer.
But, as Rosenmeyer adds, "this would be bloodless metaphysics" (p. 155) if Euripides had not seen that "man is both
beast and god, both savage and civilized,... The double nature of man is what the play is really about; ....
where man shelves the tools of reason and social compact
and abandons himself to instinct and natural law" (pp. 155,
157).

      With regard to the subject of a possible truth in the
works of Euripides, Arrowsmith observes:

> Euripidean theater is complex and uncomfortably
> strange,...Its premises...are unlike, and almost
> the inversion of, those of the traditional Greek
> theater. Typically it likes to conceal the truth
> beneath strata of irony because this is the look
> of truth: layered and elusive. For the same rea-
> son it presents its typical actions as problems and
> thereby involves the audience in a new relation,
> not as worshipers but as jurors who must resolve
> the problem by decision. But because the problem
> is usually incapable of outright resolution, is in
> fact tragic, the audience is compelled to forfeit
> the only luxury of making a decision--the luxury
> of knowing that one has decided wisely. (p. 30)

And scholarly Werner Jaeger, who approaches the dramatist
in a similar but more specific way than Arrowsmith, tells
us that Euripides "knew everything; no idea which ever came
into a human mind, sublimely religious or frankly frivolous,
was strange to him; and he could not chain himself to one
rationalist dogma" (Paideia, Vol. I [New York, 1945], 350).
He made Hecuba who had ceased to believe in the old deities
pray to a vision of the First Cause, Jaeger continues, but
we cannot "conclude that Euripides himself had a cosmic
religion, a faith in the ultimate justice of the world-process."
At the same time he presents the gods as real and powerful,
Euripides denies their existence and power. Hence the am-

biguity and, as Jaeger argues, the deep skepticism from
which flows the "vast resignation with which he views all
human acts and thoughts. " "He makes no attempt to follow
earlier poets in justifying the ways of God to man. ... Man is
now no longer able and willing to abandon himself to any view of
life which does not make himself... the ultimate standard.
And so this development ends with a paradox: at the moment
when his claim for freedom is loudest, man realizes that he
is completely unfree" (p. 354).   While insisting the religious
motif is subordinate and while defending Euripides against
attacks by those who charge him with his heroes' remarks,
Jaeger could not stress more forcefully the great knowledge
Euripides possessed on the irrational elements in the human
spirit.   Recognizing that no one has plumbed the problems
of religion more deeply than Euripides, Jaeger thus explains
why the world of Euripides is without faith.   But then, with
a personal reprieve for Euripides to which Browning might
not have objected, he questions: "Surely it is impossible not
to feel that, having understood so much and having seen so
deeply and sceptically into his age and his own soul, he
learnt how to praise the joy of humble faith in one of the
religious truths which pass all understanding, simply because
he himself had no such happy faith?" (pp. 355-356).   Understanding of this nature lends little credence to Altick's and
Loucks's belief that Browning may have been advocating "an
Arnoldian 'religion of humanity'" (p. 352) through his Euripides.   Or to their idea, also expressed by Honan, that Browning's Euripides is asking, "Why not a return to paganism?
My age... [was] less racked with doubt and misgiving" (p. 351).

       All in all the similarities one finds, or thinks he has
found, between Browning and Euripides must have weighed
heavily on the poet's decision to inject the Greek pagan into
The Ring and the Book.   Browning thought correctly that
Euripides was a lonely man but incorrectly that he was un-
popular and unappreciated.   He sensed in the ancient drama
that the time had resumed for a renewed struggle between
man and God, that Euripidean characters are instinctively
and irresistibly led to constant analysis and argument, and
that Euripides was a serious teacher (despite Jaeger's qualifications).   But with too sympathetic a bondage to the Greek's
delight in his own virtuosity, his superior psychological and
naturalistic bent, Browning perhaps missed the keen intellec-
tualism of play and playwright.   The evidence Jaeger provides
that "defenders of modernism always rallied round the name
of Euripides" (p. 338) is illuminating, even if Jaeger somewhat shades his argument by concluding with perfect certainty

that Euripides was an out-and-out intellectual because of the
strong family resemblance among the intellectualists he puts
on the stage.   In seeing the casualties Euripides mirrors of
his disruptive time--destruction of classical drama, of the
old mythical cosmology with the culture it sustained, and of
the sense of community in the city-state--Browning could
have compared them with casualties of his own age, even
those of his Pope's.   Yet Browning may still have misplaced
a great part of the skepticism of Euripides, especially that
directed at irrationality, not rationality; this I think Browning may also have done for St. Paul.   Either way, as Sir
Henry Jones argues, an unavoidable paradox of Browning's
poetry is his strange confidence in rationalizing the irrationality of human thought.   That Browning's admiration of Euripides was genuine and his imitation unconcealed seem substantiated.   But we should also remember that Browning could
have come to his practices and malpractices entirely on his
own, or with the aid of a composite Greek, which is precisely what he makes of the Pope's Euripides.   Conjured up not
altogether unlike Aristophanes' Aeschylus, Browning's Euripides is granted authorship of the noblest of all Hellenic
thought--"Some 'Know thyself' or 'Take the golden mean!'"
And much that Browning was reading into Euripides he had
beforehand read out of St. John, St. Paul, or Platonic sentiments such as the following:

> We have found, they will say, a path of speculation
> which seems to bring us and the argument to the
> conclusion, that while we are in the body, and
> while the soul is mingled with this mass of evil,
> our desire will not be satisfied, and our desire is
> of the truth.   For the body is a source of endless
> trouble to us by reason of the mere requirement of
> food; and also is liable to diseases which overtake
> and impede us in the search after truth: and by
> filling us so full of loves, and lusts, and fears,
> and fancies, and idols, and every sort of folly,
> prevents our ever having, as people say, so much
> as a thought.   For whence come wars, and fight-
> ings, and factions?   whence but from the body and
> the lusts of the body?   For wars are occasioned
> by the love of money, and the money has to be ac-
> quired for the sake and in the service of the body;
> and in consequence of all these things the time
> which ought to be given to philosophy is lost.   More-
> over, if there is time and an inclination toward phil-
> osophy, yet the body introduces a turmoil and con-

fusion and fear into the course of speculation, and
hinders us from seeing the truth; and all experience
shows that if we would have pure knowledge of anything we must be quit of the body, and the soul in
herself must behold all things in themselves: then
I suppose that we shall attain that which we desire,
and of which we say that we are lovers, and that
is wisdom; not while we live, but after death, as
the argument shows; for if while in company with
the body, the soul cannot have pure knowledge, one
of two things seems to follow--either knowledge is
not to be attained at all, or, if at all, after death.
For then, and not till then, the soul will be in herself alone and without the body.   In this present
life, I reckon that we make the nearest approach
to knowledge when we have the least possible concern or interest in the body, and are not satu-
rated with the bodily nature, but remain pure until
the hour when God himself is pleased to release us.
And then the foolishness of the body will be cleared
away and we shall be pure and hold converse with
other pure souls, and know of ourselves the clear
light everywhere; and this is surely the light of
truth.   ("Phaedo," The Dialogues of Plato, trans.
B. Jowett, I [New York, 1889], 392-393)

As would be expected, the intuitive tie between Browning and
Euripides did not long go unnoted by his commentators.   Nor
did whatever weak claim Browning held on mysticism evade
comparison with the finest expressions of Euripidean mysticism.   As has often been said, the permanent key to both
men may with assurance be placed in their realism and their
devotion to truth.   But not until our own turbulent days have
scholars so described Euripides that they seem in many ways
to be verifying the reading Browning made largely on his own.

I have never quite cared for the pall Browning's philosophical and religious verse or Sir Henry Jones's Browning
as a Philosophical and Religious Teacher casts over the last
twenty years of the poet's career, but they are outspoken
verse too few critics read and a formidable book which seem
to defy a satisfactory way through which Browning may be
extricated from the admissions of his own pen.   Up to the
present time, our best hope for the weakening of both forces
rests in the activity of Philip Drew and Norton B. Crowell,
the inactivity of the "Coleridgeans," who will have to show
that Browning followed Pauline and Platonic dualism and was

actively familiar with the Wordsworth-Coleridge notion that
we must use our total consciousness to obtain knowledge.   It
is surprising that Philip Drew thinks it possible in a brief
article to rescind Jones's "incalculable influence, " but he
pretends to ("Henry Jones on Browning's Optimism, " The
Browning Critics, ed. Boyd Litzinger and K. L. Knicker-
bocker [Lexington, 1967], pp. 364-380).   Deposing, as he
should, all dramatic elements as proof of Browning's own
thought, Drew says that Jones makes no attempt to consider
the whole of Browning's writings on religion and philosophy;
consequently, too few of the pertinent poems are examined
and too many of the isolated lines are exploited in disregard
of the main line of thought.   But Drew is wrong, and if one
could not prove he has wrestled with various parts of Jones's
book, he might conclude that Drew had not read the book
from beginning to end.   In closer conformity with Jones's
stipulated objective--that of dealing with the later poems and
Browning's agnosticism concerning knowledge--it may be said
that Jones pushes Browning into an occasional extremity of
statement for which a more reasonable explanation may be
submitted.   Yet "in the boldness of his affirmatives and neg-
atives" Browning must be held responsible for the statements
unless their meaning can be shown to be less extreme than
Jones makes it.   What other major poet, and Browning very
much wanted to be a major poet, has allowed himself the
freedom of exposing all his doubts, hopes, and premonitions
in open forum?   Hence the unfortunate practice which enabled
Hoxie Fairchild and George Santayana to hang mischievous
slogans on Browning's slenderest branches.

    And Drew is wrong in saying Jones adopts paraphrases
and simplifications of Browning's lines in order to erect an
abstract of the poet's thought so that he may proceed to de-
molish it.   Before abstracting the thought, if he does in a
particular instance, Jones has normally written a whole chapter in which he deals in depth with each of the topics which
reappear in the so-called abstract (the table of contents reveals this).   It cannot be missed, though Drew at first denies
it, that each chapter is built on a plan whereby the development of Browning's thought is carefully outlined and often
praised, his poetry fully analyzed and admirably appreciated;
indeed, almost all of Drew's initial charges are retracted at
the end of his essay.   Contrary then to Drew's early unsubstantiated generalizations, Jones limits his study strictly to
the philosophical poems, and he does not admit need for a
broader approach to his study or fail to comment discerningly
on the strength of Browning's great body of poetry.   Jones

pointedly says the poet and the philosopher cannot be answered by the same arguments, but he then proves that
Browning avidly elects philosophical discourse (so does Browning himself).   Jones is not concerned always to avoid recognition of men as individuals, as in a footnote Drew confesses;
and Jones, as Drew generously admits later of Chapters VI
and XI and of Jones's full treatment of the poet's theory of
love, illuminates poems and provides excellent analyses
throughout the volume in a manner which bespeaks complete
familiarity and understanding.   With the possible exception
of Paracelsus, Jones nevertheless sees from the beginning
in Browning's poetry latent signs of doubt concerning the
validity of human knowledge, and this judgment he also bases
on a broad representation of the poet's writing.   So Drew is
on very unsure ground when he permits himself to accuse
Jones of "setting a snippet from one poem against a snippet
from another," or to misapply Jones's language as he does
with "I do not stay to enquire," when his own best answer is
often, "But this is not so," period.

     Perhaps the best illustrations of snipocracy are Drew's
own.   After a little more than six printed pages, he writes:
"So much for Professor Jones's presentation of Browning's
'philosophy': I turn now to his attempts to refute it."   Then
with less than a half page given to "a central passage of the
book" (pp. 237-41), he grows more interested in considering
Jones's treatment of "Browning's difficulty in reconciling perfect knowledge with moral responsibility" (p. 372) and quotes
the following unitalicized sentences:

> It is impossible to conceive how the conduct of a
> being who is moral would be affected by absolute
> knowledge; or, indeed, to conceive the existence
> of such a being.   For morality, as the poet insists,
> is a process in which an ideal is gradually realized
> through conflict with the actual--an actual which it
> both produces and transmutes at every stage of the
> progress.   But complete knowledge would be above
> all process.   Hence we should have, on Browning's
> hypothesis, to conceive of a being in whom perfect
> knowledge was combined with an undeveloped will.
> A being so constituted would be an agglomerate of
> utterly disparate elements, the interaction of which,
> in a single character, it would be impossible to
> make intelligible. (Jones, pp. 291-292; quoted by
> Drew as pp. 310-311)

In an acknowledged side issue, and a step beyond Drew and
Browning's belief "that the failure of knowledge is a necessary condition of the moral life, " Jones here briefly argues
that Browning's strict view in "Rephan" admits of a very
easy refutation because it takes us beyond all possible human
experience and value of assertion.   Yet Jones's paragraph is
turned into nonsense by deletion of the italicized sentences.
Neither Browning (by quotation) nor Jones is here saying that
"we cannot conceive moral responsibility coexisting with complete knowledge and must therefore suppose that lack of certain knowledge is a necessary condition of moral development
and thus is not irreconcilable with the idea of a just God"
(p. 372).   Jones is saying that with Browning's insistence
upon process, that is, conflict and development, perfect
knowledge would have to be combined with an undeveloped
will.   This is the being so constituted as "an agglomerate
of utterly disparate elements" that he would, incidentally, be
without interest, even in a God, just or otherwise.   On the
same page Drew summarily challenges Jones's philosophical
acumen: "In short he points out a celebrated metaphysical
dilemma. "   But that is not the philosopher's orderly way of
putting it down.   He says, "We are thus confronted with
what seems to be a contradiction: a trust and distrust in
knowledge" (Jones, p. 270).   Then, after doing justice to
the conflicting element, he shows by analogy with moral and
natural life that it is inconsistent and irrational of Browning
to distrust knowledge completely because of man's inability
to know everything.

A third and last example of Drew's method might be
considered an outrage, if it did not provide an opportunity
to demonstrate how formidable Jones's arguments really are
in the three paragraphs from which Drew quotes:

> In morality (as also is the case in knowledge) the
> moral ideal, or the objective law of goodness,
> grows in richness and fulness of content with the
> individual who apprehends it.   His moral world is
> the counterpart of his moral growth as a character.
> Goodness for him directly depends upon his recog-
> nition of it. ...   In morals, as in knowledge, the
> mind of man constructs its own world.   And yet,
> BOTH ALIKE, THE WORLD OF TRUTH AND THE
> WORLD OF GOODNESS EXIST ALL THE SAME
> WHETHER THE INDIVIDUAL KNOWS THEM OR
> NOT.   HE DOES NOT CALL THE MORAL LAW
> INTO BEING, BUT FINDS IT WITHOUT, AND

THEN REALIZES IT IN HIS OWN LIFE.   The moral law does not vanish and reappear with its recognition by mankind.   IT IS NOT SUBJECT TO THE
CHANCES AND CHANGES OF ITS LIFE, BUT IT
IS A GOOD IN ITSELF THAT IS ETERNAL.   (pp.
280-281)

BEING INDEPENDENT OF MAN, CAN IT THERE-
FORE BE INDEPENDENT OF ALL INTELLIGENCE?
CAN GOODNESS BE ANYTHING BUT THE LAW OF
A SELF-CONSCIOUS BEING?   IS IT THE QUALITY
OR MOTIVE OR IDEAL OF A MERE THING?
MANIFESTLY NOT.   ITS RELATION TO SELF-
CONSCIOUSNESS IS ESSENTIAL.   With the extinc-
tion of self-consciousness all moral goodness is
extinguished.

The same holds true of reality.   THE QUESTION
OF REALITY OR UNREALITY OF THINGS CANNOT
ARISE EXCEPT IN AN INTELLIGENCE.

Now, as Drew rearranges the thought of three consecutive
paragraphs from Jones, this quotation without the capitalized
words does seem "indistinguishable from the subjectivism
which Jones criticized in Browning, although it will be observed that the sentence I [Drew] have italicized runs counter
to the rest of the argument" (p. 372).   And as the sentence
italicized by Drew admittedly runs counter, so do the capitalized thoughts.   Drew understood well enough that Professor
Jones is talking about the moral law and intelligence, the
necessity of knowing, not about subjectivism.   In these and
other of his elliptical replies, Drew scarcely convinces us
that Jones's production of logical dilemma "shows not the
confusion of Browning's thought but the unsoundness of Jones's
method" (p. 371).

It may be hoped, however, that Drew will renew the
investigation he tired of much too quickly. [4]   With the kind
of well-ordered and spaciously documented grounds he incorrectly denied Jones, he has the task of showing wherein to
Browning "the individual [is] the very foundation stone of all
knowledge. "   Wherein Browning "constantly makes the distinction between certain knowledge and religious faith, " and
wherein Jones persists in misunderstanding Browning's vital
distinction.   Wherein Browning continually insists on the need
"for each individual to discover the truth for himself. "   The
statement Drew makes at the beginning of section V of his

essay is not proof he has shown that Jones's method is de-
fective, his effect infinitely harmful. Indeed Drew's explanation of Browning's belief that nothing can be proved sounds
much like Jones's superior comments on the same matter.
But the point is something else: on the assumption that nothing can be proved, Browning accepted love as a human and
divine attribute; on the same assumption, he made knowledge
a purely human attribute. As frankly as Drew, Jones asserts
that in the great body of Browning's earlier poetry the philosophical and religious speculations are "not an impulsive and
emotional denial of man's intellectual responsibilities but a
constant awareness of his intellectual limitations" (p. 379).
Drew forgets, however, that in Jones's most succinct and
summary paragraph he is judging only the late poems:

> If he acknowledges that the highest revealed itself
> to man, on the practical side, as love; he does
> not see that it has also manifested itself to man
> on the theoretical side, as reason. The self-
> communication of the Infinite is incomplete; love
> is a quality of God, intelligence a quality of man;
> hence, on one side, there is no limit to achieve-
> ment, but on the other there is impotence. Human
> nature is absolutely divided against itself; and the
> division, as we have already seen, is not between
> flesh and spirit, but between a love which is God's
> own and perfect, and an intelligence which is
> merely man's and altogether weak and deceptive.
> (Jones, p. 288)

In response to Jones's analysis of Browning's theory of
knowledge, Drew does not satisfactorily answer a charge
which is the product of a study so prolonged and so scrupu-
lously undertaken that "the world's leading Browning scholars"
(p. 389) may rightly consider it detailed, sympathetic, profound, judicious, and brilliant. And once Drew's irritation--
as was undoubtedly the case with DeVane, Charlton, Raymond,
and Tracy--is partially assuaged, he generously concedes an
irrationality in Browning's optimism as well as in his ethical
and metaphysical speculations.

Effectively objecting to Jones's manner of preempting
the poet's words of meaning Browning must have intended
them to convey, Drew could also have contrasted this practice with the liberty Jones takes in expanding the meaning
of his own words. For, as Drew says, "love" to Browning
comes almost to stand for everything that is valuable in life,

and "knowledge" as utilized in the many casuistic poems is
not the knowledge Browning wished to honor.   But Browning
did write much too loosely about love, the head or heart,
and the heart-sickening limitations of knowledge.   And though
Drew tries admirably, he does not prove that Jones refers
to "nescience" in La Saisiaz merely as if it were a theory
of knowledge, when he says Jones fails to see that the thought
actually occurs as a postulate in an unresolved debate between Fancy and Reason (p. 370). [5]   There is more to the
use of "nescience" than either Drew or Jones expresses,
and the confusion may be confounded by a more nearly
"main-line" thought on the subject of hope, which falters
badly before the Arch Fear of an unknowable hereafter.   Yet
it remains imperative to seek for fuller explanations of many
of Jones's tightly woven thoughts: for example, what is the
difference between Jones's "priority of the heart" and Browning's "reliance in the heart"?   (p. 312) wherein specifically
did Browning believe human knowledge different in nature
from the knowledge of God? (pp. 299, 325) wherein did
Browning not assume an intuitive power of knowing right
from wrong?   (p. 297) why could not the relation of knowledge and conduct be more adequately discussed? (p. 295)
and what does Jones mean by "the faith, which he professed,
was not the faith that anticipates and invites proof, but a
faith which is incapable of proof"? (p. 322)   These questions
or similar ones both Drew and Crowell dwell on, and they
should not let them go, even though Jones may have given
the last word in Chapter X, The Heart and the Head.   Drew's
belief that Browning was content to indicate a disharmony
where Jones imposes a rigid pattern is also essential to
meeting Jones, and Drew's two references to Coleridge may
be a leap others have delayed too long taking.   Browning
knew as well as Jones that the "heart," symbolically interpreted, "is the intensest unity of the complex experiences of
a whole life, " (p. 309) while "reason" is taken merely as a
faculty which invents arguments and provides evidences.
Even though in his late poetry Browning catapulted his
thought into a verbal truancy Jones will not permit us to
forget, it does not seem logical, if philosophically sound,
for Jones in an important argument to deny Browning full
acceptance of "I know Him whom I have believed" (p. 306).
If, in all Christian literature, there is an ultimate expression of the total man's faith, it must be these words.   Here
Browning's mature judgment and the body of all his poetry
seem to rise to his defense.   If, therefore, as Jones so
forcefully argues, Browning is given in old age to a nescience
which grew with unaccountable rapidity and dumbfounding pro-

portions from earlier days, we still have, as Jones reminds us, the poetry of the poet which counts. Perhaps, as exemplified in the Pope's monologue, Browning feared more and more a new age of doubt. The creation of Guido alone is sufficient evidence to establish within Browning's own nature a struggle between belief in the reality of evil and the illusion of evil. And the determination not to still his own intellectual opposition to a changing world proves he continued to rely on his own mind, even though the gloom of his outlook upon the knowledge of others is not to be dispelled by thoughts of his better days. One might wish that with reference to Browning's theory of evil he had taken the advice he imputed to Euripides: "And least inquisitive where search least skills, / I' the nature we best give the clouds to keep" (1758-59). It will not be an easy task to disprove much of what Jones says, but whatever the effort scholars will come short of success if they fall back on Browning's being a poet and consequently unprepared for philosophical backbiting. He was neither philosopher nor theologian, but he was permanently interested in a philosophy and a religion of life he both coveted and intensely wished to share with his readers.

That Drew finds the substance of Jones's book distasteful is not to be regretted. By thinking of one of the most serious unresolved issues of Browning criticism, he joins the "Coleridgeans" in their dissent with Jones and, for better or worse, Crowell in his defense of Browning. Much less disposed than Drew to contradict Jones in a rational manner, Crowell sets the philosopher up as a sworn enemy to his hero Browning and an evil cohort of A. C. Pigou. Nevertheless, Crowell may be on the trail of a weakness in Jones's position earlier critics were overpowered by his orderly documentation and logic into slighting. Crowell should be read for his treatment of an area of research which may rightly become the richest field for contemporary criticism of The Ring and the Book. He would open, if only by a hairsbreadth, the gate to perhaps the one remaining major dilemma of the poet's life and art, and this act is better than Drew's attempt to fix and lock it. His division of study is no more assured of success than Drew's, but he may have instituted the beginning of a serious and prolonged investigation of Browning's intellectual agnosticism which will prove or disprove Jones's conclusions.

There is no need to illustrate the exaggerations of Crowell's language, but it should be shown that the same practice overtakes his method and thought. Like Drew, he

documents least when the urgency is greatest, but more
rashly and from a single quotation he jumps oftener to such
statements as "It is significant that Browning never actually
says that evil is illusion" (The Convex Glass, p. 53); "It is
significant that not once in anything Browning wrote is there
the slightest support for Jones's belief that he must have
found religion and morality in conflict" (p. 164); "The central idea in Browning [is] of the endless search for truth,
the ultimate goal, along with love" (p. 195); "There is no
injunction that all men agree on the nature of truth or God"
(pp. 219-220). Such words as "inept," "lamentable," and
"disastrous"; such phrases as "memorable imperception,"
"bemused by Jones," "sign of Jones," and "grand source of
error"; such generalizations as "This passage, which seems
perfectly clear, has proved inscrutable since its composition"
and "If scholars hold that Browning intends to convey the
theme that since man has only partial truth he should scorn
truth and give up the struggle" (pp. 200, 196)--all of these
combinations stipulate that beyond Crowell's partisanship is
a pugnaciousness which authorship of three books should have
cured. Though several paragraphs of my Essay Three are
devoted to the subject, Crowell wishes I had said something
about Browning's holding "knowledge" to be relative and always imperfect, consequently recognizing that his own interpretations were relative, imperfect, and individual. No more
than Langbaum does Crowell remember that Browning's fact
which falls like a stone in a pool was not the unstable element in the poet's illustration (I. 840); that it was the re-
fractory feeling for fact which went astray. Crowell would
like to retain my interpretation of the metaphor, Smalley's
ambiguity on fidelity to fact, and Langbaum's theory on relativistic truth, but this is all to the side, if he can prove
Jones wrong.

In his chapter on Browning's optimism (pp. 161-181),
Crowell, who seems to be writing independently of Drew, di-
rectly challenges the thought of two paragraphs by Jones on
Browning's belief on morality:

> But now comes the great difficulty. How can the poet
> combine such earnestness in the moral struggle
> with so deep a conviction of the ultimate nothing-
> ness of evil, and of the complete victory of the
> good? Again and again we have found him pronounce
> such victory to be absolutely necessary and inevita-
> ble. His belief in God, his trust in His love and
> might, will brook no limit anywhere. His convic-

tion is <u>invincible</u> that the power of the good subjects
evil itself to its authority.   (1899, p. 112; Crowell's
1902 edition drops italicized words)

But what of its moral consequences? Religion,
when <u>fully manifested,</u> is the triumphant reconciliation of all contradictions.   It is optimism, the justification of things as the process of evolving the
good; and its peace and joy are just the outcome of
the conviction, won by faith, that the ideal is actual,
and that every detail of life is, in its own place,
illumined with divine goodness.   But morality is
the condemnation of things as they are, by reference to a conception of a good which ought to be.
The absolute identification of the actual and ideal
extinguishes morality, either in something lower or
in something higher.   But the moral ideal, when
reached, turns at once into a stepping-stone, a dead
self; and the good formulates itself anew as an ideal
in the future.   So that morality is the sphere of
discrepancy, and the moral life a progressive realization of a good that can never be complete.   It
would thus seem to be irreconcilably different from
religion, which must, in some way or other, find
the good to be present, actual, absolute, without
shadow of change, or hint of limit or imperfection.
(1899, p. 114; Crowell's 1902 edition substitutes
"thoroughly consistent" for italicized words)

In his reply to these two passages Crowell seems to get to
the crux of the dilemma Jones established between Browning's
religion and morality.   Like Crowell but with far less assurance, I find Jones's definitions of religion and morality at
odds with my own personal definitions.   That religion is optimistic for the individual seems clear enough; but that "its
peace and joy are just the outcome of the conviction, won by
faith, that the <u>ideal is actual,</u>" it has never occurred to me
to take seriously.   "There <u>is</u> such a thing as faith," Crowell
responds, "and mystery has often heightened piety, not abol-
ished it" (p. 164).   And I understand Crowell to be drawing
a sharp distinction between "the faith" of the philosopher and
of the religious person.   In Part V of his essay Drew reaches a somewhat similar opinion of this aspect of Jones's
thought: he believes that the weakest light of <u>Browning as a</u>
<u>Philosophical and Religious Teacher</u> is directed "on the ex-
tremely difficult point of the relation of Browning's metaphysical and epistemological views to his religious beliefs"

(p. 378). Many readers of Chapter X of Jones's book will
disagree and insist that Jones writes exhaustively on the matter, but the same chapter does reveal that Jones may have
attributed to Browning religious practices of the period the
poet had outgrown with the writing of "Saul. "[6] Yet the critics who convincingly and finally resolve the problems Browning left for Jones to elucidate will have to know Browning as
well as Jones did, an exacting assignment for all who did
not grow up in the milieu of Browning's poetic composition.

Perhaps only those scholars who believe Browning was
familiar with the thought of Coleridge, [7] and who do not ask
the same explanation for the presence of evil in the world,
will be able to disprove the Jonesian position on Browning's
agnosticism concerning human knowledge.   Their informal
arguments which are quite faithfully held approximate the
arguments Jones presents in his Chapter X and, though it
is not always remembered, he too is advocating a philosophical solution to Browning's dilemma albeit directly from the
Germanic origin.   Indeed, he follows German idealism so
closely that Drew chooses to condemn all of Jones's philosophical writing on the basis of his "defending Hegel by at-
tacking those who found Idealism simply a collection of 'pale
and vacant general ideas'" (p. 371).   Jones, who apparently
never considered his book an attack on Browning, therefore
deserves a better hearing than his detractors have yet been
willing to grant.   And only a constant progress with Jones
through the first nine chapters will make The Heart and the
Head chapter fully representative of his unusual cogency.
Jones opens the last chapter of his book by saying Browning
"means right--that, a child may understand, " and he closes
the chapter with probably the strongest expression of faith to
be found in all of Browning's poetry.   Throughout his book
Jones praises Browning for not compromising either his optimism or his faith in God, but he regrets that Browning
saw no way to compromise between morality and religion,
especially since Browning allowed movement in both faith and
morality.   Jones does apply the strictest definitions for Browning, and he does not always remain the philosopher himself
when discussing theology.   Some of the negative charges
against Jones seem valid, but in a just court of inquiry they
would not establish in Browning the wholesome respect for
human thought and speech Crowell and Drew would like others
to recognize.   If what Jones says in defining religion and
morality is philosophically correct, it still does not seem
to accord with the religious attitudes of any number of people.   But it is also possible that the dependence of these

people upon knowledge is of the same illusory significance Jones attributes to Browning's later years.   Faith can be proved to the satisfaction of the faithful, and the intellect, they seem often to believe, is also involved.   What Jones seems to ask of Browning is a rational conversion of the Pope's "isoscele deficient in the base" into an equilateral triangle, with God and man related in strength, intelligence, and love.   What Browning, the poet, seems most intent on is leaping over the philosopher's stool:

> --Ask Plato else! And this corroborates the sage,
> That Art, --which I may style the love of loving, rage
> Of knowing, seeing, feeling the absolute truth of things
> For truth's sake, whole and sole, not any good,
>   truth brings
> The knower, seer, feeler, beside, --instinctive Art
> Must fumble for the whole, once fixing on a part
> However poor, surpass the fragment, and aspire
> To reconstruct thereby the ultimate entire.
>   <u>Fifine at the Fair</u>, xliv

Notes

1.   To be added to the examples given in the essay of the Pope's condemnation of individual Christians and all mankind are lines 354, 385, 423, 577, 673, 717, 926-930 (951), 965-985, 1014, 1035, 1061, 1214-15, 1234-38, 1241-42, 1297-1300, 1321, 1541, 1617, 1650, 1661-63, 1821-24, 1834-38, 1876-77, 1888-95, 1948, 1963-65, 1977, 1998-2001, 2114.

2.   One of Cook's strangest arguments pertains to his under-standing of Christian idealism: "[The Pope's] investigation of the Guido-Pompilia tragedy has shown him that he moves in a world in which the ideal of that [ecclesiastical] system is worlds away from realization" (pp. 200-201).   Nor is it improper to call attention to his use of "worlds away, " though he misconstrues the implication.

3.   Even more severely critical of Browning's practice, the anonymous author referred to in Essay Two, note 2, writes: 'He jumbles up its comic and tragic sides, and illustrates them by the first metaphors which come to hand, with the indifference of nature planting a hedgerow with nettles and honey suckles, roses and toadstools. "

4.   His <u>The Poetry of Browning</u> (London, 1970) does not

seem to fulfill the need for objective approach. With Chapter 9, which is a continuation of the now twice reprinted
1964 essay (Chapter 8), Drew supposes that in discussing
Browning's faith in God he is further answering Jones, but
Jones--who places less restriction on the poet's faith than
Drew--writes instead about Browning's loss of faith in human
knowledge. Drew also supposes that the Pope's judgment of
Guido is made while he speaks his monologue; that since
"there is no trace in his speech of respect for the Church"
(pp. 227-228), Pope Innocent contemns it; and that Euripides'
pointed question is no question at all, but a charge of corruption against the Church (pp. 229-230).

5.   For specific comments on nescience and theory of knowledge, see Jones, pp. 222-231, 326-327.

6.   Passages which indicate Jones may have associated
Browning too closely with the ordinary religious opinion of
the day appear on pages 298, 299, 307, 323, 327-328.

7.   A loyal "Coleridgean, " Maurice B. Cramer reminds us
that Maisie Ward brings Browning's "position close to Coleridge's in Biographia Literaria" ("Maisie Ward and Browning
Biography: A New Era, " Modern Philology, 86 [February
1971], 294-300).

BROWNING'S COMPLETE USE OF THE WORD TRUTH
IN THE RING AND THE BOOK

Thought to mean fact unless noted as absolute (A),
poetic (P), ironic (I), or uncertain (?)

BOOK I (THE POET)

1. I had mastered the contents, knew the whole truth
   Gathered together, bound up in this book,   I. 117f

2. So, in this book lay absolutely truth,
   Fanciless fact, the documents indeed,   I. 143f

3. This is the bookful; thus far take the truth,
   The untempered gold, the fact untampered with,
   The mere ring-metal ere the ring be made!...
   .... Was this truth of force?
   Able to take its own part as truth should,   I. 364ff

4. Truth must prevail, the proverb vows; and truth
   --Here is it all i' the book at last, as first
   There it was all i' the heads and hearts of Rome
   I. 413ff

5. I took my book to Rome first, tried truth's power
   On likely people. "Have you met such names?
   "Is a tradition extant of such facts?   I. 423ff

6. From the book, yes; thence bit by bit I dug
   The lingot truth, that memorable day,   I. 458f

7. After the day when, --truth grasped and gained, --
   The book was shut and done with and laid by
   I. 471f

8. Vex truth a little longer:--less and less, (?) I. 658

9. Lovers of dead truth, did ye fare the worse?
   Lovers of live truth, found ye false my tale?
   (P) I. 696f

195

10.   Well now; there's nothing in nor out o' the world
       Good except <u>truth</u>: yet this, the something else,   (?)
       What's this then, which proves good yet seems untrue?
       This that I mixed with <u>truth</u>, motions of mine
                                                   L 698ff

11.   Why did the mage say, --feeling as we are wont
       For <u>truth</u>, and stopping midway short of <u>truth,</u>   (?)
       And resting on a lie, --"I raise a ghost"?   L 742ff

12.   --No dose of purer <u>truth</u> than man digests,   (A)
       But <u>truth</u> with falsehood, milk that feeds him now, (A)
       Not strong meat he may get to bear some day--
                                                   L 830ff

13.   Say, Half-Rome's feel after the vanished <u>truth</u>;
       Honest enough, as the way is: all the same,
       Harbouring in the centre of its sense
       A hidden germ of failure, shy but sure,
       To neutralize that honesty and leave
       That feel for <u>truth</u> at fault, as the way is too....
       So leads arm waveringly, lets fall wide
       O' the mark its finger, sent to find and fix
       <u>Truth</u> at the bottom, that deceptive speck. L 847ff

14.   --All for the <u>truth's</u> sake, mere <u>truth</u>, nothing else!
                                                   L 881

15.   Next, from Rome's other half, the opposite feel
       For <u>truth</u> with a like swerve, like unsuccess, --
                                                   L 883f

16.   Find the accused ripe for declaring <u>truth</u>. L 953

17.   The obtuser sense <u>truth</u> fails to satisfy;   L 959

18.   Even so; they were wont to tease the <u>truth</u>
       Out of loth witness (toying, trifling time)
       By torture: 't was a trick, a vice of the age,
                                                   L 981ff

19.   To unhusk <u>truth</u> a-hiding in its hulls,
       "...Henceforth find <u>truth</u> by milder means!"
                                                   L 989, 1009

20.   And ignore law, the recognized machine,...
       Framed to unchoke, pump up and pour apace

Truth till a flowery foam shall wash the world?
The patent truth-extracting process, --ha?   I. 1110ff

21. While life was graspable and gainable,
     And bird-like buzzed her wings round Guido's brow,
     Not much truth stiffened out the web of words
     He wove to catch her: when away she flew
     And death came, death's breath rivelled up the lies,
     Left bare the metal thread, the fibre fine
     Of truth, i' the spinning: the true words shone last.
                                               I. 1275ff

      Note: Used 25 times, the words fact (18) and true (7)
contribute to the impression that to Browning in Book I truth
(used 33 times) means fact or alleged fact (both demonstrable
and indemonstrable) save in 8, 9 (poetic), 10, 11, where
meaning is uncertain, and 12, where meaning as in the biblical analogy is absolute and casts a dark shadow over the
accessibility of truth through partial, misused, and falsified
facts.   The double-edge "Vex truth" in 8 suggests the Book
of Revelations, where Satan shall be loosed to deceive the
nations a little longer.

                 BOOK II (GUIDO'S HALF-ROME)

1.   (Will you have the truth?)   whereof we see effect.
                                               II. 157

2.   You take your stand on truth ere leap your lie:
     Here was all lie, no touch of truth at all,
     All the lie hers--   II. 554ff

3.   She woke, saw, sprang upright
     I' the midst and stood as terrible as truth, (I)
                                               II. 1029f

4.   Let law shine forth and show, as God in heaven,
     Vice prostrate, virtue pedestalled at last,
     The triumph of truth!   (I)   II. 1085ff

5.   "And strange disguisings whereby truth seems false,
                                               II. 1411

      Note: Used 19 times, the words fact (10) and true (9)
contribute to the impression that to Guido's Half-Rome truth
(used 6 times) means fact or alleged fact save in 3 and 4

where the use is ironic.

BOOK III (POMPILIA'S HALF-ROME)

1. <u>Truth</u> lies between: there   's anyhow a child
    Of seventeen years,   whether a flower, or weed,
                                        III.   83f

2. --let us avouch, / Since <u>truth</u> is best,   III.   296f

3. Quickened by penury and pretentious hate
    Of plain <u>truth</u>, brutify and bestialize,   III.   523f

4. "And telling <u>truth</u> relieves a liar like you, III.   607

5.   <u>truth</u> being <u>truth,</u>
    Tell it and shame the devil!   III.   611f

6. And still six witnesses survived in Rome
    To prove the <u>truth</u> o' the tale)--   III.   655f

7. Or say it were no lie at all but <u>truth,</u>   III.   662

8. How, in this phase of the affair, show <u>truth</u>?
    Here is the dying wife who smiles and <u>says</u>
    "So it was, --so it was not, --...
    Confessor Celestino groans '"T is <u>truth,</u>
    "All <u>truth</u> and only <u>truth</u>:   there's something here,
    "Some presence in the room beside us all,
    "Something that every lie expires before:...
    . . . .
    How can she render service to the <u>truth</u>? III.   791ff

9. Whom foes and friends alike avouch, for good
    Or ill, a man of <u>truth</u> whate'er betide,...
    . . . .
    Should yet maintain, for <u>truth's</u> sake which is God's, (A)
    That it was not he made the first advance, III.   885ff

10. For <u>truth's</u> sake did assert and re-assert
    Those letters called him to her and he came,
                                        III.   929f

11. --I say, --why should the man tell <u>truth</u> just now
    When graceful lying meets such ready shrift?
                                        III.   938f

12.   "If, with the midday blaze of <u>truth</u> above,   (A)
                                                      III. 1365

        Note: Used 9 times, the words fact (7) and true (2)
contribute to the impression that to Pompilia's Half-Rome
truth (used 18 times) means fact or alleged fact (demonstrable,
indemonstrable, or lie) save in 9 and 12 which suggest absolute truth.

BOOK IV (TERTIUM QUID)

1.   "Now for the Trial!" they roar: "the Trial to test
       "The <u>truth</u>, weigh husband and weigh wife alike...
       <u>Truth</u> the divinity must needs descent   (I)
       And clear things at the play's fifth act--aha!
                                                      IV. 12ff

2.   It proved to be the impossible thing itself,
       <u>Truth</u> and not sham: hence ruin to them all.
                                                      IV. 353f

3.   That in the Countship was a <u>truth</u>, but in
       The counting up of the Count's cash, a lie. IV. 492f

4.   Such naked <u>truth</u> while chambered in the brain
                                                      IV. 519

5.   "There's not one <u>truth</u> in this your odious tale
                                                      IV. 619

6.   Guido, --whose cue is to dispute the <u>truth</u>
       O' the tale, reject the shame it throws on him,
                                                      IV. 652

7.   That is, submit him to their statement's <u>truth</u>,
                                                      IV. 742

8.   Eve's... no, not Eve's, since Eve, to speak
                      the <u>truth</u>, ...
       When simply <u>saying</u> in her own defence
       "The serpent tempted me and I did eat. "   IV. 852ff

9.   Not he! the <u>truth</u> was felt by instinct here,   (I)
       --Process which saves a world of trouble and time.
       There's the priest's story: what do you say to it,
       Trying its <u>truth</u> by your own instinct too,   (I)
                                                      IV. 1006ff

10.   "Whose whole career was lie entailing lie
       "Sought to be sealed <u>truth</u> by the worst lie last!"
                                              IV. 1058f

11.   Time to confess and get her own soul saved--
       But time to make the <u>truth</u> apparent, <u>truth</u>
       For God's sake, lest <u>men</u> should believe a lie:...
       With this hope in her head, of telling <u>truth,</u>
                                              IV. 1428ff

12.   In <u>truth</u> you look as puzzled as ere I preached!
                                              IV. 1580

13.   The long and the short is, <u>truth</u> seems what I show:--...
       It seems unduly harsh to put the man
       To the torture, as I hear the court intends,
       Though readiest way of twisting out the <u>truth</u>; IV. 1618ff

       Note: Used 15 times, the words fact (9) and true (6)
contribute to the impression that to Tertium Quid truth (used
18 times) means fact or alleged fact (usually a lie) save in
1 and 9, which are ironic, and 8 and 12, which are inter-
jectional.

BOOK V (COUNT GUIDO)

1.   you want no more
       Than right interpretation of the same,
       And <u>truth</u> so far--am I to understand?...
       Whatever the good-will in me. Now for <u>truth</u>!
                                              V. 113ff

2.   I want no more impulsion to tell <u>truth</u>
       From the other trick, the torture inside there!
                                              V. 844f

3.   "Let me, a man, manfully meet the fact,
       "Confront the worst o' the <u>truth,</u> end, and have peace!
                                              V. 1391f

4.   "One more concession, one decisive way
       "And but one, to determine thee the <u>truth,</u> V. 1615f

5.   I knocked, pronounced
       The name, the predetermined touch for <u>truth,</u>
                                              V. 1628f

6.   When you dismiss me, having truth enough!
                                                V. 1681

7.   You, lords, never will you say
      "Such is the nullity of grace and truth,   (I)
      "Such the corruption of the faith,   V. 1835ff

8.   Shall see truth yet triumphant, justice yet (I)
      A victor in the battle of this world!   V. 2024f

9.   "I' the necessary process, --just a trip
      "O' the torture-irons in their search for truth,
                                                V. 2056f

      Note: Used 24 times, the words fact (11) and true
(13) contribute to the impression that to Guido truth (used
10 times) means fact or alleged fact save in 7 and 8 which
are ironic.   Guido prefers to counter the truth of others
with charges of lie, lies, wrong.

                BOOK VI (CAPONSACCHI)

1.   Burn my soul out in showing you the truth. VI. 149

2.   Let me, in heaven's name, use the very snuff
      O' the taper in one last spark shall show truth
      For a moment, show Pompilia who was true!
                                                VI. 170ff

3.   With honest hearts: they easily may err,
      But in the main they wish well to the truth.
                                                VI. 209f

4.   Nowise, to make you disbelieve me now.
      I need that you should know my truth.   VI. 341f

5.   "How should he dream of you?   I told you truth:
      "He goes to the villa at Vittiano--   VI. 590f

6.   And saw right through the thing that tried to pass
      For truth and solid, not an empty lie: VI. 926f

7.   "All by the mistress-messenger!   As I
      "Recognized her, at potency of truth,   (?)
      "So she, by the crystalline soul, knew me,
                                                VI. 931ff

8.   You must know that a man gets drunk with truth
      Stagnant inside him! Oh, they've killed her, Sirs!
                                                    VI. 1163f

9.   "To the lady's chamber! I presume you--men
      "Expert, instructed how to find out truth,
      "Familiar with the guise of guilt.   VI. 1509ff

10.   Then I took truth in, guessed sufficiently
      The service for the moment.   VI. 1570f

11.   The letters and verse looked hardly like the truth.
                                                    VI. 1734

12.   --That when at the last we did rush each on each,
      By no chance but because God willed it so--
      The spark of truth was stuck from out our souls-- (A)
                                                    VI. 1812ff

13.   Did not I say
      You were good and true at bottom? You see the truth--
                                                    VI. 1884f

14.   Conti had come here and told truth.   VI. 2036

15.   A good man! Will you make him Pope one day?
      Not that he is not good too, this we have--
      But old, --else he would have his word to speak,
      His truth to teach the world: I thirst for truth,
      But shall not drink it till I reach the source.
                                                    VI. 2064ff

16.   Forget distemperature and idle heat!
      Apart from truth's sake, what's to move so much?
                                                    VI. 2072f

      Note: Used 32 times, the words fact (13) and true (19)
contribute to the impression that to Caponsacchi truth (used
17 times) means fact or alleged fact save in 7, which is uncertain, and 12 and 15, where he, like only the poet, Pompilia, the Pope, and Celestino (if ridicule and hyperbole are
excluded) emphasizes a divine source of absolute truth.
Drunk with truth [fact], Caponsacchi counters alleged fact
with lie, lies, liars, false, falsehood.

BOOK VII (POMPILIA)

1. No father that he ever knew at all,
    Nor ever had--no, never had, I say!
    That is the truth, --nor any mother left,
    Out of the little two weeks that she lived,   VII. 91ff

2. There is the friend, --men will not ask about,
    But tell untruths of, and give nicknames to,
                                                        VII. 160f

3.   she, instead of piercing straight
    Through the pretence to the ignoble truth,   VII. 326f

4. Find nothing, this time, but was what it seemed,
    --All truth and no confusion any more.   VII. 336f

5. Then I began to half surmise the truth;
    Something had happened, low, mean, underhand,
    False, and my mother was to blame, and I
                                                        VII. 516ff

6. By one or two truths only--thence I hang,   VII. 604

7. The glory of his nature, I had thought,
    Shot itself out in white light, blazed the truth   (?)
    Through every atom of his act with me: VII. 921ff

8. Repeated the mere truth and held my tongue.
                                                        VII. 1035

9. "Even if you speak truth and a crime is planned,
                                                        VII. 1097

10. Since I say anything, say all if true!
    And how my life seems lengthened as to serve!
    It may be idle or inopportune,
    But, true?--why, what was all I said but truth,
    Even when I found that such as are untrue
    Could only take the truth in through a lie?
    Now--I am speaking truth to the Truth's self: (A)
    God will lend credit to my words this time.
                                                        VII. 1192ff

11. "Yes, come, and take a flower-pot on his head,
    "Flung from your terrace! No joke, sincere truth?"
                                                        VII. 1362f

12. "If it be truth, --why should I doubt it truth? VII. 1428

13. The neutralizer of all good and truth. (?) VII. 1596

14. Against the lightning! 'T was truth singed the lies (A)
     And saved me, not the vain sword nor weak speech!
                                              VII. 1640f

15. Therefore, since hate was thus the truth of him,
                                              VII. 1727

16. He had been here, displayed in my behalf
     The broad brow that reverberates the truth, (A)
                                              VII. 1795f

17. So, let him wait God's instant men call years;
     Meantime hold hard by truth and his great soul, (A)
                                              VII. 1841f

     Note: Used 18 times, the words true (16) and fact (2)
contribute to the impression that to Pompilia truth (used 21
times) means fact or alleged fact save that 10, 14, 16, 17
seem to mean absolute, 7 and 13 a double-edged truth.
Countering unfavorable truth [fact] with false, untrue, lies,
wrong, fault, falsehood, Pompilia is unique in using fact
only two times: 1) the fact she was compelled to cohabit
with Guido "could not be repressed" (1284); 2) the fact which
means so much is "The great life; see, a breath and it is
gone! / So is detached, so left all by itself / The little life"
(1746-48).

                    BOOK VIII (ARCHANGELIS)

1. He wants who can excogitate the truth,
    Give the result in speech, plain black and white,
                                              VIII. 107f

2. May disconcert you his presumptive truth! VIII. 397f

3. Quamvis etiam innocentum, though in truth VIII. 943

4. For who fails recognize the touching truth
    That these poor rustics bore no envy, hate,
                                              VIII. 1605f

5. Zealous for truth, a credit to his kind,   VIII. 1781

Note: Used 10 times, the words fact (7) and true (3) contribute to the impression that to Archangelis truth (used only 5 times) means simply fact or alleged fact.

BOOK IX (BOTTINIUS)

1. Less distinct, part by part, but in the whole
Truer to the subject, --the main central truth   (?)
And soul o' the picture, would my Judges spy, --
Not those mere fragmentary studied facts
Which answer to the outward frame and flesh--
Not this nose, not that eyebrow, the other fact
Of man's staff, woman's stole or infant's clout,
But lo, a spirit-birth conceived of flesh,
Truth rare and real, not transcripts, fact and false. (?)
                                          IX. 99ff

2. Say, --not to grasp a truth I can release   IX. 708

3.   Pagans held, we know,
Man always ought to aim at good and truth,
                                          IX. 779f

4. Surprised, then, in the garb of truth, perhaps,
Pompilia, thus opposed, breaks obstacle,   IX. 891f

5. (Blind as he was to truth in some respects)IX. 1033

6. As this were found at variance with my tale,
Falsified all I have adduced for truth,   IX. 1435f

7. Whom telling the crude truth about might vex,
                                          IX. 1473

8. To eliminate, display, make triumph truth!
What other prize than truth were worth the pains?
                                          IX. 1570f

Note: Used 19 times, the words fact (12) and true (7) contribute to the impression that to Bottinius truth (used 10 times) means fact or alleged fact save in 1, which accents the "central truth" a master painter captures. Like Archangelis, Bottinius counters truth [fact] with charges of false and lies.

BOOK X (THE POPE)

1. And glutted hunger on the <u>truth</u>, at last, --...
   <u>Truth</u>, nowhere, lies yet everywhere in these--
   Not absolutely in a portion, yet
   Evolvible from the whole: evolved at last
   Painfully, held tenaciously by me.   X. 226ff

2. Not so! Expect nor question nor reply
   At what we figure as God's judgment-bar!
   None of this vile way by the barren words
   Which, more than any deed, characterize
   Man as made subject to a curse: no speech--
   That still bursts o'er some lie which lurks inside,
   As the split skin across the coppery snake,
   And most denotes man! since, in all beside,
   In hate or lust or guile or unbelief,
   Out of some core of <u>truth</u> the excrescence comes,
   And, in the last resort, the man may urge
   "So was I made, a weak thing that gave way
   "To <u>truth</u>, to impulse only strong since true,
   "And hated, lusted, used guile, forwent faith. "
   But when man walks the garden of this world
   For his own solace, and, unchecked by law,
   Speaks or keeps silence as himself sees fit,
   Without the least incumbency to lie,
   --Why, can he tell you what a rose is like,
   Or how the birds fly, and not slip to false
   Though <u>truth</u> serve better? Man must tell his mate
   Of you, me and himself, knowing he lies,
   Knowing his fellow knows the same, --will think
   "He lies, it is the method of a man!"
   And yet will speak for answer "It is <u>truth</u>"
   To him who shall rejoin "Again a lie!"
   Therefore these filthy rags of speech, this coil
   Of statement, comment, query and response,
   Tatters all too contaminate for use,
   Have no renewing: He, the <u>Truth</u>, is, too,   (A)
   The Word. We men, in our degree, may know
   There, simply, instantaneously, as here
   After long time and amid many lies,
   Whatever we dare think we know indeed
   --That I am I, as He is He, --what else?
   But be man's method for man's life at least!
                                             X. 347-382

3. Low instinct, base pretension, are <u>these</u> truth?
                                             X. 513

4.   Whose appetite if brutish is a <u>truth</u>.   X. 542

5.   With all these lies so opposite God's <u>truth</u>,   (A)
                                                          X. 71

6.   What does the world, told <u>truth</u>, but lie the more? (?)
                                                          X. 673

7.   Champion of <u>truth</u>, the priest and wife I praise, (?)
                                                          X. 684

8.   Now fool's-costume: which lie was least like <u>truth</u>, (?)
                                                          X. 1133

9.   I find the <u>truth</u>, dispart the shine from shade,
      As a mere man may, with no special touch X. 1243f

10.   Yet my poor spark had for its source, the sun;
      Thither I sent the great looks which compel
      Light from its fount: all that I do and am
      Comes from the <u>truth</u>, or seen or else surmised, (A)
      Remembered or divined, as mere man may:
      I know just so, nor otherwise.   X. 1285ff

11.   whether a fact,
      Absolute, abstract, independent <u>truth</u>,
      Historic, not reduced to suit man's mind, --
      Or only <u>truth</u> reverberate, changed, made pass
      A spectrum into mind, the narrow eye, --
      The same and not the same, else unconceived--
      Though quite conceivable to the next grade
      Above it in intelligence, --as <u>truth</u>
      Easy to man were blindness to the beast
      By parity of procedure, --the same <u>truth</u>
      In a new form, but changed to either case:
      What matter so intelligence be filled?   X. 1388ff

12.   We made give way before us; solid <u>truth</u>
      In front of it, what motion for the world?
      The moral sense grows but by exercise.   X. 1413ff

13.   The loins we girt about with truth,   (A)   X. 1567

14.   How can I but speak loud what <u>truth</u> speaks low,
                                                          X. 1579

15.   Within whose circle of experience burns
       The central truth, Power, Wisdom, Goodness, --God:
                                    (A) X. 1633f

16.   '"For truth's sake,' so I said, and did, and do.
                                    (A) X. 1717

17.   "Applaud, condemn, --how should he fear the truth?
                                    (A) X. 1748

18.   "Out of the fragmentary truths were light
       "Lay fitful in a tenebrific time?
       "You have the sunrise now, joins truth to truth,
                                          X. 1761ff

19.   "While thou rewardest teachers of the truth, (A)
       "Who miss the plain way in the blaze of noon,
                                          X. 1784f

20.   Shall I wish back once more that thrill of dawn?
       When the whole truth-touched man burned up, one fire?
                                    (A) X. 1795f

21.   For how could saints and martyrs fail see truth
                                    (A) X. 1828

22.   Recognized truths, obedient to some truth
       Unrecognized yet, but perceptible?   X. 1871f

23.   But what a multitude will surely fall
       Quite through the crumbling truth, late subjacent
       Sink to the next discoverable base,
       Rest upon human nature,   X. 1888ff

24.   "So you judge, --but the very truth of joy
       "To my own apprehension which decides.   X. 1935f

25.   Who, in the interest of outraged truth
       Deprecate such rough handling of a lie!
       The facts being proved and incontestable, X. 1964ff

26.   "I' the man and master: then the wife submits
       "To plain truth broadly stated.   X. 2045f

27.   So may the truth be flashed out by one blow, (A)
       And Guido see, one instant, and be saved. X. 2127f

Note: Used 22 times, the words fact (10) and true
(12) contribute to the impression that to the Pope truth means
absolute or God's truth 11 of the 38 times he used it.   Three
uncertain usages may be transitional and point to Celestino's
sermon text, "Let God be true, and every man a liar." But
if the long passage spoken by Euripides focuses on absolute
truth, as St. Paul and St. John focus on God's truth and the
Word, impressive climactic effects are doubled in the Pope's
reasoning.

BOOK XI (GUIDO)

1.   That tries for truth truer than truth itself, XI. 23

2.   Talk away! Will you have the naked truth?XI. 83

3.   In this unmanly appetite for truth,   XI. 171

4.   At the Mouth-of-Truth o' the river-side, you know:
                                                    XI. 188

5.   And anyhow says: 't is truth; he dares not lie!
                                                    XI. 409

6.   and if I stick
      Still to the truth, declare with my last breath,
                                                    XI. 417f

7.   You two come here, entreat I tell you lies,
      And end, the edifying way.   I end,
      Telling the truth!   XI. 432ff

8.   Sirs, truth shall save it, since no lies assist!
      Hear the truth,   XI. 461f

9.   Sheer lunacy unless your truth on lip
      Be recognized a lie in heart of you!   XI. 670f

10.   Contort your brows! You know I speak the truth:
                                                    XI. 695
11.   There's that i' the tale might seem like truth at least
                                                    XI. 883

12.   He goes on, takes the flattery of pure truth,
                                                    XI. 1163

13. God bless us liars, where 's one touch of <u>truth</u>
    In what we tell the world, or world tell us,
                                              XI. 1391

14. Would not begin the lie that ends with <u>truth</u>,
                                              XI. 1430

15. I see not where my fault lies, that's the <u>truth</u>!
                                              XI. 1450

16. Procedures to no purpose! Then flashed <u>truth</u>.
                                              XI. 1530

17. And turn her <u>truth</u> into a lie,   XI. 1685

18. Will you hear <u>truth</u> can do no harm nor good?
                                              XI. 1915

19.   So the living <u>truth</u>   (I)   XI. 1975

20. Possibly true, probably false, a <u>truth</u>
    Such as all <u>truths</u> we live by, Cardinal! XI. 2140f

21. Sirs, my first true word, all <u>truth</u> and no lie,
                                              XI. 2420

    Note: Used 22 times, fact (8) and true (14) contribute
to the impression that to Guido truth (used 24 times) means
fact or alleged fact save in 19 which is ironic.

BOOK XII (THE BOOK AND THE RING)

1. The virtuous sire, the valiant for the <u>truth</u>,
                                              XII. 214

2. Here has been <u>truth</u> at issue with a lie:
   Let who gained <u>truth</u> the day have handsome pride
                                              XII. 403f

3. "Who had, as usual, the plain <u>truth</u> to plead.
                                              XII. 409

4. "What with the plain <u>truth</u> given me to uphold,
   "And, should I let <u>truth</u> slip, the Pope at hand
                                              XII. 431f

5.   "To innocency, --any proof that <u>truth</u>
    "May look for vindication from the world, (A)
                                    XII. 462f

6.   "Because Pompilia's purity prevails,
    "Conclude you, all <u>truth</u> triumphs in the end?
                      (A)   XII. 472f

7.   "In face of one proof more that 'God is true
    "And every man a liar'--that who trusts
    "To human testimony for a fact
    "Gets this sole fact--himself is proved a fool;
    "Man's speech being false, if but by consequence
    "That only strength is true: while man is weak,
    "And, since <u>truth</u> seems reserved for heaven not earth, (A)
    "Plagued here by earth's prerogative of lies,
    "Should learn to love and long for what, one day,
    "Approved by life's probation, he may speak.
                                 XII. 600ff

8.   "I answer, at the urgency of <u>truth</u>:   (A)   XII. 621

9.   Of speaking <u>truth</u>, to mouths like mine at least.
                            (P) XII. 844

10.   but here's the plague
    That all this trouble comes of telling <u>truth</u>,
    Which <u>truth</u>, by when it reaches him, looks false,
    Seems to be just the thing it would supplant,
    Nor recognizable by whom it left:
    While falsehood would have done the work of <u>truth</u>.
    But Art, --wherein man nowise speaks to men,
    Only to mankind, --Art may tell a <u>truth</u>
    Obliquely [poetic], do the thing shall breed the thought,
    Nor wrong the thought, missing the mediate word.
    So may you paint your picture, twice show <u>truth</u>,
    Beyond mere imagery on the wall.   XII. 852ff

    Note: Used 12 times, the words fact (5) and true (7) contribute to the impression that to the lawyers in Book XII truth (used 16 times) continued to mean fact or alleged fact, to the poet and Fra Celestino absolute save in the poet's famous concluding passage in which facts are raised to a more reliable acceptance through Art.

INDEX

(Complete bibliographical reference is indicated by
underlined page number or note)

213

215

"Not so! Expect nor question nor reply" (X. 347), 112,
159, 165-66; "So do I see, pronounce" (X. 1239), 167

objective ego, subjective alter ego, 72-75, 80-81
Old Yellow Book: early investigation in Arezzo (XII. 782
and Rome (I. 423), 42; evidence equally balanced, 77, 79,
93; exultation in finding, 32, 36-37, 39-41, 44, 50; occupied with since 1860-62, 13-18, 22-23 n1, 122-23; unan-
swerable questions, 41-42, 59
order, old and new, 115-16, 118, 132-33, 140-41, 147
Orr, Mrs. Sutherland, 13 n12, 14 n16, 19 n6, 24-25, 37,
62, 66-67, 93, 95, 123, 126-27, 153-55

Paracelsus, 184
Pater, Walter, 125
Peckham, Morse, 72, 75, 76, 77: Browning, a moral instrumentalist, 77; truth is fabricated, 76-77; truth wears
out, 77; "value" replaces truth, 76-77, 107, 121, 123,
132, 152
Phipps, Charles T., S. J., 151-52, 155, 159
Pigou, A. C., 163, 189
Plato, 182
pluralism, 107, 125-26
poem, creation of the long, 24-32, 37 n4, 39-55 n4, 59-60,
67-68, 73-74, 78-83, 90-91: Books II-XI the poem, 69-
70, 83; intellectual and intuitional means, 48, 57; inspiration, conception, final division, composition, completion,
line count, 10-18; invention, 25, 60, 62, 65; narrative
structure, 20-21, 72-73, 93-94, 130, 147; watershed between reason and faith, 33-34, 131
poem, theme (meaning, purpose, moral, process, premise)
of the long, 10-18, 40-41, 49, 53-54, 58, 72-73, 85, 93-
94, 97-98, 107-11, 119, 121-23, 131-33, 137, 139-40,
143-44, 147-49, 152, 154-55, 179
point of view, 45-46, 73-74, 80, 102-03, 108-10, 121, 134-
35, 137-38, 147-48, 158-59, 178-79
Pompilia, 18, 21, 41, 44, 46-47, 51-55, 59, 61, 66, 95-
96, 98, 103, 105-06, 107, 109, 113-16, 118, 122, 135,
138, 139, 142-43, 145-47, 150, 156-57, 161-62, 171;
"wherefore change" (X. 1887), 118, 142
Pope, the, 31, 33-34, 36, 40, 45-48, 57, 61, 93-99, 101,
103-05, 107-08, 110-20, 122, 129, 131-35, 138-42, 144-
47, 150, 152-53, 155-57, Essay 7 passim, 181-82, 189,
193; his "dread machinery / Of sin" (1375), 114, 116;
"educated man's" (1977), 119; "figure of fact / Beside
fact's self" (216), 112; "He, the Truth, is, too, / The
Word" (376), 49-50, 112; "I / Put no such dreadful ques-

tion" (1631), 117, 134; "Is such effect proportionate to cause?" (1536), 141, 169-76; "new tribunal now / Higher than God's" (1976), 118-19, 140; "keen dread creeping" (1254), 116; "Pleadings and counter-pleadings" (216), 110-12; "poor spark the sun" (1285), 110; "quick cold thrill" (1253), 162-63, 169; "recorded governance" (1293), 111; "Reintroduce the doubt" (1855), 215; "salvation" (1630), 116-18; "scripture yields no parallel" (1525), 139, 167-68; "There is...a tale of Thee" (1348), 139; "This terrifies me" (1547), 141, 170-71; "Thy dread play / Of operation" (1343), 116; "what of God?" (I. 582), 61, 144; "wherefore change?" (1887), 118, 142; "Who is faithful now?" (1829), 117, 134
positivism, 33-34, 40, 103-04, 109, 119

Rankean methodology, 33, 132
Raymond, W. O., 10 n1, 11-14, 18, 19 n11, 22-23 n21, 54 n1-55, 56, 100-01, 105, 124, 153, 155, 187
"Recognized truths, obedient to some truth / Unrecognized yet" (X. 1871), 116, 118
Red Cotton Night-Cap Country, 63
relativism, 40, 50-55, 60-61, 72, 74-75, 94, 100-21, 124-27, 131, 135-36, 138-39
repristination, 24-26, 29-30, 37 n4, 38 n5, 39, 50, 68-70, 72-74, 80-87, 89-90, 103-04, 126-27, 152-53
resuscitation, 43, 47-48, 73, 80, 88-89, 103, 119, 121
ring, formation of a gold, 27, 29-31, 37 n4, 38 n5, 86-87
ring metaphor, interpretation of the, 24-30, 37 n4, 39-40, 44-45, 50, 53-54, 55 n4, 64-65, 67-75, 78-83, 85-91, 94, 99, 103-04, 108-09, 122-24, 126-27, 148, 151-55
Roland, Pass of, 10-11, 14-18, 22 n18, 23 n21
Rose, T. K., 38 n5
Rosenmeyer, Thomas G., 178-79 (176)
Rossetti, W. M., 10 n2-11, 13-15, 17-20 n14, 22-23 n21, 52-53, 63
Russell, Frances Theresa, 26-27, 66, 68-69, 93, 136

St. Augustine, 34, 118
St. John, 98, 132, 139, 178, 181
St. Paul, 98, 108, 113-14, 124, 132-33, 141, 166, 171-82, 188
"Saul, " 55 n5, 151
scuttling knowledge, 47-48, 57
seed and fruit of act, 112-13, 159-60, 165-67
Segal, Erich, 176-77
"Shake / This torpor of assurance from our creed" (X. 1853), 142

100-02, 105-06, 108, 121-23, 144; evolvable, 44, 101-03, 108-12, 118-19, 121-24, 134-36, 146-47, 151-52; God's, 31, 47-50, 75, 77, 94-99, 101-02, 108-09, 111-12, 115, 119, 122, 128, 133-35, 137-38, 144-47, 150, 153-54, Essay 7 passim, 161-78; gold, 68, 70, 72; "He, the Truth, is, too, / The Word" (X. 376), 49-50, 140; historicized (institutionalized), 113-15, 119-21; human, 25, 31, 50-51, 58, 91, 94-96, 98-99, 101, 104-05, 107-08, 110-11, 115, 121-23, 125-28, 135, 137-38, 141, 144, 147-48, 150, 178-93; indexed by fact, 60-61, 103-05, 108; indiscriminately exchanged for fact, 27-28, 39-42, 45-46, 48, 56, 57 n8, 58-59, 97-98, 104, 123-24, 127-28; intuitive, 31-33, 57, 61, 90-91, 94-96, 110-11, 119, 123, 137-38, 141, 146-47; multiple use of, 27-29, 40-42, 58-59, 62, 127, 144, 149-50; partial or diluted, 31, 97-99, 108, 122, 124, 135, 137-38, 141, 144-47, 152-53; personalized (psychologized), 89, 104, 109, 113-15, 119-20, 124-25, 126-28, 135, 139, 148, 152, 176, 178- 81, 186-87; Platonic, 35, 37, 75-76, 107, 115, 128, 132, 146-47, 178-79, 181-82, 192-93; poetic, 124, 127-28, 136, 143, 146-47, 150-51, 155; relativist, 40, 54-55, 67-68, 70-71, 74-78, 94, 98-126, 132, 134-35, 137-39, 143-52, 190; search for, 31, 48, 50, 97, 99, 101, 122, 124, 126, 137-38, 141, 144-46, 181-82, 189; star-imagery, 94-98; truth of the facts, 50, 62-63, 68, 102, 119-20, 123-24, 128, 134-35, 147; The Two Poets of Croisic, 63-64; Victorian Newsletter symposium, 39, 55-56, 64-65, 99-100; vision of, 54, 97, 121-24, 131-32, 134-35, 138, 146-47, 152. See "Art may tell a truth, " "No dose of purer truth, " and "Recognized truths"
The Two Poets of Croisic, 63-64

Voltaire, 64, 118, 120, 133

Wasserman, George B. , 68, 71-75, 78-83, 85-89, 94; amalgam, 71, 73; emphasis on experience, 71-75; poet more than one consciousness, 72-73; relativism, 74-75; depersonalization, 78-82
wax and honey analogy, 37, 71, 74, 79
Wedgwood, Julia, 11 n7, 13-15, 17, 20 n14 & 15, 46-47, 61, 94
Wordsworth, William, 50, 125, 183